# School Boards in America

## A Flawed Exercise in Democracy

Gene I. Maeroff

palgrave
macmillan

First published in 2010 by PALGRAVE MACMILLAN® in the United States—a division of St. Martin's Press LLC, 175 Fifth Avenue, New York, NY 10010.

Where this book is distributed in the UK, Europe, and the rest of the world, this is by Palgrave Macmillan, a division of Macmillan Publishers Limited, registered in England, company number 785998, of Houndmills, Basingstoke, Hampshire RG21 6XS.

Palgrave Macmillan is the global academic imprint of the above companies and has companies and representatives throughout the world.

Palgrave® and Macmillan® are registered trademarks in the United States, the United Kingdom, Europe and other countries.

ISBN: 978-0-230-10758-8 (hardcover)
ISBN: 978-0-230-10931-5 (paperback)

Library of Congress Cataloging-in-Publication Data

Maeroff, Gene I.
    School boards in America : a flawed exercise in democracy / Gene I. Maeroff.
    p. cm.
    ISBN 978-0-230-10758-8 (alk. paper)
    1. School boards—United States. 2. School boards—Political aspects—United States.
3. Public schools—United States. 4. School board-superintendent relationships—
United States. 5. Education and state—United States. I. Title.

    LB2831.M235 2010
    379.1'5310973—dc22                                    2010019400

A catalogue record of the book is available from the British Library.

Design by Scribe Inc.

First edition: December 2010

10 9 8 7 6 5 4 3 2 1

Printed in the United States of America.

To Joyce

My one and only

# Contents

# Preface

When I began the research and writing specific to this book in late 2007, I was on the cusp of declaring my candidacy for a seat on my local school board. I had already spent decades observing and analyzing educational developments and events around the country. In so doing, though, I had probably not given sufficient attention to the role of the board of education, an entity that is easy to overlook. The possibility of running for a position on a school board piqued my interest in doing this book, which seemed like a logical follow-up to other books I have written about many aspects of education.

My work on the book reinforced my conviction that people ought to know more about school boards. These bodies spend a lot of the public's money, provide millions of jobs, and most importantly, help shape the future for young Americans. Yet school boards remain out of sight, garnering attention primarily when the annual budget is set. My goal in this book, as in most of my previous ones, is to reach both education professionals and serious general readers.

I didn't enter this endeavor with a plethora of preconceived notions about school boards. Some critics would abolish them. Others would trim and narrow their responsibilities. Frankly, I'm not persuaded that elementary and secondary education would be that much better if school boards didn't exist.

This doesn't mean that school boards could not do a better job of governing the districts they serve, the legal function with which they are charged. Regardless of background, almost all members come to school boards as amateurs in school system governance. They learn on the job and suffer from the shortcomings that plague novices in most endeavors. I use the word "flawed" in the subtitle of this book advisedly. There are many built-in obstacles that thwart school boards.

My time on a school board was invaluable to my work on the book, which I offer neither as a memoir based on that experience nor as an exposé of the board on which I served. This is not a book about the Edison, New Jersey, board of education. However, I draw on my board experiences where applicable to help illustrate some of my points. Authors do this all the time. At no point, though, do I refer by name to any of my town's board members, school employees, students, or anyone else associated with the Edison public schools. Nor have I violated any confidences.

I was in touch by phone, email, or in person with dozens of people throughout the country as I gathered and verified information. I quote these sources extensively, and I have crafted anecdotes and formed impressions based on what I learned. Virtually all the quotes in this book that are not accompanied by citations are ones that I personally obtained. I broadened the scope of the book through interviews with people in about two dozen states.

The subject of my focus is, indeed, the American institution of the school board. There are sufficient commonalities despite the differences to allow for such an investigation. It is therefore possible to make statements and offer observations that capture the ethos of school system governance almost wherever in the country that it occurs.

For me, already familiar with the world of education, service on a school board was unlike any other experience that I have had. It burdened me with legal and fiduciary responsibilities. It put limits on what I could say publicly about what I had learned. It thrust me—a person accustomed to interviewing others—into the role of interviewee for members of the media. It put extensive demands on my time without any remuneration whatsoever. It threw me into close and continuing contact with eight fellow board members, most of whom—most of the time—were generally cordial despite differences that arose. It exposed me to the world of politics and the infighting, gossiping, and maneuvering that unfortunately insinuate themselves into the work of what are supposedly nonpartisan positions on school boards.

Furthermore, when I was elected the board president in the spring of 2010, as I was nearing completion of this book, I got a new perspective on school board service. It was a challenging time, when millions of dollars had to be cut from our budget and an interim superintendent had to be found quickly to replace an acting superintendent who did not get hired as superintendent. It became clear that the expectations that the board president must meet and the pressures under which he may find himself far exceed what other members of the board face.

All in all, I was fortunate in winning election to the school board governing the fifth-largest district in the state, driven by both curiosity and a sense of volunteerism. I certainly did not take on this mission to write a book, but that was a happy outcome. It was a privilege to play some small role in trying to enhance the learning of my neighbors' children. The future of every student who attends a public school is at stake in the work of school boards, and there is perhaps no greater responsibility for which a man or woman can volunteer. It might sound corny, but it's true.

Gene I. Maeroff

# Chapter 1

# A Cradle of Democracy

The nation's public schools represent the ultimate expression of American democracy. They are operated by the people, for the people. They instill the knowledge and cultivate the attitudes of the next generation of Americans, serving 90 percent of the country's school-age population. A local board of education is—in its ideal form—a group of citizen-volunteers who give unselfishly of themselves, usually without remuneration, to look after the affairs of the school system and, by extension, the community. Of all the institutions in the country with jurisdiction over large chunks of money and the ability to influence the nation's future, boards of education are surely the most obscure and least understood.

Local control of schools is one of the shibboleths by which Americans identify themselves. It is a notion so deeply ingrained in our consciousness that few Americans think about it anymore, according to Chester E. Finn Jr., who said "the phrase rolls off the tongue without even engaging the mind."[1] The board of education is the personification of that attribute, an entity supposedly representing the best instincts of the public in wanting to provide for the well-being of the next generation. "School districts are perhaps the most democratically controlled agency of government," Ronald W. Rebore wrote in a book intended to serve as a handbook for school board members and a textbook for students of educational administration.[2]

The local board of education is a distinguishing feature of public schooling in the world's most affluent society, holding sway over 13,862 separate districts in the 50 states. Many other countries have national systems of education. Some observers conclude that the school board, linked as it is to its locale, is a thread that binds America's democratic fabric. It is, after all, through a democratic process that people generally choose the members of the board of education, and those members, voting in meetings open to the public, govern the schools. Education historian Carl F. Kaestle wrote that Americans' commitment to local control of schools is based partly on their idea that this makes the schools more responsive, more democratic, and more efficient. Local and state control of education, he said, connects to American "concepts of family and community," while national power "strikes many as foreign."[3]

Charles Everand Reeves, a consultant in educational administration during the first half of the twentieth century, described school boards as "bulwarks of democracy." In 1954, when the nightmares of World War II still reverberated throughout the world, he asserted that an important part of the attack on democracy by Hitler, Mussolini, Lenin, and Stalin was their seizing control quickly over the schools. "It is important to the sound maintenance of our representative form of government," Reeves wrote, "that school control continues to reside, in large measure, in the representatives of the local communities."[4]

But can it be that local control and the school board itself are as outmoded as some other old standards—the privately owned pharmacy on the corner, the Lions or the Elks, the local daily newspaper, the Oldsmobile parked in the garage, or the assumption that the bank on Main Street retains the mortgage on your home? Did the nation fool itself about the importance of having their neighbors govern the public schools or did the arrangement simply outlive its usefulness? Are local school boards "a little bit of both dinosaur and democratic symbol" as one education professor described them in the early 1990s?[5]

## The Special Role of School Boards

More of the taxes that Americans pay to their states and localities go toward schools and colleges than to anything else—public safety, corrections facilities, health services, and infrastructure. Typically, no local body has control over so much money as the school board. Public schools received $556.9 billion in revenues from local, state, and federal government sources for the 2006 through 2007 school year, according to the U.S. Census Bureau.

The neighborhood school is embedded in the national consciousness—an enterprise that fills people with memories lasting from the time that they learn to read and write until they complete their final preparation for college or the workforce. Friendships that may endure for a lifetime are formed, and it is in the public schools that many Americans experience their earliest hurts and triumphs. The institution of the public school figures for decades in most lives as the place where generations of families spent so much of their time.

Governing this enterprise is the entity vaguely known as the board of education, which some may consider the building that houses school headquarters, others may think of as the administrators in the central office, and few recognize as the half-dozen or so men and women who govern the school system. "Very few respondents, including rather sophisticated and civically engaged citizens, know very much about the role and responsibilities of local school boards,"[6] concluded a study of school boards in 1986, a finding that could be replicated today.

However obscure the board of education, its potential authority is indisputable, backed by the letter of the law and embodied in the citizens who meet periodically to take votes and go on record with decisions having to do with maintaining and constructing buildings, purchasing items ranging from boilers to paper, hiring and promoting personnel, granting medical leaves, declaring equipment obsolete, resurfacing parking lots, and, oh yes, approving textbooks and curriculums.

For more than 25 years, school reform has been a mantra of critics dissatisfied with the preservation of the status quo by school boards. Reformers speak of hiring better teachers, finding principals who know how to lead, devising curriculums to require students to do more thinking, and generally abandoning practices that have proven ineffective and unproductive. Yet, amid the many proposals for change, there is scant attention to the role of the board of education. Reformers sally forth as if school boards did not exist and as if top-down solutions could be implemented by fiat. School boards, though, despite having lost considerable authority in recent decades to state and federal officials, still have the ability to determine the extent to which reforms will even be attempted. Anyone seeking to improve schools ignores the power of school boards at some peril.

### *School Boards' Place in Democracy*

"Democracy forever teases us with the contrast between its ideals and its realities, between its heroic possibilities and sorry achievements," wrote Agnes Repplier, an essayist of the late nineteenth and early twentieth centuries.[7] It's doubtful that Repplier had public school districts uppermost in mind in making this observation, but her statement nonetheless resonates when one thinks about the schools and the manner by which they are governed. A century later, U.S. Defense Secretary Donald Rumsfeld tried to tap into similar sentiments about democracy with his controversial statements in the wake of widespread looting after the invasion of Iraq. "Freedom's untidy," he declared. "Stuff happens."[8]

Perhaps George Bernard Shaw, known for his acerbity, summed up the plight of school boards with his statement, "Democracy is a device that ensures we shall be governed no better than we deserve." Shaw directed his statement at democratic bodies generally, but other critics have been particularly harsh when it comes specifically to school boards. One of the most biting indictments was offered by Mark Twain. The great American humorist reputedly said, "In the first place, God made idiots. That was for practice. Then he made school boards."[9]

The contradictions of democracy are such that most school boards do not have carte blanche. While they represent an expression of democracy at the local level, there is frequently a tension between what school board members want and what the public desires. Therefore, not only do taxpayers in most locales vote on school budgets, construction referendums, and the composition of the boards, but they also may attend and speak at meetings of the board. In 2009, controversy erupted across the land when members of Congress convened meetings with constituents in their home districts to discuss federal health care legislation. After some of these gatherings turned into raucous verbal brawls, some people charged that the halls were stacked with activist opponents of the proposals. Hadn't anyone ever heard of school board meetings?

Democracy is indeed fragile, and the system by which men and women become school board members and the method by which they govern—ostensibly fair and rationale—sometimes represents democracy at its most vulnerable. Democracy evolves, always changing, never a finished product, and sometimes at risk. This is a theme of Sean Wilentz's majestic study of the sweep of American democracy through the decades from Washington to Lincoln.[10] Few safeguards promote the public welfare to guarantee that those who ascend to public positions of authority, including members of school boards, are knowledgeable and dedicated individuals who will carry out their duties diligently. John Adams, as a founding father and as president, famously distrusted the masses, according to Wilentz, and worried about whether democracy empowered them to too great an extent. Some critics are concerned that the very democracy that opens service on school boards to everyone may be the undoing of some boards.

Nevertheless, some observers are not troubled by the absence of expertise in educational matters among members of school boards. The author of a book sponsored by the National School Boards Association, an organization that champions the role of school boards, found it remarkable that ordinary citizens control school boards and other major institutions, a situation he considered an underpinning of democracy.[11]

The system, depending as it does on citizen volunteers, ordinarily provides few direct supports to school board members—a flaw, but not one unique to school boards. One could similarly criticize other public bodies and the people who serve on them. Almost everywhere in this country, members of town and city councils labor without adequate support for understanding and delving into the expensive and vital issues that come before them. Members of zoning boards and other such public bodies, supposedly representing the public interest, may, in fact, sometimes place the concerns of real estate developers and others above those of the public. And, as the case of disgraced former Illinois governor Rod Blagojovich sadly reminds us, even government at its highest levels may bequeath a betrayal of the public interest.

So, maybe the question is whether we should expect anything more of school board members, volunteers distracted by full-time jobs, than we do of other public servants. This is how democracy functions in the United States. School boards with their strengths and weaknesses are no worse, and often better, than the many other governmental entities that spend the public's money and provide crucial services. Did the federal government over the many years of the Iraq adventure and the expenditure of hundreds of billions dollars do any better?

Two scholars of education present the mission of education in the broad context of democracy, "Education has special responsibilities in democratic societies because all the decisions underlying public institutions are subject to ongoing review. Each new majority can amend the constitution, changing the laws and shifting public funding to new priorities, undo checks and balances, and allow values of liberty and tolerance to wane. Education is essential, then, to give each generation an understanding of the principles and institutions that support democratic society."[12]

Literacy and democracy go hand in hand. Teaching children to read for meaning is the most important task facing schools. An informed and literate populace is essential to the preservation of democracy. The public schools figure mightily in this equation. Their failures are society's failures, and a local school board that does not place this responsibility over all others is derelict in its duties. Yet, despite local control of schools, all too many children never become fluent readers. Perhaps this represents a mockery of democracy.

### The History of School Boards

The forerunners of public schools were established in the New England colonies in the seventeenth and eighteenth centuries. Colonial leaders, influenced strongly by religious precepts, called for the education of children so as to counteract Satan, the great deluder. They reasoned that people who could read the Bible would not have their heads turned by the attractions of evil. And so it was that churches and religious groups played a major part in establishing the first schools. The cultivation of religious faith more than the preservation of democracy figured in these efforts.

A law enacted in 1647 in Massachusetts—just a generation after the arrival of the Pilgrims, who left Europe in search of religious freedom—mandated that each town establish a school. Essentially, it was up to the town to finance and oversee its school, which generally led to the formation of a committee to carry out these tasks. Given the manner in which they evolved, it is no accident that many towns in New England still call their school boards "school committees."

In the beginning, there was no such person as a school superintendent, and the committees oversaw both policy and administrative functions. Those were the days when school boards actually operated the schools, a responsibility that would now be frowned upon. School board members "examined and selected the teachers and decided upon their salaries, determined the length of school terms, secured wood for fuel, had school buildings repaired, visited classes, and even examined the pupils."[13] And so it was with these many responsibilities that school committees had dozens of members, a function of both the amount of work they did and the wish to pursue democratic goals by making the schools as responsive as possible to the town. Laws enacted in Massachusetts in 1826 and 1827 made school committees independent of towns and local government, paving the way for the autonomous school districts that now exist in most states.

By the mid-nineteenth century, school boards had evolved further, shedding their administrative role by placing many of their responsibilities in the hands of professional superintendents. Having their friends and neighbors on the boards "provided democracy in education, meaning self-rule by elected representatives of the people," wrote education historian David Tyack, who said that some states had as many as 45,000 local school trustees, often outnumbering the teachers.[14] By one estimate, the country still had 765,186 school board members (at an average of six members per board) as recently as 1930, when there were 127,531 school districts.[15]

The number and size of school boards shrank during the twentieth century, but the existence of a panel of citizens charged with governing the public schools continued to inspire confidence in many Americans that the schools adhered to a democratic tradition. The fact that some of those very same boards acted until more than halfway through the twentieth century to bar African Americans and disabled students from many of the public schools raises questions retrospectively about democracy, questions that most school boards conveniently left unaddressed.

One factor that potentially links school boards to the exercise of democracy is that the majority, more than two-thirds, preside over districts of fewer than 2,500 students. Theoretically, like the traditional New England town meeting, school board elections and meetings in such systems remain close to the people. The disparity in the size of school districts can be seen in the fact that only 2 percent of them have enrollments of more than 25,000 students each.

## Connections to Perceptions of Community

A sense of community is built on many characteristics. Everything from encountering neighbors in the supermarket to turning out for the annual Fourth of July fireworks helps forge community. The public schools, too, figure prominently in bringing people in a particular locale together around a shared sense of purpose. The schools that children attend are an essential component in fostering a sense of community. The very fact that the schools hold sway over a youngster's safety and security for almost as many hours each day as parents do puts schools in a class of their own. Moreover, what transpires in classrooms helps determine the future prosperity of a community. No entity other than the family has so great a role in shaping the nation.

A conscientious and hardworking school board recognizes that its decisions affect the quality of the community. A good school board continually takes the local temperature, trying to gauge the dreams and aspirations of residents. The board strives to prepare members of the next generation to take their place in the community. On the other hand, some school boards may do little more than go through the motions, putting the system on automatic pilot. A school board unable to keep children out of harm's way, for example, where drugs, gangs, or violence invade schoolyards and corridors, can contribute to the demise of a community. Likewise, a school board that breeds dissension can fracture the unity of the community.

Controversy may consume the school board itself. This happened in a rural district in eastern California, where for probably the only time in the state's history an entire school board was recalled in 2009 and each of the five members replaced. Big Oak Flat-Groveland Unified School District, the site of the tumult, is less than a half hour's drive from one of the most peaceful spots on earth. But even the serenity of nearby Yosemite National Park could not soothe the unrest after a popular math teacher was fired and students at Tioga High School, applying what they said they had learned in civics class, helped lead the recall of the school board.

Disputation seemed to be in the water in Big Oak Flat-Groveland, which had seven superintendents in eight years when Mari Brabbin arrived in 2008 to take her combined position of superintendent-principal at the system's other high school, Don Pedro. Perhaps the sprawling geography of the school district and the far-flung nature of its population led to the divisions. The district has 500 students scattered over an area as large as Los Angeles Unified School District, where the enrollment is the nation's second largest.

The school board backed the superintendent unanimously in dismissing the teacher over an allegation that he had committed plagiarism as a college student. He denied the charge, as did his alma mater, California State University at Fresno. The superintendent and the school board would not back down and restore his job. "I was never satisfied that I got to the bottom of the reason for firing him," Richard C. Paddock, a former *Los Angeles Times* reporter who covered the story for the newspaper, told me. "It didn't make that much sense to me." Apparently, it didn't track well with voters either. Seventy percent of them turned out four months after the teacher's dismissal to oust all the school board members. It's called democracy.

### What the Research Shows

How much does a community gain by having a good school board, and conversely, how much does it harm a community to have a bad school board? A difficulty in trying to answer this question has to do with sorting out cause and effect. It is not unreasonable to expect a desirable community to have a good school board nor to expect that an undesirable community will have a bad school board. A study carried out under the auspices of the Iowa Association of School Boards looked at this issue. An examination of student achievement data found that members of school boards in high-achieving districts were significantly different in their knowledge and beliefs from their counterparts in low-achieving districts. These kinds of differences showed in administrators and teachers, as well.

School board members and educators, too, in the high-achieving districts held to higher standards for students and were less likely to accept excuses for low achievement. They were more knowledgeable about teaching and learning issues and could cite specific examples of how goals were attained. High-achieving districts were more apt to use data and other information to monitor student progress. The boards in such districts were more amenable to professional development and more likely to create supportive workplaces for staff. Finally, the school boards in high-achieving districts had better connections to their communities.[16] Given that some critics of school boards would abolish them, one wonders whether the advantages that a good school board confers could be realized in the absence of local control of education.

In addition to making a difference in the schools, a good school board may benefit a community in other ways as well. A school board that can ensure high quality in the schools may pay dividends that affect the value of real estate and the quality of life in a community. This, at least, was the finding of a literature review by the RAND Corporation. "There is powerful evidence," RAND concluded, "that the quality of a school or a school district, as measured by average test scores, is positively associated with housing values."

RAND found a 0.5 to 1 percent increase in average property values for each 1 percent increase in reading or math scores. Researchers unsurprisingly observed that homeowners were willing to pay more to live in a community served by a school or school district of high quality. In turn, if homes in desirable school districts sell for more and if they are reassessed to reflect the higher values, then it follows that good schools can increase tax revenues, according to RAND. Moreover, if schools help make a community more desirable, the locale will draw more affluent people and even sales tax revenues will grow as such residents can afford to spend more with local businesses.

There is yet another way that RAND examined the data, concluding that good schools can lead to "substantial reductions in major crimes." The researchers found double-digit reductions in murders, assaults, motor vehicle thefts, and arson for each one-year higher-average educational level in a community. Some of that reduction can spill into neighboring communities, but on the other hand, neighboring communities can provide perpetrators for crime in the district that has the higher educational achievement, the report theorizes.[17] All in all, the RAND study, like the one in Iowa, does not differentiate between cause and effect. Few observers, though, would reason that making schools better—as school boards (not alone) can help do—would not redound to a community's desirability.

### Challenges to Notions of Community

Confusion about what the school board owes its community can contribute to the disenchantment of some citizens. Thomas L. Alsbury, a professor who studied school boards and superintendents, said that most board members don't believe that they must base their actions on the wishes of the people. They envision themselves as *trustees* rather than *delegates* of the citizenry. He maintained that such a view was more acceptable in former years, when school board members were elite leaders who saw themselves standing above and apart from the larger community. But a transformation during the last generation, as less elite people came to sit on school boards and as issues grew more complex, made school board membership more problematic. Alsbury wrote, "When teachers unions became a political force in board elections after the 1970s, coupled with a simultaneous increase in community ideological purity and diversity, and a decline in general community involvement in school boards, local special-interest group politics increased and focused more on protectionism."[18]

Whatever the reasons—lack of interest, too many demands on their time, a sense of detachment from the public schools—the decline in community involvement is seen in the low attendance of the public at meetings of the board of education. Many times the audience barely outnumbers the board members and top staff assembled at the front of the room. This absence of public participation is underscored at meetings around the country in school auditoriums filled with empty seats. Democracy demands that school boards conduct their business in full view of the public, but the public appears disinclined to take advantage of this opportunity for an unimpeded view.

The public is losing its psychic sense of ownership of the schools. Some of the loss is illusory, and some is very real. An increase in childless households and the growing portion of elderly Americans inevitably leads to detachment from the schools in homes where no one feels a direct connection to the public schools. Moreover, the replacement of homogeneity by diversity means that school boards ask some residents to pay school taxes in behalf of students with whom they may not readily identify.

The public schools are among the harbingers of demographic change. Increasingly, school systems are becoming symbols of America's expanding diversity. At least one of every five kindergarteners today has a foreign-born parent. School boards should be sensitive to such shifts and attempt to keep the public schools responsive to new needs while continuing to engage households without children in school. Public schools can affect the ability of people of different backgrounds to live together. School boards have more potential impact in this regard than most people realize.

John Dewey, education's leading philosopher, wrote during the great migration to the United States early in the twentieth century that it was incumbent on the educational enterprise to apply to its endeavors the ideas and ideals of a democratic society. He envisioned the role of the school as balancing the various elements in the social environment so that "each individual gets an opportunity to escape from the limitations of the social group in which he was born and to come into living contact with a broader environment."[19] School boards are in a position to make that happen 100 years later, in the midst of a second ingathering.

It is not easy, though, for local school boards to function in the midst of such change. School board members become mechanics trying to recalibrate an aircraft engine while the plane is in flight. Sometimes it becomes incumbent upon boards to build community where it scarcely exists, where people live side by side in splendid isolation. The self-rule of democracy, in which the populace comes together in the name of the common good, weakens when people turn inward and go their separate ways. School boards, for example, cannot readily rally citizens in behalf of the public schools when some of them resent the fact that public schools serve students who are not citizens or whose parents used illegal means to enter this country.

### Instilling Democratic Values in Students

Board members should never lose sight of the extent to which schools affect the attitudes of the young people who sit in their classrooms. School boards have the ability to further democracy. Margot Stern Strom, president and executive director of Facing History and Ourselves, maintained in 2008, on the sixtieth anniversary of the Universal Declaration of Human Rights, that Americans ought to reflect on the ability of education to prevent mass atrocities and to advance individual freedom and dignity. She pointed to an extreme example of the contrast in national leadership to make her point.[20] During the 1930s and the first half of the 1940s, she said, Franklin Delano Roosevelt saw education as a vehicle for keeping freedom alive and Adolf Hitler saw the schools as places for indoctrinating the young with his hateful philosophies. "Democracy cannot succeed unless those who express their choice are prepared to choose wisely," said Roosevelt. "The real safeguard of democracy, therefore, is education."[21]

Literature and social studies are curricular staples, essential to democracy. Students learn about freedom and liberty in novels and in books of nonfiction. They gradually gain the ability to contrast forms of government. They may become discerning observers of democracy's challenges, identifying the tweaks and adjustments that can strengthen democracy. "What our schools must do is teach young people the virtues and blessings of our democratic system of government," historian Diane Ravitch wrote in the wake of the 9/11 attacks. "Our ability to defend what we hold dear depends on our knowledge and understanding of it."[22] School board members must distinguish between indoctrination and education. They should recognize that instruction will best serve students when young people learn to question and probe the tenets of democracy. School board members should read and become familiar with the books that students read.

In addition, school boards promote democracy when they ensure that students and their parents receive fair treatment. Parents should have the opportunity for input. Educators should mete out discipline evenly. Students should have the chance to enroll in courses that will help them grow intellectually. Social settings in schools ought to enable students to participate without embarrassment. Schools should be places that reinforce democratic beliefs and school boards can help make that possible.

# Chapter 2

# The School Board's Impact on Student Learning

Under the guise of democracy, each state is free to set standards for its students and those standards may be as low as the state wishes. The federal government does not dictate standards for learning. The No Child Left Behind law, enacted at the beginning of this century, required public school students to meet state standards, but the fact that some states called for low standards got insufficient attention. There was nothing to prevent an individual local school board from lifting its standards above those in the rest of the state, but scant incentive to do so given that its schools might face sanctions for not meeting the higher standards.

Most Americans don't realize the extent to which this approach differs from the practice in many other parts of the world, where national bodies set standards and then, national examinations determine the extent to which students have met the standards. Observers could argue endlessly about whether the approach in the United States is more democratic in giving so much leeway to the states and to the school districts in those states. Finally, in 2010, there was a move to get the states to adopt common academic standards, a voluntary process that eventually could lead to more uniformity throughout the country.

Slowly but inexorably, policymakers have accepted the idea that the United States needs common standards and that each state should move in this direction. Some policymakers and educators are fed up with the idea that in the name of states rights a student in Louisiana need not learn algebra as well as a student in Massachusetts or that a student in Alabama need not learn to comprehend what he or she reads as well as a peer in Minnesota. They reject the notion that it is more democratic for students in one state to know less about science than their counterparts in another state.

School boards have not been without parameters. With every state having standards of some sort—promulgated by the state education department or a state board of education, or both—local school systems have had guidance. Standards take two forms. First, content standards describe the broad material to be covered, grade by grade, subject by subject. Second, performance standards, usually in the form of state-sponsored assessments, set the bar that students must reach grade by grade in each of those subjects. Committees of educators, adhering to the broad outlines of the standards, create curriculum for individual school systems, and board members essentially apply their rubber stamp.

## Responsibility for Student Learning

Taking responsibility for student learning is surely one of the most problematic tasks of school boards. Most states give school boards some say in this area, but what does the average citizen who serves on a school board know about curriculum and instruction? What gives school board members the knowledge, for instance, to approve textbooks, an authority that usually rests with them?

I was intrigued upon assuming my seat on a school board to discover that we were asked to approve the textbooks and curriculum guides for individual courses. Of course, committees of educators had already reviewed and recommended the curriculum and these materials. Typically, the educators measure the books against criteria that call for them to determine the ancillary materials that will accompany a course and to examine format, content, and teachability, as well as whether the book presents material in a nondiscriminatory manner. School boards tend to act compliantly on matters of curriculum and instruction, performing a pantomime of local control in the tacit name of democracy. I wonder how many school board members anywhere take the time to examine these books and curriculum materials.

The few times that the public hears about the involvement of the school board in approving curriculum and textbooks comes when controversies erupt. The handling of evolution, arguments over new math, or conflicts on the role of phonics in reading instruction occasionally take center stage. Otherwise, school boards approve curriculum guides and books and materials without anyone paying heed.

Speaking as one school board member, I wouldn't be able to tell a good physics textbook from a bad one or decide whether a calculus curriculum guide gives students adequate exposure to the subject. I do know something, though, about reading instruction and American history, and I did ask to have a look at materials that teachers had reviewed in these areas, among others. I didn't object to their choices; I was merely curious. One of my board colleagues, a chemistry teacher in a neighboring district, voluntarily looked through the textbook that a faculty committee had recommended for this subject. I suspect, though, that most members of the board—except possibly some on the curriculum committee—do not bother to inspect the textbooks or curriculum materials that they approve by voice vote.

What are the limits of democracy? What does it mean to the democratic process to vest school board members with authority over instructional pursuits? Does this make the public schools more responsive to the populace? I doubt it.

Most school boards are filled with citizen volunteers who lack expertise beyond the source of their livelihoods or what they might learn from an avocation. They come from all walks of life. School board members in the United States are largely unpaid part-timers without personal staff to whom they can turn for input. Two-thirds of them receive no board salaries, and another almost 10 percent get less than $2,000 a year from this work, meaning that about four of five school board members earn little or nothing for the job.[1]

### Boards Have Differing Levels of Responsibility

The substantial amounts that some large districts pay their board members are the exception. Until 2007, Los Angeles considered board service a part-time position and paid each of its seven members $26,347 a year. Then, a commission decided that those who held their positions as their only employment should receive $45,637 annually, equivalent to the beginning teacher salary. Board members who had outside employment continued to get the lower salary. All members of the Los Angeles board got the same health benefits as full-time district employees, as well as retirement contributions. They also could use district vehicles.

Each board member in Los Angeles had an administrative assistant to perform clerical duties and another position to which the member could appoint someone for purposes that the member determined. Each member had an office budget of approximately $215,000, which most spent on personnel. Two board members used this fund to maintain and staff field offices in their geographic districts. Salary levels for all of these positions were set by the district and ranged from about $25,000 to $80,000, with full benefits for assistants who had more than half-time assignments.

Having assistants makes board members in Los Angeles or anywhere else less reliant on the superintendent for research and information. There is a good chance that most of the nation's school board members, having no such aides, sometimes end up ill-informed and vote on matters on which they lack a full understanding. Adding to their difficulties, school board members may be pulled into non-instructional pursuits, attending to issues involving the physical plant, collective bargaining, budgets, personnel decisions, and law suits. This may leave them without sufficient time to delve into academic matters.

Yet school boards differ from district to district, even within the same state, and it is difficult to generalize about how they carry out their work. Some school boards, for instance, may set policies determining how to group students for instruction and how many levels of a course the schools will present. School boards may approve offerings of Advanced Placement courses and set policies for laboratory facilities for science courses. Thus, school boards have opportunities to influence various aspects of teaching and learning in ways that differ from district to district.

School boards across the country focus more on curriculum and instruction than ever before. Concern about student achievement drives this attention. The beginning of this trend can be traced to 1983, when the federal government released a report, *A Nation at Risk*, deploring the condition of American education and warning of dire consequences if change did not occur. A campaign to increase academic requirements and put more rigor in the curriculum followed.

The first President Bush convened an Education Summit for the nation's governors in 1989, trying to increase influence over education at the state and national levels. In 1994, President Clinton backed Goals 2000, an effort to raise national achievement by the end of the century. The second President Bush persuaded Congress to embrace No Child Left Behind, with its penalties for public schools that failed to make adequate yearly progress. President Obama quickly moved to tie federal education grants to his version of school reform. No school board could possibly have missed the message that extended over two decades. While the nation's school board members did not react uniformly, they all increasingly felt the heavy hand of government on their shoulders.

### Denver's Effort to Act Responsibly

Some school boards face greater challenges than others when it comes to student achievement. What made Denver different was the progress that the school system made after the board of education became resolute in its determination to attack academic difficulties. Around the middle of the first decade of the 2000s, the school board coalesced into an effective unit that tackled three major problems facing the district: low test scores, a high dropout rate, and an ineffective program for English language learners. "We rallied around student achievement because at the end of the day that's what our school board believes it's elected to do," Theresa Pena, the board president, told me.

The Denver Public Schools (DPS) were able to make progress because a stable and informed seven-member board collaborated with an ambitious superintendent to fashion bold plans to deal with seemingly intractable problems. Consultants conferred with board members and the superintendent on strategies and approaches to support promising changes even in the face of controversy. So it was that the school board, which in many other big cities has been an obstacle to improvement, became a fulcrum upon which the superintendent balanced his efforts to remake the public schools.

Observers agreed that Superintendent Michael Bennet was able to make progress because, for the most part, school board members aligned themselves with his efforts and backed him even in the most disputatious of times, for example, when he closed some of the city's worst-performing schools. This degree of co-operation was not guaranteed given the vagaries of an elected school board and the turnover that inevitably occurs on such a body. The board and the superintendent benefited from the backing they received from influential local foundations and from community leaders who had been cultivated and attracted to a reform agenda.

Bennet's initiatives might not have been possible with a feuding board or one on which individual members spent much of their time looking out for special interests or posturing. This is a system that from the middle to the late part of the decade strengthened its pioneering, but still far from perfect, ProComp teacher incentive plan; sought to raise the quality of its instructional staff; removed principals deemed unsuccessful and gave raises to principals judged most successful; and set out against some community opposition to promote charter schools and greater choice for students and their parents. The local teacher union, ruffled by some of the board's positions, endorsed candidates to run against sitting board members, a largely futile move as the voters mostly rejected the union's candidates.

Denver's board of education struck a reformist pose simply in hiring Bennet, a top aide to the city's mayor without formal credentials for running a school system. Early on, Bennet took on the task of making sense of an often-impenetrable budget, gaining sophisticated understanding so that he could explain the intricacies to others and render it more transparent. One measure of his success is the fact that Colorado's governor tapped him in 2009 to replace a departing U.S. senator from the state. His chief financial officer moved up to replace him as superintendent, permitting the school board to maintain continuity in the district's leadership.

One idea that Denver's school board members—most of whom went through training sessions with the Center for Reform of School Systems (CRSS)—said that they got from consultants was a way to circumvent the Sunshine law so that they could discuss matters in private and try to reach consensus before voting. Rather than gathering as a full board, which would have violated the law, board members would frequently meet with Bennet and his top staff in pairs so that they could get a better understanding of the issues. To a large measure, one board member told me, the training by CRSS changed the board's vision for the school system. In effect, the board gave the superintendent cover for some of the most grueling tasks that he assumed in an attempt to raise academic achievement.

DPS became a system that made better use of data to pursue improved instructional outcomes by monitoring performance and holding personnel accountable for results. It instituted a common curriculum and developed curriculum guides in core subjects. There was even a report in 2009 that identified early warning signs, based on the records of dropouts, to allow the district to do more to retain students in school. The Council of the Great City Schools gave approval to the school board's work in progress in a 141-page report issued in 2009. The report credited efforts up until that time for "substantial gains in student achievement." It stated, "The school district now has in place many of the components that one finds in some of the nation's most rapidly improving urban school districts."[2]

But the school system had by no means completed its task and the report reminded readers that in spite of its improvement, "the district remains below statewide averages on most academic measures."[3] Statistics gathered by *The Denver Post* newspaper at the end of 2009 showed that despite an improved graduation rate, only 52.7 percent of students got their diplomas on time. Moreover, even with an increase in college-going, 56 percent of Denver's high school graduates had to take remedial courses once they reached campus.[4] The school board could rightfully take a portion of the credit for the gains, but further academic progress might be in jeopardy without continued vigilance and commitment by a mostly united school board.

## Affecting What Gets Taught and How

Lodged firmly between the school board and the curriculum and books it approves are those empowered to convey that material—the teachers. They shut their classroom doors, pursue their work out of sight of other adults (even their colleagues), and determine what gets taught and how it happens. The classroom is sacred territory, normally restricted to students, their teacher, and a handful of others who make cameo appearances in support of the instructional program. Collective-bargaining contracts may place restrictions on the right of principals to observe teachers for purposes of evaluation. In many places, a principal must inform a teacher in advance and not just drop in unannounced to conduct such an observation.

Even board members may be barred from entering classrooms under normal circumstances, precluding the folks who oversee the school system from watching the lessons unfold. Board members are not expected to form opinions about how well or how poorly individual teachers perform. A board member seeking to visit a classroom to observe instruction can run into a closed door. Teacher union leaders in some districts contend that a board member—even one who has been employed in education—has no legal authority to watch teachers. Moreover, many teachers are understandably uneasy about having board of education members—their nominal employers—watch them carry out their work. Some board members may not care because they have no interest in seeing instruction and even if they did so they might lack the background to gain insights into what they observe.

Classroom instruction therefore may be invisible to members of school boards. This is amazing when you think about it. The various responsibilities of board members come together in the student-teacher relationship. Yet except for special occasions, board members in some districts have no first-hand knowledge of what transpires in this relationship. Schools may invite board members into classrooms for isolated events—the third-grade Halloween celebration, Poetry Day, Dr. Seuss's birthday, or a high school chemistry demonstration. Such staged occasions are hardly typical of the day-to-day instructional program, though.

All of this is not to say that school boards do not affect instruction. They have policy jurisdiction over a number of factors that impact on teaching and learning. With the aid of educators, board members may weigh policies for imparting the various subjects at each grade level. They can enunciate objectives. Then, relying on the testing program, measure progress and see if the schools reach the marks they have set. What counts most is whether students learn what the school board and community expect of them. A book aimed at the nation's school board members recommended, "You as a board member cannot control teaching through curriculum guides, training, supervision, evaluation, or any other device . . . All you have to do is control learning."[5] The policy-setting function of school boards gives them some authority in this regard.

*Framing the Right Policies*

School boards may set policies and reach bargaining agreements pertaining to the sizes of classes and of schools, the workloads of teachers, the availability and use of computers, and the point in the curriculum at which teachers present certain material. They have some leeway as to which subjects the schools offer in each grade. Notably, boards in some places have moved algebra down into the eighth grade from the ninth grade on the supposition that students will then be able to complete a more rigorous sequence of math courses in high school. Some educators regard algebra as a "gateway" course to higher achievement in all courses, believing that it trains the mind and inculcates good academic habits.

The state board of education in California in 2008 mandated algebra for all the state's eighth graders, not leaving the decision to local school boards. The debate over the California policy should remind members of local school boards throughout the country to exercise care in using their authority. Critics argued that many of California's eighth graders would not be ready for algebra and that schools would have to dilute courses to accommodate those students. Some studies, in fact, suggest that enrolling students in algebra earlier than usual may increase failure rates in such courses.[6] It is a controversy not unlike one involving school boards when they turn their attention to policies for admitting students to Advanced Placement courses that are supposed to offer college-level work. More than half of a sampling of Advanced Placement teachers said that "too many students overestimate their abilities and are in over their heads."[7]

School boards also may have a say in the number of hours in the school day and the number of school days in the academic year. Most states mandate the minimum number of days in the school year, often 180, but some school boards may choose to exceed the minimum. Their power over the clock and the calendar is something that school boards should take more seriously. Two researchers who looked at the effects of school closings due to snow days found that the lost instructional time led students to score lower on reading and math assessments than peers in other districts that did not lose as many days to closings. They estimated that more than half of schools failing to make adequate yearly progress in third grade under the No Child Left Behind law would have met the requirements if schools had been open on all the scheduled days.[8] This finding raises questions about whether school boards do enough to ensure that their districts devote sufficient time to instruction.

Admittedly, more time does not necessarily translate into more learning. One variable is how well teachers use the extra time. Students spend a great deal of their time in school on housekeeping activities—shutting down one task and getting ready for another. Furthermore, depending on the inclination of the student and how the teacher organizes instruction, what appears to be instructional time may actually be lost when students are bored, distracted, or disengaged.

A school board that aims to maximize the time available for learning has options in its policies. The process can begin with an investment in professional development that helps teachers get the most out of instructional time. It may continue with a policy calling for a program of summer assignments and mechanisms to support students during this lengthy vacation so that young minds remain involved with learning. Many school boards, though, limit their options by agreements they write into collective-bargaining contracts. As bargaining has evolved, school boards have, for example, surrendered some of their control over the length of the school day and the school year.

A notable way in which a school board could make more time available for learning at a crucial point in a child's development is by decisions affecting prekindergarten and kindergarten. It all depends on how much a school board is willing to spend and how much classroom space it has available. The federal government requires districts to offer prekindergarten to children eligible for special education, but a school board may also include regular education students in such classes. Furthermore, it may determine whether such children begin at age three or age four and whether the program operates for a half-day or a full day. These are all matters of policy.

A similar issue arises for a school board when it comes to kindergarten. Only 14 states require youngsters to attend kindergarten. Schools boards have considerable latitude in whether to make kindergarten a half-day or a full-day program. A school board that spends money on good prekindergarten and kindergarten programs will probably find that fewer students end up in special education, more read on grade level, fewer become subject to disciplinary measures, and ultimately, more continue through to their diplomas. This is an investment in instructional time that school boards must weigh against other possible uses of the same funds.

School boards, though, are not always free agents when it comes to decisions about kindergarten and many other matters affecting teaching and learning. Massachusetts was typical of many states when growing financial pressures in early 2009 forced school boards to consider whether they could afford to continue offering full-day kindergartens in a state that requires only a half-day. Three-quarters of the state's school systems voluntarily had full-day programs, in many instances charging parents fees for the extra half day.

Some school boards canceled plans to implement full-day programs and others enacted fees for the programs. "State financial assistance is at risk and inflationary costs for schools are higher than for some other areas," said Glenn Koocher, executive director of the Massachusetts Association of School Committees. "So, where does the school committee get money to fund full-day kindergarten?" He put some of the blame for the lack of adequate funding on the state for what he said were costly mandates, "It is a rancid regulatory climate that just keeps getting worse."

Class sizes, too, are supposedly within the control of school boards. It is a matter of hiring enough teachers and building enough classrooms to have fewer students per teacher. This is one area in which the teacher union would be glad to co-operate. The idea of more jobs for teachers and relieving some of their burdens appeals to teacher unions. More importantly, it can allow teachers to give more attention to each student. On the other hand, school boards can more readily hold expenses in check when they let class sizes increase and do nothing to reduce the sizes.

*English Language Learners*

High among the challenges facing school boards are those involving English language learners (ELL). More than 5 million youngsters, living in homes where usually little or no English is spoken, often struggle to make their way through a curriculum that may be incomprehensible to them. The federal government has declared that schools must serve such students, but largely leaves it to school boards to determine how to do so.

Unprecedented numbers of immigrants, both legal and illegal, flooded into the United States during the last generation. These newcomers, overwhelmingly from Central and South America, dispersed themselves into towns and cities across the country that formerly had few non-English-speaking residents. The number of Hispanic students in elementary and secondary schools doubled from 1990 to 2006, accounting for 60 percent of the growth in enrollment.[9] In Boston, of all places, Hispanics became the largest segment of the enrollment in 2009, accounting for 38.1 percent of the students and edging out African Americans.[10]

The number of ELL students is particularly large in such states as California (1,568,738), Texas (601,588), and New York (192,053). But some states once considered out-of-the-way locales for immigrants have also seen large influxes. There are, for example, 64,238 English language learners in Minnesota, 92,176 in North Carolina, and 63,740 in Oregon.[11] An irony of the situation is the fact that most of the children are American citizens, having been born in the United States to immigrant parents. Schools sit on the frontline in determining what shape democracy will take and whether these children will grow into adults fully able to participate in civic life and possessing the skills for gainful employment. The future of democracy in the United States depends on the outcome and on how well school boards respond to these challenges. In many ways, the federal government does not recognize the burdens that the schools carry as the lead agencies bearing this heavy responsibility.

School boards may choose between curricular approaches that stress either bilingual education or English as a Second Language (ESL). In the first instance, students begin their education mostly in their native tongue and gradually, usually over several years, transition into instruction that contains more and more English. ESL, on the other hand, involves special lessons in English to impart the language and teaches all the subjects in English, with the student's native language playing no role in instruction. School systems trying to figure out how to address the needs of these students must repeatedly test them to determine their command of English and place them at levels corresponding to their needs.

Even at this late date, unanswered questions remain about the methods that best serve English language learners. School boards do not have clear guidance about what to do and researchers still address these questions. *Education Week*, in a special issue on English language learners, put it this way, "What they have yet to nail down is how to help this vulnerable and challenging population of students over the learning hump that comes later in elementary school; how to teach higher-order reading skills, such as comprehension; how to teach adolescents who are new to English; and how to boost achievement in academic subjects other than English."[12]

Sometimes, for reasons having little to do with education research, school boards lose the right to make decisions about how best to deal with such students. In Massachusetts, for instance, voters approved a ballot initiative in 2002 banning transitional bilingual education in the schools. Afterward, the enrollment of students of limited English proficiency increased in special education from 15.3 to 19.5 percent and the high school dropout rate among such students grew from 6.3 to 12.1 percent.[13] In 2010, the federal government began a compliance review of ELL practices in the Boston public schools based on suspicions that the system was not properly serving the language needs of students from non-English-speaking backgrounds.

School boards across the country had to contend with No Child Left Behind regulations that required them to break out achievement data for students of limited English proficiency. Districts faced sanctions if students did not show adequate yearly progress. No matter how much success districts enjoy in moving students out of this subgroup, though, there will likely be new English language learners to replace them. Scores on the National Assessment of Education Progress serve as a reminder of the gaps between English language learners and other students.

## The School Board's Effect on Achievement

School boards, even with the limitations placed on them, have an awesome responsibility when it comes to student learning. Think about it: If the board of education blows it, kids may reach adulthood unequipped to function in society. Democracy itself is at stake. E. D. Hirsch Jr., who led an effort to get schools to help students master a common core of knowledge, said that such an attainment is "a prerequisite to something equally profound in a democracy—a sense of community and solidarity within the nation."[14]

I doubt that any school board deliberately shortchanges students on their learning, but some clearly are negligent. There are many ways in which a school board may stumble if it fails to see the obstacles in its path. A school board may not hire and tenure the best teachers. It may approve the appointments of principals who lack leadership qualities. It may expect too little of students. It may expect too much of students. It may not pay enough attention to individual schools where achievement lags. It may not do enough to engage parents in reinforcing learning. It may not buy appropriate textbooks. It may not build a culture of learning in all of its schools.

Some critics maintain that school boards are not sufficiently aware of trends in education and, lacking such information, neglect to take steps that could improve outcomes for students. Concern of this sort spurred Oklahoma's state board of education to direct the state superintendent to create formal channels to provide local school boards with data on dropout rates and the numbers of students who enroll in remedial courses at the college level. Official policy in Oklahoma now dictates that principals of secondary schools must review and discuss at a local school board meeting the annual certified dropout reports that the district has submitted to the State Department of Education. In addition, principals are to discuss with local school boards the college remediation rates, subject by subject, for their graduates. These data are collected by the Oklahoma Regents for Higher Education.

Such an approach may remind board members that some districts do not educate students to the fullest extent. Board members in these locales could benefit from such a reminder. More than 60 percent of students enrolling at the country's two-year colleges and 20 to 30 percent at four-year colleges take remedial courses.[15] These facts ought to embarrass school boards. Sometimes it is not within the purview of the school board to offer programs that deal with every student's needs and prepare more of them for college. But school board members who reflect deeply on this problem may support policies that lead to better guidance, implementation of work-study programs, stronger literacy instruction at the secondary level, and formal tutoring.

One night during the public comment session at a meeting of the school board on which I sat, a district resident came to the microphone and asked why one of our district's two high schools had a much higher rating than the other. He referred specifically to the rankings in *New Jersey Monthly* magazine, but the disparities in student achievement between the two schools were evident in other ways as well. One high school had 27 National Merit semifinalists, the most in the state that year, and the other had only two. The resident mentioned that the perceived differences played out in lower real estate values in the south end of town, served by the high school with lower scores.

The questioner was told that all the board could do was assure equal inputs for the two high schools—the same curriculum, teachers of similar quality, the same amount of money spent on programs, and the like. "The result," said the board spokesman, "is nothing we have control over and, therefore, is nothing we can fix."

I wondered to myself whether our school board or any other fulfills its responsibility if it doesn't try to exert control over educational outcomes and fails to address differences in achievement. These goals, for example, underlie the federal government's Title I and special education programs, which provide extra assistance for needy students. Granted that the lower-achieving high school served the side of town where households tend to have lower socioeconomic standing, but is that a reason for a school board to deny responsibility for boosting achievement? Experts agree that a school board's main role, after hiring the best superintendent available, is to govern and set policies in ways that maximize academic achievement for every pupil.

### When a Board Overlooks the Children

The Halifax County school board in northeastern North Carolina was one that clearly failed its students when it came to teaching and learning. Statistics showed in 2008 that only 31 percent of third graders, 32 percent of fourth graders, 22 percent of fifth graders, 28 percent of sixth graders, and 15 percent of seventh graders performed at or above the proficiency level in reading. Halifax County is a poor, mostly rural place where the school board seemed to accept lack of achievement as a way of life among its 4,500 students.

The situation grew so bad that by 2009 Superior Court Judge Howard Manning called it "academic genocide." The crux of his finding was the following, "Halifax County Public Schools children are suffering from a breakdown in system leadership, school leadership, and a breakdown in classroom instruction by and large from elementary school through high school."[16] Judge Manning called on state officials to "exercise command and control" over the public schools of Halifax County. The judge cited a landmark ruling by North Carolina's Supreme Court in 1997 that held that every child in the state was entitled to "a sound basic education."

An agreement that the school board was pressured into signing after the judge's condemnation allowed the state board of education, at the direction of Gov. Bev

Perdue, to intervene during the 2009 through 2010 school year. The plan called for three weeks of professional development for principals and central office personnel, two weeks of professional development for teachers, 12 full-time master educators to help teachers improve instruction, three school transformation coaches, a district transformation coach, and consultation with the state department of public instruction on use of federal and state appropriations. The school board stayed in place, met regularly, but had vastly reduced powers.

## *Getting It Right for Children*

The classic Lighthouse study by the Iowa Association of School Boards, mentioned earlier, found that members of boards that bolster education consistently express their belief that all children can learn, rejecting such excuses as poverty, lack of motivation, and lack of parental involvement. By contrast, boards in districts where achievement flounders are stuck in the status quo and have members who expect it to take years to see improvement in student achievement.[17] Board members everywhere would do well to see themselves as change agents, asking continually how the school system is doing and how it can perform better. Such a formula can benefit every school board, whatever the level of achievement and whatever the accomplishments.

When the state legislature in Georgia was prompted in 2009 to draft a statute after the school board in Clayton County had utterly neglected its duties and achievement languished for years in the district of more than 50,000 students, the act stated, "The motivation to serve as a member of a local board of education should be the improvement of schools and academic achievement of all students."[18]

It is more difficult to boost achievement once students reach high school, but school boards may take steps earlier to influence outcomes at the end of the process. A school board may decide, for example, to offer preschool to children who will reap the greatest benefits. It can collaborate with parents to enrich out-of-school experiences. It can bolster literacy instruction in the early grades. It can staff the neediest schools with excellent veteran teachers, not newcomers. It can provide better professional development.

Every student won't be a top achiever by high school, but chances are that attainment will rise. Rather than take the position that school boards have no control over outcomes, it might be more accurate to say that a board has the ability to set priorities. No school board ought to accept the proposition that demography predetermines outcome. It is the duty of each school board member to do all possible to lift every student out of mediocrity. School boards can have more effect on achievement than many people think. Boards that choose to get involved in improving student outcomes may through their policy-setting role use the testing that state and federal authorities require to highlight needs and to marshal the needed resources.

"Advocates and practitioners of standards-based reform must become more proactive in understanding school boards' crucial role," urged Michael D. Usdan, the former president of the Institute for Educational Leadership. "A persuasive argument can be made that . . . comprehensive school reform will only succeed if it is predicated upon a sustained, co-operative, trusting relationship among parents, school and district staff, and the school board."[19] Sometimes, though, co-operation and trust are in short supply among school board members when it comes to judgments about school reform.

### The Math Wars in Ridgewood, New Jersey

Controversies involving teaching and learning can erupt when school boards least expect them. This happened in Ridgewood, New Jersey, an upscale suburb of towering trees and expensive homes, in the middle of the first decade of the 2000s. In Ridgewood, a village of some 25,000 souls, they called it "the math wars." What occurred was a rather bellicose affair for a place where the excellent music program that begins in the third grade culminates in high school with three symphony bands, two jazz bands, and various vocal opportunities. The board of education was attacked and forced to defend the mathematics textbooks students used in several of the elementary schools, where educators had more or less taken it upon themselves to introduce a hands-on math curriculum.

Critics charged that the books were not sufficiently demanding and that the books encouraged a "constructivist" approach that did not imbue students with the fundamentals. Some parents who raised questions about the math program claimed they were patronized by teachers who told them that the issue was one for professionals to decide. A campaign against the school board was conducted via the Internet, at board meetings, through letters to the editor of the local weekly newspaper, and even by innuendoes against the board president and his family. The Internet helped foes of the math textbooks spread their concern and sustain their campaign. A site entitled The Ridgewood Blog continually attacked the "reform math" that critics said undermined learning. An Internet site created by the Concerned Parents' Math Committee solicited signatures for an online petition to restore the "tradition of excellence in K-8 Math Education in Ridgewood."

"They were telling falsehoods to make it appear more widespread than it was," Mark Bombace, the president of the school board at the time, said afterward about the petition drive and the contention that the disputed program was used throughout the school system. "The board had known that scores were lagging at Travell [one of the elementary schools that used the disputed textbooks]. We were surprised that this went beyond a few local parents."

The controversy accelerated during the 2006 through 2007 school year, which the superintendent said would be his last before retiring. The turmoil over the math textbooks reached the point that some parents told their children not to do homework because the parents didn't approve of the methods in the books. So, some teachers began to provide one kind of instruction in the schools while sending home traditional homework. Meanwhile, the board carried out a search to replace the superintendent.

Once the board selected a successor, critics of the math textbooks delved into his background and posted critiques on the Internet. They asserted that his history as a superintendent in Long Island, New York, indicated that the prospective superintendent would likely be a math reformer. They sent him letters and made phone calls imploring him to reject the job. A reception scheduled by the school board in June to introduce the new superintendent to Ridgewood was unexpectedly canceled, just weeks before he was to assume the post. Bombace explained that the man had withdrawn. The school board, which had spent $20,000 on the search, now resorted to appointing an interim superintendent.

Controversy continued to enmesh Ridgewood during the 2007 through 2008 school year. Bombace told me that he allowed himself to become a lightning rod for the attacks to spare his fellow board members some of the grief, helping to keep the board unified in the face of the criticism. He later looked back on the situation with relief over the fact that Ridgewood has only five members on its board of education, which he said made it easier to close ranks than if the board had seven or nine members and more possibilities for disagreement. In January 2008, Bombace presided over a special meeting of the school board featuring an open discussion of the math program. Principals of Ridgewood's various schools explained the history of math instruction in the district, described the balance between traditional math lessons and newer methods, and discussed the thinking skills students need in math to prosper in a future of global competition.

Six months later, by the end of the school year, Bombace, a captain in the village's fire department, had not run for reelection to the school board and a new superintendent, Daniel Fishbein, was chosen. Fishbein, superintendent of a smaller but similarly advantaged New Jersey district, was a Ridgewood resident with five children in the district's public schools, affording him a perch from which to observe the controversy as an uninvolved parent.

To place the brouhaha in Ridgewood in context, it is worth noting that during the 2007 through 2008 school year, more than half of the students at five of the district's six elementary schools scored at the *advanced* proficiency level on the state mathematics assessment and at the sixth school, Travell, 48.5 percent reached this exalted level. By comparison, 35.4 percent of the elementary students in New Jersey attained advanced proficiency. Furthermore, *New Jersey Monthly* magazine rated Ridgewood High as the seventh best high school in the state in its annual ranking.

During Fishbein's first year as superintendent, a process led by a planning team went forward to find a new textbook series to replace the three different series used in the six elementary schools. The district held two large meetings for teachers and parents in the fall of 2008. The planning team read research, solicited input from experts, and listened to testimony from textbook vendors. The team whittled the choice down to four math textbook series and then made the books available for public inspection. Most of those who bothered to examine the textbooks were apparently teachers, not parents.

Finally, the team selected the series favored by the teachers, not a Singapore math approach that was the first choice of parents. The team asserted that its choice offered balanced skills, concepts, and problem-solving and that it provided resources for enrichment and additional practice in each lesson for all levels of learners. When the school board accepted the recommendation near the close of the school year in 2009, only a smattering of parents attended the meeting. At least one voiced support for the choice, at least one opposed it, and another just asked some questions. It looked like the math wars were depleted of ammunition. But appearances are not always what they seem. Ten days after the board approved the new math series, The Ridgewood Blog criticized the research behind the books and said that the school board had been insufficiently curious about the cost of implementing the new program. There was reason for the school board to remain vigilant.

### When Curricular Controversies Erupt

Issues of faith or morality often figure in curricular disputes. Some school board members have no compunction about delving into the curriculum when social issues are at stake. Evolution offers the best example in this respect, with school boards throughout the twentieth century and into the twenty-first century trying to dictate what students should learn about human origins. Almost 100 years ago, Americans were held rapt by the Scopes "monkey trial" in Tennessee that pitted two of the country's most prominent citizens against each other as counsels to the opposing sides. William Jennings Bryan, former Presidential candidate, argued that science teacher John Scopes degraded human beings and denied God by telling students that they were descended from apes. Clarence Darrow, the lawyer known for representing unpopular causes, took the position that students should have benefit of modern scientific findings. This is the battle without end.

Critics of evolution tried more recently to give their approach a scientific aura by labeling it "intelligent design." They hoped this euphemism would win approval from the courts. Board members of the Dover Area School District in Pennsylvania, for instance, ordered ninth-grade science teachers to read aloud a statement offering an alternative explanation called intelligent design for the origin of life when they spoke of evolution. A federal court declared in 2005 that the school board's action had violated the First Amendment of the U.S. Constitution. The eight board members who issued the mandate were defeated in their effort to win reelection by candidates who denounced the requirement.

The State Board of Education in Texas, facing somewhat similar pressures in 2009, voted 13-2 to abandon a mandate that called for science teachers to present the strengths and weaknesses of scientific theories of evolution. Ultimately, a compromise ordered teachers to offer students a variety of scientific theories on human origins. Advocates of the teaching of evolution viewed the change as making instruction less favorable to creationism than it had been, but still worried that it called evolution into question. The standoff is an uneasy one that affects books and curriculums. School boards get caught in the middle, especially when directives from the state level compel them to act in one way or another. Louisiana exemplified this challenge when it enacted a law in 2008 permitting teachers to use supplemental textbooks to enable students to critique scientific theories of evolution.

Evolution is not the only controversial area in the curriculum. Some school boards have insinuated themselves into instructional areas by outlawing books when they do not approve of the language or the subject matter. The Newman Crows Landing Board of Education in rural California dropped *Bless Me, Ultima*, a Chicano coming-of-age novel, from a required reading list in 2009. It was an echo of an earlier intervention on the other side of the country. The board of Community School District 25 in the heart of New York City's Borough of Queens banned *Down These Mean Streets*, a coming-of-age autobiography of a Puerto Rican, a generation earlier. I covered that story for *The New York Times*. In both instances, the language was just too raw and offended school boards that seemed to believe they acted in behalf of their local communities.

One of the nation's most notorious incidents of this sort, involving a school board's selection of textbooks and supplementary reading materials, arose in West Virginia's Kanawha County Public Schools. The dispute spanned almost the entire calendar year of 1974. The school board routinely adopted the books and materials for the English language arts courses at a March meeting. A dissenter on the five-member board took steps to make the public aware of the content of the books and materials, which few people had bothered to examine while they were available for inspection at the county public library before the board's adoption.

Soon, 12,000 people signed a petition opposing the books, which they said provided negative depictions of family life, religious belief, and the American political and economic systems. The board agreed to set up a public committee to provide input on the future selection of schoolbooks. This response proved insufficient in a county in which cultural sensitivities were sharply divided between the urban population of Charleston and residents of the rural hollows east of the city. Religious fundamentalism, patriotism, and long-standing feelings of powerlessness among the poorer eastern part of Kanawha County fueled the dispute.

Unrest simmered throughout the summer of 1974 and by fall a clerical group denounced the reading list. On September 4, more than 3,000 miners walked off their jobs in sympathy with opponents of the books. Protests and boycotts escalated, finally turning violent. The board closed schools for a week in mid-September, hoping to defuse the anger of people who felt that their views had been ignored. The board even voted to withhold the books, pending review by a citizens' committee. In October, the president of the board of education resigned and in November officials issued arrest warrants for the superintendent and three board members, charging them with contributing to the delinquency of minors by authorizing the use of un-American and un-Christian books. The board capitulated to the protesters before the end of December, agreeing to return the books to the publishers and setting new procedures for textbook adoptions.

School boards are by no means the only entities that become parties to such disputes. Teachers, principals, librarians, and superintendents probably banish books more often than school boards do. It's just that such incidents have larger consequence when they involve school boards. The irony is that board members ordinarily do not seem to care all that much about the many books that they adopt almost without comment, scarcely giving a thought to what they contain and how they will influence children.

# Chapter 3

# Expenditures

## Huge and Uneven

How many other enterprises in the United States have annual budgets of more than $560 billion? Boards of education are in a class by themselves and few citizens seem aware that these entities—controlled by a handful of their neighbors—oversee so much money. Many people don't realize as they pay their local taxes that the greatest portion of the bill underwrites the public schools. It matters not whether a household uses those schools or ever used the schools.

School boards in 34 states are independent, developing their own budgets and levying taxes to support those budgets. In nine states school boards depend on another level of government, typically a municipality or county, to levy taxes, and school boards in these states may or may not have power over their budgets. Thirty-five states have caps on taxes and 12 states have caps on spending,[1] thereby restricting the financial latitude of school boards. Thus, a crazy quilt of arrangements blankets the nation's school districts and creates differences among school boards in the authority they exercise over budgets and taxes.

School expenditures in most localities end up as the only public outlays on which citizens may vote. Perhaps this makes the schools a more democratic undertaking than other areas that consume tax dollars. Americans cast ballots to determine who represents them in Congress, but have no direct say on spending for defense, Social Security, welfare, or unemployment benefits. They vote for members of the state legislature and cannot determine how those lawmakers spend money for, say, prisons or highways.

However, citizens in most locales can approve or reject the budget that their school board proposes. For this reason, school taxes are different from other taxes. The vast squandering of tens of billions of dollars by the federal government hardly reaches the consciousness of the average taxpayer, who has had no say in that spending. The very same taxpayer may bellyache, though, about $5,000 earmarked in the local school budget to send fifth-graders to an overnight, outdoor nature activity.

Worst of all, local property wealth deeply impacts the funds available for elementary and secondary education. School boards must contend with the fact that the same tax rate will not produce identical amounts of money for public schools from district to district. Almost two generations of lawsuits against these inequities have barely made a difference in the way that states fund education. Inequality in public education in the United States is rooted in a long history of differences in the resources marshaled for individual students.

The direst fiscal conditions since the Great Depression exacerbated the situation during the final years of the first decade of the twenty-first century. School boards serving all sorts of schools, from those in poor inner cities to those in advantaged suburbs, struggled to balance budgets without undermining support for student achievement. Some boards faced the loss of property tax revenues as homes went into foreclosure and businesses collapsed. Taxpayers everywhere, enduring personal financial pressures, resisted property tax increases. Meanwhile, multiyear contracts with teachers and other employees mandated outlays that school boards could ill afford.

School systems felt the impact in ways large and small. The school board in Los Angeles voted by a four to three margin to lay off thousands of teachers and other boards asked some employees to accept pay furloughs. Montgomery County, Maryland, asked teachers to forgo scheduled raises. Class sizes rose in some districts as boards hired fewer new teachers. Advanced Placement courses were threatened in Orange County, Florida. The state superintendent in South Carolina raised the prospect of four-day school weeks to save money on operations. Washington, DC, accumulated unpaid bills for textbooks and custodial supplies dating back three years.

In districts across the land, school boards looked at libraries and athletics as budgetary lines from which to squeeze savings. Charges for school lunches increased, some field trips became virtual, and school officials asked parents to provide more of the supplies for their children. Fiscal shortages manifested themselves even in television drama as the fictional Dillon High School of "Friday Night Lights" endured a struggle over whether to spend money on new textbooks or on an elaborate new scoreboard for its highly touted football team.

Congress, riding to the rescue like the white-hatted cowboy in an old-time Western, funneled billions of dollars in stimulus money into the states, with the public schools among the beneficiaries. School boards in some districts used these funds to avoid laying off teachers. The school board on which I sat spent stimulus dollars to help compensate for money cut from our budget by the state education commissioner after taxpayers rejected our budget. For all school boards, no matter how they used stimulus funds, the aid was stop gap and could not be counted on as a permanent source of sustenance to feed hungry budgets. School boards were up against the wall in 2009 and 2010 as they viewed future financial commitments.

## Scant Relief for the Neediest Students

Given these fiscal pressures, the American dream remains a distant mirage for some students. They attend classes in shabby buildings lacking proper facilities and have teachers who may not be equipped to offer them a quality education. The courses carry familiar titles, but they are as empty of content as a cherry pie in which someone has neglected to include the fruit. How strange it is that one country allows such variations in the education of its young! And often, there is little that an individual school board can do to rectify the situation.

Some students start behind and trail forever, even if they ultimately receive diplomas, which may be largely worthless documents. These students get a truncated form of education, leaving them unprepared for higher education or for the world of work. The inequities, having a corrosive effect, tend to reflect class, race, ethnicity, and geography. They militate against success in college and, ultimately, diminish adult opportunities. The impact extends beyond the individual. Society pays the price in costs for welfare, the justice system, and lost tax revenues.

Even life expectancy is affected, with poorer Americans, inevitably the less educated, living shorter lives than those who are more affluent.[2] Members of local school boards in poor communities sit at the nexus of these woes, chastened by the realization that their options for serving the children are severely limited. As they struggle with debilitating fiscal issues, these school boards must try to fend off the toll that poverty, crime, family dysfunction, and the lack of constructive role models take in children's education.

"Geography Matters: Child Well-Being in the States," a report that documents these failures, uses 11 indicators of child well-being to record the condition of youngsters state-by-state. A child fortunate enough to be born in Vermont, New Hampshire, Massachusetts, Minnesota, or Washington—the five highest-ranking states—is more likely to benefit from prenatal care, less likely to be poor, and less likely to die in childhood, for example, than in Texas, Oklahoma, New Mexico, Mississippi, or Louisiana—the five lowest-ranking states. "The state they live in should not adversely influence the life and death of children—but it does. Such inequalities affect all Americans, rich and poor alike, and weaken both our economy and our democracy," the report said.[3]

Educational inequities destroy human potential. Consider the fact that one of every 100 adults in the United States was in prison during 2007. The figure, the highest rate of incarceration in the world, was greatest for groups that get the worst education—one in 15 adult black men and one in 36 adult Latino men. Studies show that the prison population suffers from higher rates of illiteracy than the general population, a not inconsiderable factor in their turning to unlawful behavior. The states spent $44 billion in tax dollars on corrections in 2007.[4]

The link between bad education and troubled lives is inextricable. Tom Carroll, president of the National Commission on Teaching and America's Future, identified a relationship between expenditures for prisons and those for education. "States and localities that are attempting to control crime by spending more on prisons would be better off spending more on schools," he said. "Texas, California, and Florida, for example, hold the highest state prison populations, while at the same time they fall below the national average on providing opportunities for educational success."[5]

*Within States, Across States*

For a generation, much of the attention given to educational inequity has focused on funding disparities within states, instances in which one school system might spend two or three times as much on each student as a neighboring district. Essentially, these gaps reflect differences in property wealth. Geography is destiny in education—property wealth can vary greatly from district to district. These differences limit the ability of school boards to improve the lot of their students.

"In many states, where you live is what you get," stated an article in an academic journal. It continued, "When we have a public education system where, quite literally, people with enough money move to a community where their children will get the best education, we create incredible gaps in achievement among students throughout the nation—especially minority and low-income students."[6] Robert H. Frank, a Cornell University economist, maintained that a reason housing prices soared before the bubble burst was that "the best schools are in the most expensive neighborhoods."[7] Some parents, for the sake of their children, were moving to school districts they couldn't afford.

The states with the highest average expenditures tend to have some of the greatest spending disparities among their districts. This happens because some of these wealthy states have large numbers of school systems, some of which are rather small.[8] One way to make spending throughout a state more equal is to make the state one large school district, a step that only Hawaii has taken. A move in this direction is the creation of such county-wide school districts as exist in Florida, North Carolina, and Maryland. In general, the fewer school districts into which a state is divided, the narrower the range of spending among districts.[9] Many states have funding formulas for public schools that attempt to overcome some of the disadvantages for schoolchildren in poorer districts. Seldom, though, do these formulas produce equity, as school board members in these locales very well know.

Three interrelated factors—capacity, willingness, and effort—shape the future for schoolchildren in the United States. Financial support for students is, essentially, left to serendipity. School boards in some districts of limited wealth simply lack the capacity to do more for their elementary and secondary pupils unless they put a tremendous burden on their taxpayers, a step that many boards are loath to take. Children who happen to live in these places are put at great disadvantage. The capacity to spend is, of course, greatest in districts with the most property wealth per child. The willingness of citizens to tax themselves determines how readily they will make use of the district's property wealth. Effort figures into the equation when citizens in a less wealthy school system tax themselves more heavily than those in a wealthier district in order, for instance, to produce the same amount of money.

Spending disparities among states, while less discussed, are no less consequential. One researcher, law professor Goodwin Liu, found that "disparities between states account for more of the variation in district per-pupil spending nationally than do disparities within states,"[10] and that even eliminating disparities within states would not achieve equality because "the enormous disparities across states would remain."[11] During the 2005 through 2006 school year, for example, when the average expenditure in the school systems of the United States was $10,615 per pupil, some states were well above this figure and others were well below. New Jersey ($16,587), New York ($15,837), and Connecticut ($15,219) were at the top and Utah ($6,629), Idaho ($7,343), and Oklahoma ($7,623) were at the bottom.[12]

The dramatic effects of this pernicious pattern can be seen in the fact that the highest-spending school districts in some states do not spend as much as the lowest-spending districts in some other states. Not counting the outliers—the 5 percent of districts at either end of the spectrum in each state that spend the most and least money—per-student revenues in Mississippi's highest-revenue district, for instance, were lower than the per-student revenues in the lowest-revenue districts in 24 other states. While Mississippi's plight was the worst, a similar pattern existed in such states as Oklahoma, Alabama, and Idaho, where the highest-revenue districts per-student were exceeded by the lowest-revenue districts, respectively, in 16, 13, and 9 states.[13]

### The Stubborn Persistence of Inequities

Education Trust, an advocacy group for equity in education, found in its annual analysis of spending on elementary and secondary education that equity *decreased* in 16 states between 1999 and 2005. This finding came from comparing the resources of school districts serving the highest percentages of low-income students and students of color with districts serving the lowest percentage of such students.[14]

Attempts by school boards to address differences are not wholly effective. When the federal government started to aid the public schools in a substantial way with Title I of the federal government's Elementary and Secondary Education Act, it provided supplemental funds for the education of impoverished children. This program, authorized by Congress as an extension of President Lyndon B. Johnson's War on Poverty in 1965, continues to this day. Many people assume that Title I helped to overcome funding inequities, but this has not entirely been the case.

The allocation formula enabled Title I to reduce educational inequality within states, but not across states. This occurred because, in part, the formula provided more per-pupil aid to states that already spent more on each student. For instance, Arkansas had 1.6 percent of the nation's impoverished schoolchildren in 2001 but got only 1 percent of Washington's Title I allocation. Texas had 11.9 percent of the poor schoolchildren but got only 8.5 percent of the money. Meanwhile, looking at two high-spending states, Massachusetts had 1.5 percent and Pennsylvania had 3.2 percent of the country's poor schoolchildren and received, respectively, 2.2 and 4.2 percent of the funds.[15]

Rachel B. Tompkins, president of the Rural School and Community Trust, made a similar point: "For the past six years, two of the four formulas used to distribute federal Title I funds have systematically discriminated against small, high-poverty school districts. These formulas use student weighting schemes intended to direct more funding to districts with the highest concentrations of Title I students, but they allow two alternative methods of weighting . . . Small districts never benefit from number weighting."[16]

*Uneven Outcomes*

Another way to reflect on inequities, rather than focusing on finances, calls for looking at outcomes for students. One of the best measures of achievement is the federal government's National Assessment of Education (NAEP), which the U.S. Department of Education calls "the nation's report card." Children in some states, most of which have low per-pupil spending, achieve only modest scores on NAEP tests.

Fourth-graders in 2007 ranked highest in reading (in descending order) in Massachusetts, New Jersey, New Hampshire, Vermont, and Virginia—all above the national average in per-pupil spending. The lowest scores, from the bottom up, were in Louisiana, Mississippi, California, Arizona, and Nevada—all below the national average in spending. In mathematics, fourth-graders scored highest (in descending order) in Massachusetts, New Jersey, New Hampshire, Kansas, and Minnesota—all above the national average in per-pupil expenditures. The lowest scores, from bottom up, were in Mississippi, New Mexico, Alabama, California, and Louisiana—all below the national average.

One has only to examine high school graduation rates to see how much difference locale makes in outcomes. While urban high schools may graduate little more than half of their students, high schools in suburbs—just over the city line—may award diplomas to at least 80 percent of their students. "The fact that just half of those educated in America's largest cities are finishing high school truly raises cause for alarm," stated a report on graduation rates. "And the much higher rates of high school completion among their suburban counterparts—who may literally live and attend school right around the corner—place in a particularly harsh and unflattering light the deep undercurrents of inequity that plague American public education."[17]

The educational terrain of the United States is pockmarked with achievement gaps. Policymakers and school board members find it easier to maneuver around those gaps than to stop and try to close them. Test scores attest to the chasms that separate groups of students. There are gaps between racial and ethnic groups, between rich and poor students, between city dwellers and those in suburbs, and among geographic areas of the country. School finances often are a major factor figuring in these differences. The No Child Left Behind law forced schools to focus on achievement gaps by requiring them to disaggregate test results so as to reveal differences among racial and ethnic groups, as well as among disabled students and English language learners.

### Money Makes a Difference

Money makes a difference or else school boards serving high-achieving school systems wouldn't spend as much as they do. Lack of money contributes to achievement gaps when some students have highly qualified teachers and others do not. Often, the students with the greatest needs get the least experienced teachers, sometimes as a result of collective-bargaining contracts that give veteran teachers preference in choosing where to work. Money matters when some schools have better instructional materials and more access to information technology than others. James B. Hunt Jr., a North Carolina Democrat, and Thomas H. Kean, a New Jersey Republican—both former governors—asserted that hiring highly qualified teachers and retaining them is a key to improving schools in some of the most difficult settings. "Hiring in hard-to-staff schools is a revolving door," they wrote. "High-poverty urban schools lose about twice as many teachers each year as low-poverty schools."[18]

Sarah Saxton-Frump grew up in the prosperous New Jersey suburb of Summit, attended a private school, and earned her Ivy League degree at Brown University. Then, when she joined Teach for America and was sent to teach social studies at a high school in Brownsville, Texas, she had her epiphany. She might as well have ventured to a distant planet. She discovered the connection between poverty and inferior education. "For 60 percent of them," Saxton-Frump wrote of her ninth-graders, "English is not their first language. If nothing changes, half of them will drop out of high school by the time they're 18. The students who do graduate will likely perform at an eighth-grade level. I suspect only 35 of my 148 students will go on to college; maybe five will leave Brownsville."[19]

Good intentions of school board members are no substitute for sufficient funds to hire qualified teachers and to keep classes small enough for them to make a difference. Richard M. Nixon recognized this imperative and sought to do something about it more than a generation ago. He appointed a commission on school finance that issued a report in 1972 urging the federal government to help the states wipe out funding imbalances. The administration considered imposing a new national tax to yield enough money for Washington to assume as much as a quarter of the cost of local education. But soon afterward, President Nixon had to shift his focus to the growing scandal over a break-in at an office building and had little time or energy to devote to educational matters. Succeeding administrations never glanced at the prospects with which Nixon had flirted.

On the other hand, while equity in funding is a laudable goal, inputs, however lavish, do not guarantee outputs. Equality of opportunity remains problematic when school boards in some places spend money ineffectually. Some districts with the lowest achievement also are the most dysfunctional when it comes to using resources wisely. Their ills are systemic, and strategies to help them operate more efficiently and more productively ought to accompany any additional infusions of aid. A report on the world's best performing school systems by McKinsey & Company, a consulting firm, concluded that the most important features in those places were getting the right people to become teachers, developing them into effective instructors, and ensuring that the system is able to deliver the best possible instruction for every child.[20] School boards should play a role in this process.

The urgency of the situation is underscored by projections showing that youngsters of racial and ethnic minority backgrounds, who tend to be the least affluent Americans, will soon make up a majority of high school students in a number of states. About 40 percent of those under the age of 18 in the United States are members of these groups. In a trend that began with the high school graduating class of 2005 and will continue through the class of 2015, there will be an increase of 54 percent in Hispanic graduates, 32 percent in Asian/Pacific Islanders, 3 percent in blacks, and 7 percent in Native Americans. Meanwhile, the number of white non-Latinos receiving diplomas will decline by 11 percent. A report setting out these data calls on schools and postsecondary institutions to reach out more assertively to serve these students.[21] Underscoring the changes and their implications for education was the estimate that some time in 2010 non-Hispanic white women would for the first time account for a minority of all births in the United States.[22]

### Spending More Effectively

School boards both sustain and are victims of an ineffective system of school finance that makes it difficult to trace the impact of spending, especially at the classroom level. It is a system not of the making of school boards, but they stick to a conventional path that may not redound to the best advantage of the students they serve. School boards oversee budgets, year after year, with little knowledge of the cost effectiveness of their spending. Both the most hard-pressed districts and the wealthi-est would gain if school board members had more business acumen.

Look at the budget if you want to know where a school board places its val-ues. It expresses in dollars and cents the priorities of board members about what counts most to them. In many districts, the board devotes a growing portion of the budget—as much as $4 of every $5—to the salaries and benefits of staff. It is good to treat educators and other employees well, but it means less for other pursuits. The days of school boards paying penurious salaries to their educators are long gone in many parts of the country, though the public does not always realize the extent of the improvement in the pay and benefits of teachers. "They think that teachers earn, on average, far less than is actually the case," wrote the authors of one study. As a matter of fact, when respondents to a survey found out how much school districts actually spend on their pupils they were less inclined to support increases, though half of those surveyed nonetheless continued to back higher school spending.[23]

The classroom figures first and foremost in the thoughts of most school board members, but they have to get students to those classrooms and that accounts for a portion of the spending. The coat of yellow paint that became the standard in 1939 marks the ubiquitous presence of school buses on roads and highways across the United States, a fact of life that causes many a morning and afternoon traffic jam in towns large and small. Pupil transportation is a $17.5-billion-a-year item for the nation's school boards, averaging $692 per student transported.[24]

The cost of vehicles, maintenance, and personnel has a place in the transporta-tion budgets of almost all school systems. Most districts buy their own buses and hire their own drivers, but private companies under contracts provide about one-third of the transportation, mostly to larger districts. Altogether, some 55 percent of elementary and secondary schoolchildren ride to school in these vehicles, some youngsters in rural regions traveling dozens of miles each day. With big money at stake in the school-busing business, criminality is an ever-present threat that may be invisible to most school board members. In New York City, for instance, nine companies were identified in 2009 in a federal investigation as having paid bribes that allegedly led officials to overlook safety violations and falsified billing.

Sixty percent of the states mandate that districts provide pupil transporta-tion, often specifying the distance that a pupil must live from school to be entitled to service. In turn, all but five states help local school boards pay the expense, but—whether from local funds or state coffers—the money originates with the taxpayers. School boards each year must devise budgets that absorb rises in fuel costs, increases in salaries and benefits for drivers, and higher prices for vehicles. In most locales, school boards provide buses even for students attending nonpublic schools as a result of federal court decisions. About a half-million school buses travel some 4 billion miles a year carrying America's students to and from school. Among the occasional nightmares for school board members are the bus that has an accident, the bus that gets lost, the bus on which bullies intimidate students, and the bus on which a driver or attendant molests a child.

Food, too, figures into the budgetary concerns of school boards. In most districts, school boards provide not only meals for students but also dining and storage facilities, kitchens or preparation areas, and a staff to get food ready and then to clean up afterward. The U.S. Department of Agriculture (USDA) is the big player in this endeavor, reimbursing school boards—according to federal statistics—to the tune of $9.3 billion a year for providing 5.2 billion lunches to 31 million youngsters of elementary and secondary age. In addition, USDA gives schools $1 billion annually of surplus food, approximately 15 to 20 percent of what schoolchildren consume. *USA Today* charged in December 2009 that millions of pounds of the beef and chicken that schools receive from the USDA wouldn't meet the standards of fast-food restaurants. The federal government promised to investigate the allegations.[25]

President Harry S. Truman signed the law establishing the National School Lunch Program (NSLP) in 1946, and it has grown and thrived since then, just like the hundreds of millions of students who have benefited from it. An effort to ensure adequate nutrition for even the country's poorest children is a cornerstone of the program, which provides free lunches to those from the lowest-income families—up to 130 percent of the poverty level—and reduced-price lunches to children from families with incomes up to 185 percent of the poverty level. Districts that participate in NSLP may charge up to about $3 for lunches served to children who don't qualify for the federal subsidy and then collect a reimbursement of 25 cents for each meal served to such students. The law does not allow participating districts to make a profit on the program.

Students from families in such programs as the Supplementary Nutritional Assistance Program (formerly called Food Stamps) and Temporary Assistance for Needy Families (TANF) receive automatic enrollment in the school lunch program through direct certification. Other families fill out applications on which they self-report their income. The law permits school districts to audit 3,000 or 3 percent of applications, whichever is smaller, and to request such documentation as pay stubs. Thirty percent of the audited applications for subsidized lunches during the 2007 through 2008 school year could not be verified because families did not respond to the requests,[26] a fact that raises questions about the eligibility of some of the 97 percent of unaudited participants.

The business side of a school board's operations may not be as important as the academic side, but teaching and learning cannot thrive without a solid and sustainable fiscal base. Education is a business. And it is up to school boards to pay as much attention to that side of their activities as to the instructional side. School boards that serve the largest districts spend the most money. Thus, it was encouraging that the Council of the Great City Schools, a Washington-based group comprising 67 of the country's biggest school systems, carried out a multiyear effort to help its member districts improve their business practices.

The council's Performance Measurement and Benchmarking Project dealt first with the development of detailed analyses and key indicators that pertain to transportation, food services, maintenance and operations, and procurement. The goal was to develop measures for financial management and general accounting for these areas. The work later extended to business operations, finance, human resources, and information technology. It was the first time that the group developed such indicators for school districts and collected relevant data from the nation's urban public schools, according to the council. It became possible, for instance, to say of big-city systems that, on average, the districts transported students at a median cost of $988 per child—more than the national average—or that the average custodial workload was 23,501 square feet and the cost of maintenance and operations per square foot was $3.22.[27]

It is not unusual for men and women to join school boards with a professed interest in holding down the growth in taxes. Given that intent, they should evince a concern with the business side of their school systems and not leave these matters almost exclusively to the business administrator and the superintendent. Fiscal data are of such magnitude and complexity that school board members could make important contributions if they had a better grasp of the business side of their responsibilities.

### Linking Outlays to Outcomes

School boards bear only part of the blame for the lack of precision in their spending habits. In most cases, they follow formulas laid down by state officials who may know even less about what public schools get for their money than members of school boards. Statutes and regulations from the state may dictate staffing levels, class size limitations, and certification requirements for employees, as well as hours, days, and months that school must devote to various learning tasks. "State leaders have a fundamental choice to make," said one of the most important reports yet on school finance, "whether to continue tying funds to administrative structures, employee groups, and programs or to give schools money in ways that allow experimentation and continuous learning about what is possible given many alternative uses of funds and what works in different situations."[28]

This six-year school finance study by 40 experts, underwritten by the Bill and Melinda Gates Foundation, set down these four recommendations for school spending linked to the constant improvement of students:

- Driving funds to schools based on student counts, perhaps weighted with extra funds for disadvantaged students, so that the principal is responsible for managing and allocating money within the building

- Linking data about uses of funds to student outcomes so that alternative methods of delivering instruction can be compared on the basis of costs and effectiveness
- Encouraging innovation and experimentation with funds, based on what works and what does not
- Holding schools and districts accountable for student performance and continuous improvement. The central office should be able to analyze outcomes and find or develop more productive methods, staff, and school providers.[29]

"Money is used so loosely in public education—in ways that few understand and that lack plausible connections to student learning—that no one can say how much money, if used optimally, would be enough," the study concluded. It called for more transparency in expenditures and more analysis to link student characteristics, teacher attributes, instruction, costs, and student results.[30]

This means that school boards should, paradoxically, have both more and less control over their funds. They should have greater latitude for drawing up budgets and allocating monies to individual schools based on student performance. At the same time, they should be constrained from using instructional funds in ways that do not demonstrate sufficient cognizance of performance and cost benefit analysis. A small minority of school boards already operate in this manner, by design or by accident. The vast majority of school boards, though, continue to cling to tradition when it comes to how they spend the taxpayers' money.

Marguerite Roza, a member of the team of scholars that prepared the report on school finance that I just described, argued that typically school districts do not trace the money into the classroom. She said doing so—at the high school level, for instance—would enable districts to identify relationships among priorities, spending, and outcomes; clarify relative spending on discrete services and the organizational practices that influence the deployment of resources; and establish the cost of high school services as a necessary precursor to identifying whether there are better ways to provide some services."[31] When school board members make decisions about high school courses, which generally are more expensive than instruction at the lower grades, it would be desirable, for instance, to have authoritative knowledge about what courses cost most and why. This does not mean that boards should abandon such courses when budgets tighten, but it will provide insight into how, why, and where to set priorities.

### A Need for Greater Oversight

Considering the amount of money involved, there is curiously little oversight for the spending of school boards. Members approve expenditures and receive summaries of bills that the district has paid and checks that have been cut. Yet school board members are amateurs in the world of finance and the information they get can be voluminous and overwhelming. There is just so much they can reasonably do to keep tabs on expenditures. The school system's business administrator bears primary responsibility in this area. A diligent business administrator is a boon to any school board, almost as valuable as the superintendent. This person, easily overlooked by the public, is the fiscal motor that keeps the district humming. Laws in most states require financial operations of school boards to be audited, providing another layer of oversight. But the Enron travesty and the adventures of Bernard Madoff demonstrated that audits do not guarantee efficiency and integrity.

Some states audit the fiscal affairs of school districts and some do not. New York State stopped doing so in the 1970s, when the near financial collapse of New York City and problems in other parts of the state ended the practice except for spot checks. A new law in 2005 provided funds to hire additional auditors, enabling the state to resume audits of school districts. Passage of the law was spurred by a scandal in the upscale school system in Roslyn, on Long Island, where a court convicted the superintendent and his co-conspirators of stealing more than $11 million from the district. The school board seemed as surprised as the taxpayers by the thievery.

It didn't take long after auditors went back to checking on school district expenditures for them to discover, as revealed in 2009, that the system in Niagara Falls overpaid 272 employees by more than $500,000 by incorrectly sending an extra check to each of them. Also, five districts could have saved a total of $212,000 on electricity bills by having people shut off computers at night. In another district, laptop computers had been used to play casino games and visit pornography sites.[32]

When it comes to fiscal mismanagement of the public schools, no place beats Detroit, where the school board—like the local industry—seems to have been asleep at the wheel. The situation deteriorated so greatly that the district, after running a deficit for seven straight years, was flirting with a $300-million deficit when the state intervened in 2009 to appoint an emergency financial manager. Some members of the elected school board objected when the financial manager hired a chief academic officer and intruded in other ways into areas that board members thought were their domain, but the board was hardly in a position to complain. "The schoolchildren of Detroit are being deeply affected academically by the chronic inability of the district to manage its finances," said Mike Flanagan, Michigan's state superintendent of public instruction.[33]

Enrollment declined as many of the families that could afford to flee Detroit did so, triggering a drop in per-student state aid, and putting the school district in danger of following General Motors and Chrysler into bankruptcy. Robert C. Bobb, the financial manager sent in by the governor, found hundreds of unauthorized expenses and employees on the school system's payroll in positions not even listed in the budget.[34] Bobb, a former city administrator in Washington DC, spoke of the "rampant waste, fraud, and abuse" common in the Detroit school system.[35] In 2008 and 2009, the system cut jobs by the hundreds. By 2010, Detroit—with its falling population and financial losses—was in the process of reducing by half the number of schools that had existed in 2005. Detroit's mess epitomizes the harm that a negligent school board can inflict on a district and its children. Fortunately, the situation is an anomaly, but it exemplifies the downside potential of shoddy governance.

School boards have a monumental responsibility when it comes to monitoring the funds under their aegis. Even the most honest and well-intended members can easily make mistakes or fail to discern the errors of others. Board members have to keep their eyes not only on revenues from local taxpayers but also on sizable allocations from state and federal sources. The budgets over which individual school boards preside run from the millions to the tens of millions to the hundreds of millions and even to the billions in a few very large districts.

Large sums present temptations that some people, even school board members, cannot resist. In a case working its way through the courts even as this book was completed in 2010, a board member of the Broward County Public Schools in Florida stood accused of one count each of extortion and bribery and five counts of honest services fraud. She had allegedly accepted funds from federal agents posing as consultants for building contractors to steer contracts their way. Perhaps most surprising is that fiscal abuses and mistakes do not occur more frequently. School board members themselves seldom are charged with wrongdoing. Given the sizable amounts of money involved, this says either that the nation is fortunate in the people chosen to govern its school districts or that oversight should be a lot more extensive.

### Capital Expenditures

School boards spend money not only on annual operating budgets but also on construction and renovation—capital expenditures. Such outlays generally involve borrowed money and in most places, school boards must get voter approval to sell bonds for construction. The school board needs money not only to cover the actual cost of the construction but also to pay interest on the borrowed money. Fortunately, the federal government planned to set aside as much as $14 billion in its stimulus package for school modernization and repairs, but this was one-time assistance.

One of the greatest financial burdens facing school boards is the cost of accommodating new students that residential construction brings into a district. The revenues that school systems derive from the additional property taxes they collect seldom offset the cost of educating extra students. Some states and localities require real estate developers to provide funding for the new schools needed to serve the added students, but in other places, there is no such mandate and school boards have no recourse but to ask taxpayers to support the construction of new school facilities. This is a challenge to school boards. Citizens may assume that districts will always have the space to accommodate students. But this is simply not the case and especially in these difficult economic times, the possibility exists that school districts will have outdated and inadequate facilities. Without enough space, school systems may cram their enrollments into existing classrooms, raising class sizes to the breaking point.

Inadequate space may mean that pullout sessions for special education students or counseling take place in cramped, windowless spaces built as storage closets or that libraries become classrooms. A lack of wiring stifles technology and a shortage of laboratories may handicap science. Gym classes may be squeezed into areas in which the usual games and activities have to be abandoned. So what is a school board to do? Working with the superintendent, the school board sends out mailings and holds a series of meetings, trying to convince taxpayers that the district desperately needs to pass a referendum. Good luck! It's hard enough to win approval for the annual school budget. Taxpayers may view new construction as a luxury that students can forgo.

"A board may find itself in the unenviable position of having to defend itself to its community for proposing a new facility that some community members do not think is needed," said author Robert W. Flinchbaugh. "When a board has made it known that it is thinking about building a new facility, it can cause itself and its chief executive officer considerable grief if it is has not put the idea before the public early on."[36] I saw this happen on a board on which I eventually served when a proposal was rushed and put before the public with little advance notice. It was destined to stir controversy given that the plan called for constructing an elementary school on the playing field of an existing middle school—money was not spent to acquire land for construction—and the site potentially created a traffic nightmare and had questionable drainage. Voters rejected the referendum.

The new, more frugal economy that has emerged from the recession led to the creation in one state of the Massachusetts School Building Authority to try to rein in school construction costs. This could mean fewer public schools with such amenities as swimming pools and skating rinks; better bidding procedures and construction management systems; a centralized clearinghouse for best practices in school construction; and possibly, designs used for multiple projects, which would lessen the cost of architectural fees. The effectiveness of this approach remains to be seen, but it is clear that replicating the Taj Mahal of public schools will be a receding option for many school boards.

More energy-efficient buildings are apt to be higher on the agenda of school boards in Massachusetts and elsewhere. Some boards may seek certification for their buildings from a new nonprofit organization, the U.S. Green Building Council. The group's LEED certification (Leadership in Energy and Environmental Design) will endorse projects that include energy savings, water efficiency, emissions retention, indoor environmental quality, and stewardship of resources. New school construction also now faces the financial burden of complying with security provisions mandated by government at the federal and state levels after 9/11. Schools and other public buildings must incur the expense, for example, of bollards and similar physical barriers to block vehicles from being driven into entrances and structural elements to resist collapse.

The likelihood of passing a referendum can be affected by the time of the year that a school board decides to hold the balloting (April is best), whether it is a renovation (which fares better than new construction) or an addition, whether it contains facilities for athletics (the least successful item), and, of course, the amount of money requested (under $10 million attracts more support than more than $10 million).[37]

Should they get enough votes to pass a referendum, school board members, few if any of whom are experts in construction, take on fiduciary responsibility for spending tens of millions of dollars for services about which they have little more knowledge than they do about how to get a space vehicle to Mars. They can and do use tax revenues to hire consultants, but nevertheless the board of education retains the legal authority and responsibility for the entire process. It is enough to frighten a conscientious board member into inaction.

Consider just one step that comes early in the process, the hiring of an architect and the evaluation of his or her proposals. How can taxpayers be sure that the architect is the most qualified person for the job and how do all the board members know that the selection has been done in an impartial manner? What plan is best and how should an amateur—which virtually every board member is when it comes to building a school—have confidence in the plan? And so it goes through the entire process until students enter the completed building for the first time.

# Chapter 4

# Jobs, Jobs, Jobs

School boards are job machines. This is especially true in some small towns and suburbs, where the school system is a major, if not the largest, employer. School boards perform as gatekeepers in such places, opening doors to lifetime employment, pensions, and health benefits for the chosen few. Jobs are available on all levels as school systems hire not only certificated educators but secretaries, lunchroom workers, teacher aides, security officers, bus drivers, crossing guards, custodians, groundskeepers, and a host of other nonprofessionals. Many such positions do not require a college degree and provide a kind of security seldom found any longer in private sector employment. As a matter of fact, Paul E. Peterson, a government professor at Harvard University, wrote that the number of pupils for each member of the support staff declined from 58 in 1960 to 43 in 1970 to 27 in 2005.[1] Jobs on the support staff, in other words, proliferated at a faster rate than enrollment.

Thus, school systems may hire staff even as enrollment falls or, at least, at a rate faster than enrollments expand. The New York City school system illustrates this phenomenon. It added 1,075 principals and assistant principals during the first seven years under mayoral control, when the budget increased from $13 billion to $22 billion. During this period, the system's million-plus enrollment declined, but the district created many new small schools, requiring additional principals. Also, the system hired employees in its burgeoning accountability department to measure the performance of students and schools. At the other end of the salary spectrum, public schools in New York City added 4,500 more aides to oversee lunchrooms, corridors, and school yards. To be fair, expenses for special education and pension obligations soared during the years that Mayor Michael R. Bloomberg controlled the system.[2]

Positions in school systems and other sectors of public employment became even more coveted when the country began shedding jobs at the rate of a half-million a month in 2008. Private employers fired and laid off workers as companies struggled to survive in a shrinking economy. By July 2009, the U.S. Department of Labor said there were six job seekers for every opening in the United States, the bleakest ratio in the almost 10 years of tracking such numbers. But government at all levels was largely insulated from this phenomenon and the health benefits and generous retirements offered by school systems became ever more desirable. School boards hold the keys to the kingdom for some people.

On the other hand, some noneducator jobs in public schools are not as attractive as others. The huge federal government program that subsidizes lunches and breakfasts for schoolchildren, for example, requires hundreds of thousands of food service workers. Some receive wages directly from school systems; contractors who operate the programs pay others. Their median hourly pay in New Jersey in 2007 was $8.15. Sixty-four percent worked for contractors and received no benefits. Moreover, unlike regular school employees including secretaries and custodians, lunch aides working for contractors got no pay for school holidays.[3]

## Jobs for the Favored

School board members and other influential people who want friends and relatives hired can often make that happen. It is de rigueur in some districts for board members and others, especially political figures, to pass along resumes to the superintendent. Everyone will say that the superintendent has no obligation to hire these people, but almost certainly, such candidates get the kind of attention that those who submit applications through regular channels do not. Until not many years ago, some politicians in Delaware County, a suburb of Philadelphia, gave some superintendents lists from which to hire candidates and some school boards, not wanting to alienate powerful figures, readily acceded to this patronage.

Individual members of school boards may be unaware of the ways that favoritism manifests itself around them. The employment rosters of some districts are laden with relatives, as if the school system itself gave birth to entire families. Mothers and fathers, sons and daughters, aunts and uncles, and cousins already on the payroll try to get relatives hired. It is not terribly different from the federal government's chain migration policy that permits immigrants, once they become citizens, to petition for the admission of relatives.

The superintendent ultimately recommends candidates for employment, but lower-level employees, too, may influence the hiring process. Central administrators, principals, teachers, secretaries, custodians, and others already working in the system may tell friends and relatives of openings and promote their candidacies. This is not to say that candidates who attain positions this way are necessarily unqualified. Such people may be as qualified as a half-dozen other candidates. It's just that those half-dozen other candidates don't have anyone stirring the waters in their behalf.

One of the more egregious examples of favoritism in hiring occurred in the Montour School District, just south of Pittsburgh. Throughout the 1990s and into the 2000s, the school board apparently carried out and participated in the widespread practice of hiring relatives and friends of board members and of giving jobs to politically connected individuals. At one point in 2003, an investigation by the *Post-Gazette* newspaper found that 16 percent of the district's employees were related to the district's current or former employees or to school board members. At least six of 19 new teachers hired just the previous fall were children of current or former board members or of employees.[4]

The hiring abuses came to light when the district's public relations director filed a federal civil rights law suit after losing her job. She eventually settled her claims in exchange for a payment of $135,000. Former and current employees testified in depositions filed in behalf of their ousted colleague that the town's Democratic committee chairman played a prominent role in the district's hiring procedures. One former administrator stated in a deposition that some board members met with the party boss at his home or at a restaurant to discuss school board issues. A current employee testified that the party boss reviewed teacher applications at the school system's offices every two or three months.[5] Outraged citizens formed the Montour Taxpayers Organization to push for reform, creating a rebellion that prodded four of five board members whose terms expired in November 2003 not to run for reelection.

There is yet another backdoor through which people obtain jobs in some school systems and this approach bears fewer fingerprints and is more or less hidden from sight. Some ranking officials will scratch each other's backs. Rather than award a position in their own school system to someone whose appointment might raise eyebrows, they will ask an official in a neighboring district to provide the job. Somewhere down the road, there is apt to be a quid pro quo.

Not only may these various circumventions of the system be unfair, they can undermine meritocracy and lead to the employment of less-than-well-qualified workers at all levels. School systems may end up with employees who are not suited for the positions they occupy. The board shapes the future with every job it fills. Almost all the certificated personnel it appoints will attain the equivalent of guaranteed lifetime employment. Each poor hire will be a weak link in the chain of instruction. This fact is probably not fully considered by some school boards. "Oh, he's so-and-so's son and old so-and-so was a good old boy so we might as well give his son a job," someone says. The effects on education may be minimal when it comes to nonprofessional, out-of-the-classroom positions. But the same kind of influence leads to hiring teachers and sometimes even administrators who are not the best candidates for the jobs. The school board, knowingly or unknowingly, plays a role in this process as it officially approves all appointments.

Other factors, too, might interfere with the school board's ability to adhere to proper policies in filling posts. Under a long-standing arrangement, for example, Philadelphia's Board of Revision of Taxes (BRT) had appointive power over 78 clerical positions paid for out of the school budget. The positions were nothing more than patronage to reward party workers and their families, depriving the school system of $3.8 million annually that it could otherwise have spent to greater effect. "The setup has proved impervious to attacks by reformers, who've been complaining about BRT patronage since Philadelphia was run by Republicans," reported an article in 2009 in *The Philadelphia Inquirer*.[6]

Theoretically, a school board's vast power over hiring seems to imply that it may, if it chooses, exercise close scrutiny over the filling of each position. But this is unlikely in a sizable district. "A board alone has the authority hire teachers," Charles J. Russo, an authority on education law, wrote by way of example, going on to say that "It is impractical, if not impossible, for a board to be actively involved in the process of hiring all new teachers." The board, he said, "must rely on its administrative staff to make recommendations concerning the suitability of prospective teachers. Then, even if a board's approval is merely a formality, it will have carried out its legal mandate."[7]

A school board could inject greater integrity into some hiring decisions, particularly for principals and central administrators, by giving parents and other taxpayers a say in the process. Having them on committees to screen and interview candidates might lead to more transparency and reduce opportunities for favoritism and patronage simply because outsiders would witness the process.

*Restrictions on Hiring*

Credentials count in determining the candidates whom school boards approve for educational positions. Regulations in almost all states, by and large, limit entry to those who gain certification by completing prescribed courses of study, which vary according to whether the person seeks to teach at the elementary or secondary level, work as a guidance counselor, principal or as a superintendent, or occupy some other professional post.

School boards, in other words, do not have a great deal of latitude if they want to hire nontraditional candidates into certificated ranks, particularly as teachers. Few board members complain about this situation, but many critics of public education say that school boards should consider candidates who have not pursued the usual paths. Some states have alternate routes that permit school boards to offer jobs to a limited number of people with less traditional qualifications, ordinarily with a proviso that they take education courses once hired.

Organized teachers argue that their occupation is a profession and not just anyone can walk into a classroom and teach. They point out that people without proper credentials do not fly commercial airliners or perform surgery. On the other hand, some of the nation's most coveted private schools, not restricted by regulations affecting public schools, have faculties made up of teachers with no formal credentials and families have no compunction about paying college-size tuitions to send their children to those schools. Such a program as Teach for America provides young liberal arts graduates of selective colleges—without the usual credentials—to teach in public school systems that have difficulty attracting enough teachers. Increasingly, Teach for America grounds them in pedagogy, but nothing as extensive as graduates of schools of education receive.

An interesting program to hire teachers of math and science, two of the most difficult fields to staff, began in New Jersey in 2009, during the worst days of the recession. The tri-state region surrounding New York City, the heart of the country's financial industry and an area hit hard by the cutbacks, ended up with thousands of people who lost jobs in banks, brokerages, and other financial service companies. Lucille E. Davey, New Jersey's education commissioner, and Ada Beth Cutler, education dean at Montclair State University, reasoned that many of these men and women worked with numbers and knew math even if they had gotten degrees in such fields as business, finance, accounting, and marketing.

Thus, New Jersey launched Traders to Teachers, a program that the state legislature approved to enable displaced financial services professionals to become math teachers. Ordinarily, people coming out of the business world would have been ineligible to join public school faculties. This 18-month waiver of the usual requirements permitted them to start out teaching either algebra or geometry.

Traders to Teachers was scheduled to use $200,000 in federal funds to prepare four cadres of 25 candidates each as math teachers. The future math teachers had to spend four days a week in classes at Montclair State for three months as well as a day a week working in a public schools under mentors, who were retired math teachers. At least two people applied for each opening and those accepted had to pass a math test, write an essay, spend two days under observation in a public school classroom, and be interviewed about their experience in that classroom. Some math professors and some high school math teachers expressed reservations about the candidates' qualifications and asserted that the program would dilute standards. Cutler insisted, though, that it would be rigorous and cautioned that without such nontraditional approaches the public schools might never have enough able math teachers.

A sacrosanct hurdle that school boards seldom try to overcome in collective bargaining is the presumption that school systems should pay the same salaries to all teachers with equal experience and the same number of graduate credits. This practice is not followed elsewhere in the professions. In higher education, for instance, faculty members in some disciplines receive substantially more than colleagues in other disciplines. Teacher shortages in math, science, computer technology, and some other fields could be ameliorated by differential pay, but teacher unions want no part of it.

School boards could try to bolster quality by hiring candidates primarily from outstanding teacher training programs and by expecting them to have top grades, sparkling academic records, and solid recommendations. Few school boards, though, are inclined to direct their administrators to analyze the hiring policies of their districts and to review research that identifies factors that might increase prospects for finding the most promising candidates. A study from the National

Bureau of Economic Research suggested that attention to a collection of attributes might lead to hiring more effective candidates. The researchers collected information on such factors as candidates' pedagogical content knowledge, cognitive ability, personality traits, and self-efficacy. The factors had a modest but statistically significant relationship with student and teacher outcomes, particularly in regard to student test scores. Such research, further refined, might someday point school boards toward more effective hiring practices.[8]

Sometimes prejudice, too, constrains hiring, though this probably happens a good deal less today than in former years. Apparently, preferences based on gender may still be alive and well in some places. A senior researcher for the New Zealand Council for Educational Research found in her country that boards of governors or trustees—the counterpart to American school boards—favored male candidates for principalships in primary schools. This was so, she stated, even when men had lower academic qualifications.[9] School boards in the United States are probably more sensitive than ever before to their own biases and generally try to guard against actions that might result in lawsuits.

*Payments to Vendors and Fees for Professionals*

Finally, there are payments that school boards authorize to a host of people who are not actual employees of the district. The larger the district, the more money the board pays to outside individuals, professional partnerships, and vendors who provide goods and services. While some of these people and companies may receive far more than the district's average employee, the district generally has no obligation to put them on the permanent payroll as it does with regular employees, or to provide them with benefits.

Among the professionals receiving fees are lawyers, physicians, psychologists, social workers, architects, engineers, and occupational and physical therapists. The school board may at the beginning of each school year approve a stated fee for each of these professionals, who then charge the district whenever they render service. The big money for the architect usually comes when structures are built or renovated and the architect gets a commission based on the cost of the construction. New Jersey allows school boards to engage some of these professionals under no-bid arrangements on the presumption that it is in the best interests of districts to do so.

New Jersey's education commissioner sought in 2008 to head off abuses in fees that school boards pay to law firms by setting down regulations requiring, for instance, that lawyers set budgetary maximums for legal services and that boards pay only for services performed at written request. Local school boards found such requirements onerous, unreasonable, and little more than a device to increase paperwork.

School boards also approve payments for a host of goods and services from vendors who supply everything from paper, uniforms, athletic gear, copiers, boilers, and cleaning compounds. Some of the larger bills involve vendors of books, computers, transportation, and food services. Speaking from experience, I found it virtually impossible as an individual board member to know that everything was on the up and up when it came to payments that the board approved for professional fees and vendors. I received dozens of pages showing records of payments each month, but I could do little to assure the public that we spent their tax dollars with probity and efficiency.

The potential for abuse can be seen in a couple of recent criminal cases involving vendors that ended with prison sentences for the perpetrators. An audit by a forensic accounting firm revealed that the Wake County Public School System in North Carolina was ripped off to the tune of at least $3.8 million between July 1, 2002, and December 31, 2005, through kickbacks and phony bills involving employees of the school district and a transportation parts company.[10] The collusion was carried out mostly through hundreds of invoices for amounts of less than $2,500 that did not have corresponding purchase orders.

In another case, concluded in 2009, Utah's Davis School District was defrauded of $4 million in a textbook purchasing scheme involving a wife who was the system's director of federal programs and her husband, a former Title I specialist for the state education department. "They were entrusted to be mindful stewards of limited educational dollars," said a special agent from the Internal Revenue Service. "Instead, they became selfish, greedy criminals who put their own interests before the well being of our children's education."[11]

### Conflicts of Interest

Conflicts of interest on the part of school board members may affect hiring and promotions. In this regard, school board members tend to be no better and no worse than other officeholders. Although all school boards do not follow the same rules when it comes to ethics, it seems reasonable to prohibit a member from awarding a job to a close relative, from having a role in evaluating or promoting a relative already working for the district, from being part of a negotiation or voting on a contract with a union of which the person is a member, from using his or her board position to win contracts from the district or to help others do so, from using privileged information for financial gain, and from accepting what a reasonable person would regard as a bribe.

Regulations in New Jersey went in the wrong direction in 2009, when the state department of education loosened its policy to allow a district to hire a board member's immediate relative after demonstrating that the district had conducted a thorough search for the position and the board member's relative was the only qualified and available candidate. Ethics is not simply a matter of legality. The question for a board member to ask himself or herself is how the public will perceive a given act. It is all but impossible to codify and prohibit every possible ethical violation that a member of a school board could potentially commit. Better yet, each school board member should have a conscience meter that sounds an internal alarm when he or she is about to step over an invisible ethical line.

A conflict of another sort arises when someone attains a position as a board member in a district in which his or her relative already works. Obviously, the new member did not use a board position to get the relative hired. Yet once on the school board, the new member certainly has a stake in seeing his or her relatives prosper in the system.

I was elected to a school board on which I sat with a retired teacher from our school system—whose wife and two sons worked for the district—and a current teacher from a neighboring system. In addition, another board member was the son of a former teacher in our system and yet another was the husband of a teacher in the district. On top of this, the acting superintendent had a wife working in our system. By and large, they were all perfectly fine individuals, as much committed to board service as anyone else, but on an ideal school board, members would have fewer encumbrances.

To provide the appearance of impartiality, the law may require—as it does in New Jersey—that a board member with a relative employed by the system abstain from discussing or voting on matters that would affect the relative. Wouldn't it be simpler, though, to ban from service on school boards those whose immediate relatives work for the system?

When I ran for the school board on a slate with two other candidates we made a point of emphasizing that none of the three of us had relatives employed in the district, and we vowed that we would not hire any relatives during our watch. My partner, an experienced substitute teacher in another school district, wanted to apply on her own to work as a substitute teacher in Edison. It took some heavy persuasion on my part to dissuade her from seeking a substitute's job in the district even though it would have been perfectly legal. I wanted to avoid even a hint of a conflict.

I had been a school board member for a mere two months when an assistant superintendent asked me about a teenager who had shown up at school headquarters in the company of an adult who told officials that "Gene Maeroff has promised" him a summer job. I was astonished by this story; I didn't know the teenager, whose name was recited to me, and I certainly had not promised him a summer job or sent him in search of such a position, nor would I. My inquiries revealed that the boy lived a block from me, though I did not know the family. It turned out that another neighbor, an acquaintance to whom I had not spoken about the situation, took it upon herself to drive the young man to school district headquarters and to announce that the boy was there at my behest, ready to start the job that I had supposedly promised him.

*Other Ethical Breaches*

New Jersey has a school ethics commission that reviews complaints about the conduct of school board members. Three decisions that the commission rendered in October of 2008 typify possible violations—trying to get someone hired, trying to get someone fired, and micromanaging. The commission censured a former school board member who while on the board had pressured the superintendent and members new to the board to provide a job in the district for his wife. The commission recommended a six-month suspension for another board member who had tried to get the principal who supervised his wife, a physical education teacher in the district, fired. The commission censured another board member who, despite not being part of a board bargaining team, had attended a meeting when the team was in a delicate negotiating position, an action that the commission decided could have compromised the board's position.[12]

Education at all levels offers abundant opportunities for favoritism in employment. Where jobs are available, there will always be those who want to pull strings or have strings pulled in their behalf. Higher education is no less exempt from such indiscretions. Some members of the board of Suffolk University in Boston, which, believe it or not, had the second highest-paid president in the country from 2007 through 2008 academic year, were discovered to have financial relationships with the university as lobbyists and publicists.[13] Not long afterward, first the University of New Mexico and then Roger Williams University in Rhode Island allegedly attempted to hire the sons of the institutions' presidents. Around the same time, it became known that the North Carolina State University provided a job to the wife of a former governor who had influenced the selection while he was governor.

Sometimes the money to be made through education leads wrongdoers down devious paths as when an audit by the state comptroller in New York State found a host of violations in the 8,300-student Liverpool Central School District, including ethical and legal breaches involving the nine-member school board, a former superintendent, and other high ranking administrators. Among the violations were diversions of monies raised by student groups to buy office furniture, cell phones, and other items to benefit school officials; the bypassing of the disbursement process to route funds to a nonprofit corporation; payments to a law firm totaling $660,000 without soliciting written proposals; and inflation of a superintendent's income to boost his pension benefits.[14]

School boards rely on their human resources and personnel officers to protect taxpayers from another kind of crime, the one that results when men and women who work for school systems misrepresent themselves to boost their chances of getting positions. Education orients itself toward credentials and one expects that officials will scrutinize credentials, yet school systems occasionally find themselves victimized by charlatans with phony or at least questionable degrees. Not only may bogus degrees lead to jobs, but they also may result in raises and promotions as the pay scales of school systems are conditioned on credentials. These wrongdoers, in effect, steal from the taxpayers.

One notorious case occurred in 2008, when the *San Francisco Chronicle* reported that an area superintendent falsely claimed on his resume to hold certain degrees. The man had been named superintendent after the school board paid for a search and for a background check on him. He resigned from his $150,000 post. Another newspaper, the *Asbury Park Press* in New Jersey, revealed just a month earlier that another superintendent and his two top aides had received doctoral degrees from an alleged diploma mill. The school board had paid the tuition costs for the three administrators and then gave them raises based on their spurious degrees. Ultimately, they agreed to stop using their doctoral titles and surrendered their raises. Shortly thereafter, the state legislature, with the support of the New Jersey School Board Association, moved to pass a bill to prevent school employees from obtaining raises, promotions, or tuition reimbursements for advanced degrees from nonaccredited institutions.

### Tenure: Lifetime Job Security

The prospect of lifetime employment means that much is at stake each time a school board hires a new employee. The legislature in New Jersey enacted the nation's first law awarding tenure to teachers in 1909. Until then, teachers across the country were hired and fired arbitrarily as many school boards, administrators, and politicians used jobs in schools to promote nepotism, favoritism, and patronage. Supporters of tenure hoped that it would protect teachers from caprice and lead to a more professional force of educators. Everything has not changed, though. A former chancellor of the New York City Public Schools told me of his discovery that a teacher had been denied tenure because he wouldn't change the grade of the son of a board of education member.

Today, job protection for teachers is almost universal, though there has been a trend in some states to avoid the term "tenure" and to speak instead of due process provisions, which have essentially the same effect. Furthermore, tenure-like job protection in the public schools has been extended in some places to employees other than regular teachers, including, for instance, custodians. Legislators in New Jersey in 2010 bestowed what is called "tenure-like" protection on paraprofessionals who assist teachers in Title I-funded programs.

The law states that paraprofessionals cannot be dismissed or reduced in compensation during the term of their contracts except for "good cause" and made them eligible for hearings in either eventuality. The bill was just one more thrust in the ribs of school board members who want the freedom to decide on the status of paraprofessionals without the interference of lawmakers.

Laws in most states dictate that employees spend several years, most often about three, on a tenure track before receiving tenure. Supposedly, employees prove themselves during this period. Principals and supervisors observe and evaluate untenured teachers, ostensibly rooting out along the way those who show the least promise. Ideally, an induction program during these years would help novices learn their craft and strengthen their instructional abilities.

### The Disadvantages of Tenure to the Work of School Boards

A school board officially grants tenure, but this can be little more than confirming an attainment over which board members have little or no control. In the first place, the board more or less automatically votes to hire candidates whom the superintendent recommends. Then, the board usually has little to do with the process as new teachers pass through a probationary period. And finally, the person receives tenure, again virtually automatically, after a specific period specified by the state. Tenure is good for adults. The question is whether tenure is good for the children who sit in the classrooms of these teachers. Critics of the public schools speak frequently about how difficult it is to get rid of incompetent teachers.

Some people—not necessarily school board members—would like factors besides time served to determine who gets tenure. Joel I. Klein, the schools chancellor in New York City (where, essentially, there is no school board), and his boss, Mayor Michael R. Bloomberg, wanted students' test scores considered in tenure decisions. They indicated that scores alone should not be the determining factor, but that test results should be among a number of factors weighed. Bloomberg and Klein ran into a roadblock in Albany, where the teacher union has a potent lobbying machine, when they sought legislative approval for this idea. Finally, in the spring of 2010, helped by the need to make a change to qualify for federal Race to the Top funds, New York's state education department reached an agreement with the statewide teacher's union for an evaluation system to include consideration of student scores on state and local examinations. The evaluation of both tenured and non-tenured teachers, as well as principals, would also rely on observations by trained evaluators. Educators rated as "ineffective" twice in a row would be considered for termination.

The time it takes for teachers to gain tenure in most states is absurdly short and scarcely long enough to confirm emphatically that a teacher is up to the task. A study by the Center for American Progress in 2008 stated that "tenure is not a rigorous bar that teachers must meet, but rather a mark of time: Teachers receive tenure as a matter of course, as long as they have put in the required number of years."[15] A survey by the National Council on Teacher Quality found that in every state except Iowa and New Mexico tenure is virtually automatic after a prescribed period on the job.[16]

Given such findings, a school board's greatest contribution as regards tenure might be to encourage the superintendent to ensure that those interviewing prospective teachers select candidates very carefully. Then, the school board has the ability to make certain that the district has a proper induction program during the probationary years to provide novices with guidance and assistance. There should also be painstaking evaluation of nontenured teachers to weed out those with least promise. Unfortunately, not all school boards recognize the need for such programs or are willing to pay for them. The results can be catastrophic for children. Researcher William Sanders, known for his value-added studies, maintained that fifth-grade students who had three very effective teachers in a row gained 50 percentile points more on a state assessment than students who suffered through three ineffective teachers.[17]

Defenders of teacher tenure insist that laws provide adequate opportunities to weed out incompetent teachers. Moreover, they argue that jobs should be protected to prevent school boards from getting rid of experienced, more highly paid teachers merely to save money. Al Shanker, the late president of the American Federation of Teachers, told me that little notice is taken of the number of incompetent teachers counseled out of the profession or who choose to leave on their own and so the low number of successful dismissals for incompetence can be misleading.

The New York City Public Schools paid a teacher performance unit made up of eight lawyers and eight administrators a million dollars a year to build cases against incompetent educators. In 2010, after two years of this effort, the school system had fired only three teachers for incompetence. Ten others resigned or retired, and nine others agreed to pay fines, accept reassignments, or both. One was deported and 50 others awaited arbitration. An additional 418 had left the system after finding out they could face charges of incompetence,[18] a development that would tend to reinforce the point that Shanker made years earlier.

Among all the possible grounds for dismissal of a tenured teacher, incompetence may be the most difficult to prove. So school boards wanting to dismiss incompetent teachers often pursue other avenues with fewer barriers. Cases of illegal behavior, sexual and drug abuse, and failure to follow directions more frequently result in dismissals than charges of incompetence. For example, while Alabama and Delaware both list incompetence as a reason for termination, they both also list immorality as an acceptable cause.

Investigative reporters from the *Los Angeles Times* in 2009 reviewed every case over a 15-year period in which a tenured school employee had been fired by any California school district and in which the employee formally contested the decision before a review commission. They found that the vast majority of firings relied on charges other than incompetence—immoral or illegal behavior, insubordination, and repeated violation of such rules as those requiring that they show up on time. In 80 percent of the cases competence wasn't a factor. Even though the districts pressed ahead with only the strongest cases, they were successful just two-thirds of the time.[19] One case dragged on from 2002, when the teacher was removed from the classroom, to 2010, when a Los Angeles County Superior Court finally ruled that the district could stop paying him. The teacher, sidelined all the while, continued to receive his salary and benefits.[20]

Job protection for teachers and other education professionals can, as was found in Los Angeles, mean getting paid for not working. Two of the most notorious examples of this policy existed in Los Angeles, where those banished from classrooms were "housed" in settings in which they did nothing, and in New York City, where unwanted teachers were assigned to a "reserve pool." In Los Angeles, the teachers—accused of such wrongdoing as sexual conduct with students, harassment, theft, or drug possession—were assigned to district offices and other non-teaching sites while their cases were pending and paid some $10 million in salaries as of the spring of 2009.[21] In New York City, some 1,400 educators whose positions had been eliminated and whom other schools did not want sat in the reserve pool. They were collecting $74 million in salaries at the beginning of the 2008 through 2009 school year.[22] In 2010, the school system and the union reached a tentative agreement in New York to speed up the hearings of the cases and to assign the teachers in limbo to perform administrative work or nonclassroom duties instead of having them do nothing.

### Paying for Legal Complications

As a result of tenure, boards of education have less leeway than private sector employers to remove employees. This is just one more factor that tends to render a school board relatively impotent. Regular attendees at school board meetings know that at some point the board will usually adjourn to a closed session to deal with personnel, legal, and confidential issues. A feature of these sessions may call for a presentation by the board's lawyer and a discussion by the board of pending legal cases involving the board as a party. Some of these matters involve attempts to dismiss tenured employees. The cost of proving a tenure-dismissal case against a board employee typically runs tens of thousands of dollars and may range into the hundreds of thousands.

The tenured employee may attempt to turn the tables on the district by claiming to have been the object of discrimination or harassment on the basis of gender, age, race, or ethnicity. Suits can drag on for months, even years, before resolution. The taxpayers of the school district, represented by the board, are forced to pay lawyers to pursue the case. The tenured employee, on the other hand, generally spends nothing out of pocket, relying on his or her union to bear the expenses.

Elaborate grievance procedures in bargaining agreements make it difficult not only to dismiss board employees, but even to reassign them to another school or another subject. Often, reassignment—called the "dance of the lemons" in New York City public schools—is the lone alternative to dismissal given the cost to taxpayers and the time demands on district officials who try to build a case. A teacher in the small Nettle Creek school district in southeastern Indiana sued the school board in 2005 after it approved her transfer from teaching Advanced Placement English to teaching seventh-grade English. The case was not resolved until 2009, when the U.S. Court of Appeals in Chicago upheld an earlier finding that threw out her allegations.[23] She had charged that sexual harassment, a hostile work environment, breach of contract, administrative retaliation, violation of just cause, and discrimination on the basis of national origin were all behind the reassignment. The district superintendent was quoted as saying that the case cost the school system $195,102 to litigate.

Legal costs, though, are only part of the financial burden that the board of education bears. Sometimes, the employee involved in the litigation has been removed or is on leave and the school board must pay a substitute to perform the person's duties, while continuing to pay the litigating employee's salary. Moreover, the administrators called to testify in such cases lose precious work time. If the case reaches a verdict and the school board loses it could be responsible for paying a sizable sum to the employee.

School boards sometimes buy off employees involved in litigation by giving them hefty amounts in out-of-court settlements to drop the suit or to resign so as to avoid further legal expenses. Such payouts may come after months or years of litigation and the school board—having been held hostage—decides it is preferable to give the employee money to end the suit. These settlements generally receive no public attention and the taxpayers do not realize that the school board spends their hard-earned money in this fashion. From the school board's perspective, though, it makes sense. The board reckons that the settlement is less costly than continuing to incur legal fees while carrying an employee on paid leave. It may also be that a school board would rather provide a settlement to an employee who agrees to drop the suit and retire as some of these litigants are not people that the board wants to send back into a school.

Members of the Council of School Attorneys, responding to a survey, picked "employee discrimination/termination" as the top legal issue facing elementary and secondary education during the 2008 through 2009 school year. "It doesn't matter whether a teacher proves incompetent in the classroom, strikes a child in anger, or is arrested for after-school misdeeds," the *American School Board Journal* commented on this issue. "The hard reality is that state tenure laws and collective bargaining agreements require school officials to jump through a series of procedural hoops in their quest to discipline a teacher."[24]

*Paying Up Even When the School Board Isn't Responsible*

Sometimes school boards face payouts for circumstances for which they are seemingly not responsible, but—like events more directly under their control—there may be costs to taxpayers either way. This happened in Loudon County, Virginia, in 2009, when the school board voted voluntarily to pay $167,621 to reimburse an assistant high school principal for expenses he incurred in a legal defense. The charges against him had been brought not by the school board, but by the Commonwealth of Virginia. The state charged the assistant principal in 2008, first, with possession of child pornography and, then, with contributing to the delinquency of a minor.

He said that he was looking into the texting of nude photos by students at Freedom High School and downloaded to his cell phone a photo of a female naked from the chest to midthigh—supposedly a student whose picture was taken by another student—with her arms crossed over her breasts. A police officer arrested the assistant principal in the school, led him to a patrol car, and handcuffed him. The assistant principal, a veteran school administrator of 29 years and past president of the Coalition of Asian Pacific Americans of Virginia, said that he had carried out the investigation of what has become known as "sexting" in conjunction with a school security official and with the knowledge of the principal.

The school board continued to pay his salary and assigned him to clerical duties outside the school building. Finally, in the last days of the school year in the spring of 2009, a Loudon County circuit judge dismissed the case. Almost three weeks later, the assistant principal wrote an op-ed article for the *Washington Post* in which he stated: "I was furious that the sheriff's department, by its own admission, had never even investigated the original incident. No one interviewed the principal until after my lawyer demanded that they do so . . . Looking back, I'm not surprised by the students' behavior. But I struggle to understand how my actions in performing my job could have been so badly misconstrued."[25]

The school board agreed. It declared that the assistant principal was charged in the course of carrying out his duties and, accordingly, voted to pay his legal bills, though the board had no obligation to do so. But matters involving school boards are often not simple, even when they aim to redress an injustice. The only lawyer on the board, Bob Ohneiser, voted against the payment. He told me that while he favored righting a wrong, the school administration had not been forthcoming with the school board in disclosing the roles of all the personnel involved in the case and that the legal fees were unreasonably high. And so it goes when school boards spend public money.

### Health Benefits, Pensions, and Other Provisions

It is not just the paycheck, but benefits, as well, that make employment in school districts and other government jobs so attractive. Generous health care coverage and pensions accentuated the difference between the public and the private sectors during the 2000s. Health care provisions for active employees and retirees have put the fiscal viability of many localities and states on an unsustainable course. Salaries and benefits for employees account for an increasing portion of spending by school boards and leaves less and less for anything else. In Edison, New

Jersey, for example, contract provisions for employees consumed 80 percent of school district expenditures. Only about one of every five dollars was left for such expenditures as transportation, technology, textbooks, athletics, and possible pilot programs to improve academics.

The contract for teachers tends to set the pattern for remaining employees—secretaries, custodians, central office administrators, and principals. Other groups may receive the same health coverage and some other provisions that teachers get so that the school board does not put itself in the position of treating different classes of employees unequally. Noneducators may even get longevity pay just as educators do, and they may have a salary guide with guaranteed steps in their pay, as well.

In addition, the contract may provide several weeks of paid sick days for teachers and other school system employees. Frequently, employees may carry over these sick days from year to year and even receive compensation at retirement for at least some of the sick days not used. Ninety percent of teachers and other government employees have paid sick days, but only 40 percent of those working in the private sector get paid sick days.[26] Of course, sick days come on top of a long summer break and the days and weeks during the school year when public schools close for various holidays and vacations. Some teachers use their paid sick days to schedule elective surgeries during the school year rather than delay such procedures until summer, when the surgery would be on their own time and the district would not have to hire a substitute.

A study by three Harvard researchers of elementary teachers in an urban system with 80 elementary schools found that teachers disproportionately took sick days on Fridays and Mondays.[27] School systems must cover classes whenever teachers are absent for whatever reason. This can prove expensive. Our school board spent $1.3 million a year on substitutes. A school system may pay other teachers stipends to cover the classes of colleagues if it does not hire substitute teachers. Teacher absenteeism is not just a financial issue. Various studies show that students may suffer academically when regular teachers are absent and the continuity of their education suffers from interruption.

Health care coverage is one of the most important benefits in elementary and secondary education. Many school boards extend this same coverage to spouses no matter how great their incomes. And, of course, the employee's children are covered. It cost my school board about $15,000 per employee to provide coverage for those with families. This comprehensive health coverage for all of our employees consumed 10 percent of the entire budget of the school board on which I served. In some districts, employees contribute very little or nothing toward the premium on their health policies and the district absorbs the entire amount, with employees responsible for small co-payments for doctor visits. Collective-bargaining units seem ready to strike to protect this arrangement. A study of teacher contracts in New York State in 2008 called health insurance "the fastest growing compensation cost for school districts" and found that the district share of premiums averaged between 85 and 95 percent.[28]

At least a dozen states, mostly in the South and the West, do not authorize collective bargaining for teachers. Curiously, school boards in these states tend to follow many of the practices contained in bargaining contracts in the rest of the country. This is not to say that teachers in states without collective bargaining have all the benefits, protections, and influence on their working conditions as their colleagues elsewhere. They don't. But they tend to have tenure or something like it, pay scales that follow steps just as in the ladder in the salary guides found in contracts, and differential increases for graduate credits and master's degrees.

Employees of school systems, like other government workers, generally receive payments in retirement that guarantee them a percentage of their salaries, defined-benefit pensions. A generation ago, most private employers paid such pensions, too. No longer. Private sector employees have had to assume greater responsibility for paying for their own retirement. In 1979, 62 percent of private-sector workers had defined-benefit plans and only 16 percent had defined-contribution plans, akin to a 401k that carries no guaranteed level of payment. By 2005, 63 percent of workers in the private sector participated in defined-contribution plans and only 10 percent remained in line for defined-benefit pensions.[29]

# Chapter 5

# A School Board's Key Employee

## The Superintendent

Above all else, a school board is responsible for hiring the superintendent. Everything flows from this decision, the most important one that a school board can make. Relations between the board and the superintendent set the tone for almost everything that happens in the school system. The relationship resembles a marriage. Board and superintendent are figuratively in bed together. Their fortunes are linked. They can decide to be accommodating partners, like a husband and wife in a thriving marriage, or they can feud and lose trust in each other. They bask in their joint accomplishments and must wend their way through the occasional and inevitable spats.

The success of such a partnership depends on continually cultivating the relationship. A superintendent who ignores the school board or who limits his or her contacts to only a few board members jeopardizes the future. The result may be little different from what happens when spouses shut down channels of communication. MaryEllen Elia, superintendent of the Hillsborough County Schools in Tampa, Florida, said that she made it a point to meet one-on-one with each school board member on a biweekly basis and spent at least a full day, on average, every week working in one way or another with board members.[1]

In the absence of collaboration and without mutual respect between a school board and a superintendent, the signals of dysfunction are recognized by other central administrators, by teachers and staff, by parents, and by the entire community. If the board inherits an ineffective superintendent or—even worse—hires a superintendent who lacks the ability to carry out the job, this may weaken the school system during the tenure of that person. The school board cannot and should not try to perform the work of the superintendent, no matter how capable the board members may be. The school board is not supposed to administer the schools and does not have the legal authority to do so. Problems in school systems often can be traced to the board trying to supersede the superintendent.

The superintendent is the chief executive of the school system, no matter how much pressure individual board members or even the entire board puts on him or her. There is a delicate balance to maintain. John Carver, a writer and consultant on governance, sums up the situation this way: "Making staff decisions trivializes the board's job, disempowers staff and interferes with their investment in their work, and reduces the degree to which the CEO (the superintendent) can be held accountable for outcomes."[2]

As a CEO, a school superintendent probably spends far more time dealing with and responding to his or her board members than a CEO counterpart in business. Corporate board members may live far from headquarters and see much less of the CEO than those on school boards, who encounter the superintendent at school and district functions. School board members also may stop by administrative headquarters to chat with the superintendent with some regularity and interact with the superintendent at various board committee meetings. James H. Lytle, an education professor and former superintendent, estimated that a superintendent spends 20 to 50 percent of his or her working time on board-related matters.[3]

An intrusive and power-hungry school board can readily violate the relationship with the superintendent. Working behind the scenes, board members may make it known, for instance, that they want certain people hired and the superintendent may very well heed them. Few members of the general public—and even other board members—will know what transpired. Differences and factions among board members may create situations that only a Solomonic superintendent can resolve. Breaks in the relationship between board and superintendent may shatter confidence and fracture lines of communication.

A superintendent who works for a board that knows and understands how to govern has an easier job. Then, the members recognize the differences between their role and that of the superintendent. Such a board acts in ways that serve the best interests of the students in the classrooms. The savviest superintendents therefore help board members build their capacity for governance. Not all superintendents recognize this part of their role. In fact, a superintendent may feel that he or she can be more effectively insulated from potential meddling by not making board members more adept in their role. This attitude, though, leaves the superintendent less effective than if the board were more capable of good governance.

A school board, while trying to respect the superintendent's role, certainly should not restrict its agenda to items of the superintendent's choosing, though the superintendent may have more of a hand than board members in shaping the agenda. When a board is purely reactive to the superintendent's agenda it raises the question of why the board exists. Surely, individual board members who keep themselves informed can use meetings to bring items to the attention of the board at large and to seek action on some of those items.

School superintendents are like baseball managers. Once they get into the network they gravitate from one superintendency to another, almost regardless of performance. More than four out of five of them like what they do, 48 percent calling the job "very rewarding" and 33 percent calling it "rewarding."[4] School boards often find it easier and less challenging simply to hire someone who has experience as a superintendent in another district than to go through the hard work of conducting a full-blown search to find the best qualified candidate even if that person may not have previously been a superintendent.

There is reason to wonder whether school boards spend enough time thinking about the characteristics they want their superintendents to possess. There are so many different kinds of issues from one school system to another that boards of education should not regard superintendents as interchangeable. The ethnic composition of the enrollment, the existence of achievement gaps among groups of students, whether or not the existing curriculum and instruction are working, the depth of the central administration, relations with the teacher union, and communication with the public, all of these factors and many more ought to determine which superintendent a board hires.

### Hiring, Evaluating and Rewarding the Superintendent

Unlike managers of major league baseball clubs, school superintendents are the highest-paid employees in their organizations. In this game, there are no star players who earn more than their bosses. There is no Alex Rodriguez educator who makes more money than a Joe Girardi superintendent. The superintendent, like a chief executive in the business world, is "numero uno" in elementary and secondary education when it comes to his or her salary.

School boards in recent years have in fact taken a page from the book of corporate boards and enriched superintendents—at public expense—to a degree unknown until the 1990s. Superintendents of large school systems routinely earn annual salaries of more than $250,000 and they may get such perquisites as a car and driver, an expense account, and possibly a temporary residence to add to the allure of their positions. There are no lucrative stock options for school boards to award to superintendents, and their salaries and perquisites may be paltry by corporate standards, but sometimes superintendents get the educational equivalent of a golden parachute when they retire. Remuneration for superintendents outside the big urban areas is more modest. The average salary for superintendents is $211,867 in systems of 25,000 or more students, $164,376 in systems with enrollments from 10,000 to 24,999, $146,402 with enrollments from 2,500 to 9,999, and $108,218 where enrollments number fewer than 2,499 students.[5]

While the analogy to baseball managers may not apply to salary differences between school superintendents and the people who work under them, there is a comparison that one may draw from the world of sports. Superintendents resemble athletic coaches in that the best of them are leaders. Maybe that is why so many school boards historically have turned to former coaches in their search for both principals and superintendents. School systems need superintendents who can inspire others and direct them down productive paths. School boards face a huge challenge in identifying potential leaders conversant in instructional issues. The Wallace Foundation underscored the importance of leadership in 2009 by providing Harvard University with a $10-million grant to set up a tuition-free doctoral program to prepare educational leaders. The program will focus on people, especially principals and superintendents, capable of bringing about major school reform.

*When Problems Intervene*

Pressures on school superintendents are enormous and while school board members should hold high expectations of these chief executives, they also should appreciate the myriad challenges facing the modern superintendent. Taxpayers increasingly resent requests to provide more and more money for education. Parents want the best for their children and grow disenchanted when they suspect that the schools do not deliver. Teachers want a say in their working conditions. Special interest groups push single-mindedly for programs that do not serve wider purposes. The news media put the superintendent under a microscope in an attempt to discern flaws.

Ideally, a superintendent—in addition to being a problem-solver—will be an instructional leader, though critics might say that is asking too much of the person at the top and that a deputy superintendent for curriculum and instruction should suffice. Yes, a superintendent without deep knowledge of curriculum and instruction may surround himself or herself with aides who provide instructional expertise, but a superintendent ideally will possess such understandings and not have to depend on others to fill in the blanks.

For these many reasons some school boards may hire search firms to identify candidates for the position of superintendent. School board members may not be adept at interviewing candidates about the esoterica of teaching and learning. On the other hand, boards may be reluctant to spend money on searches for candidates, and some boards reserve the responsibility of a search for themselves, however qualified or unqualified board members may be for such a task. Is it any wonder that some districts end up with superintendents who are poor matches for the districts that hire them? The honeymoon may not last long. Given the expense of a superintendent's salary and benefits and the person's impact on a district, $20,000 or so seems a small price to pay for a search.

A veteran superintendent, especially one advancing toward retirement, might cultivate candidates from the ranks, especially ones who display outstanding leadership as central administrators and building principals. But most often a search is in order when a vacancy looms. A school board should vet even inside candidates to see how they measure up against others. School boards hire two-thirds of superintendents into their jobs from outside the district, a practice that occurs more often in small districts, where the pool of internal candidates is more modest.[6]

The periodic evaluation of the superintendent's performance is one of a school board's major tasks. This may sound like a trivial matter, but if the board does not evaluate the superintendent, then no one else will. The superintendent is the sole direct employee of the school board. Such evaluations generally occur annually, toward the conclusion of the school year. The evaluation should not be carried out in a vacuum. At the time that the board hires the superintendent and each year thereafter, the board, with input from the superintendent, should set performance goals for the superintendent, specific benchmarks by which to measure the person. In so doing, the school board accomplishes two tasks—moving the school system forward by identifying objectives and providing a yardstick by which to gauge the superintendent's performance.

A survey by the National School Boards Association found that the three most important factors that members used to evaluate their superintendents were the board-superintendent relationship, the morale of school system employees, and the safety of students. The next two factors rated "very important" by board members were management and district performance on standardized assessments.[7] The board's relationship with the superintendent should rank very high if the parties are to work together for the betterment of the district. Some school boards may overlook employee morale, but they should not forget the role that the superintendent plays in helping teachers and others feel content in their work. Finally, a district that cannot protect its students from harm may readily lose the confidence of parents and find the entire enterprise falling apart.

Some experts take exception with the idea that school boards should evaluate their superintendents. Robert W. Flinchbaugh, an authority on school governance, argued that evaluations of a superintendent are inevitably subjective and will not necessarily motivate a superintendent. Better than formal evaluations of superintendents, according to Flinchbaugh—who is in a minority with this opinion—is to encourage self-evaluation. "If superintendents are the chief executive officers of school organizations who manage resources for the benefit of developing people, programs, and policies, how can they be evaluated when there are so many variables involved over which they have no control?"[8] This position, followed to its logical conclusion, could mean that almost no one's performance should be formally assessed.

*Charlotte: The Superintendent and the Board Pulling Together*

A superintendent may be most effective when he or she operates with the school board members as a team, a goal not readily realized. The Charlotte-Mecklenburg

Public Schools lacked such a team approach in the spring of 2005, when critics applied the word "dysfunctional" to the school board and a Citizens' Task Force convened to explore ways to improve the 133,600-student system. The report that the group commissioned with foundation aid and issued later in the year declared "a need for greater strategic policy leadership from the district's school board." It also stated that a "disconnect" between the system and the community would not be repaired by simply a "better communications plan or a set of discrete policy changes."[9] The report left no doubt that the board had to alter its approach.

Changes that might give the district what it needed loomed on the horizon. Quietly and out of sight, the school board was already undergoing training from the Center for the Reform of School Systems with a grant from the Broad Foundation. Also, in the wake of the report's release, a search for a new superintendent led to the pursuit of a candidate who seemed to possess the qualities that the task force had in mind for the school system. "Without that report, I wouldn't be here," Peter Gorman told me in late 2009, three years after he assumed the superintendency. He felt that community dissatisfaction with the system set the stage for bringing in a transformational leader.

The readiness for change of school board members as a result of their training made his ascension possible. Gorman joined them for the last stages of the training. "It helped us understand that we are a team—the board and the superintendent—and how the team could best work together," Molly Griffin, the nonpracticing lawyer who was the chairperson of the school board, said of the training in retrospect. What they learned led board members to focus intensely on policy and governance, their proper role.

A theory of action produced in conjunction with the school board's training proved a vital document, setting out a strategic approach for the board's planning, goals, policies, budgets, and actions. It gave Gorman what he considered a bully pulpit from which he and the staff could drive reform. Whenever a member of the board demurred from some of his proposals, he joked that the person was suffering "amnesia," having forgotten the approach to which the board committed itself.

One of Gorman's more controversial initiatives, stemming from the school board's embrace of improved achievement in all the district's 176 schools, was his plan for getting principals and teachers who had proved themselves to transfer to low-performing schools. Using various incentives, Gorman induced extensive staff changes at 25 schools by 2010. There was some unease over his hiring in 2009 of 100 members of Teach for America—especially for the low-performing schools—to bring the district's total force of teachers from this program to 250. Performance gains reported in the fall of 2009 seemed to show that Gorman and the board had put the system on the right track. The scores of black and low-income students on state high school exams exceeded those of their peers in most of the rest of North Carolina.[10]

By the end of 2009, though, there were questions about the ability of Charlotte-Mecklenburg to sustain its pursuit of improved student achievement. Almost all the board members who had undergone training had left the board. The future of the team approach was in question, a possible victim of the turnover that undoes some school boards that finally learn to work together.

### The Special Situation of Urban School Superintendents

Superintendents of urban school districts occupy the most precarious perches. Turnover in the position can be so quick that an urban superintendent has little time to make a mark on a school system and disappears from the job before meeting all the building principals. Harry Hodges, a commentator on issues in public administration, said decades ago that the urban school board is "one of those instruments of tortuous propensities which, beaming with unbecoming and reflected wisdom, wanders in a twilight zone between civil squander and political connivance. Undoubtedly, some future public appraisal, beyond the board's discernment, will snuff it out."[11] On average, urban superintendents served in their posts for four and half to five years as of the beginning of the 2000s.[12] The lack of continuity in the post can devastate urban districts. School boards in the largest districts sometimes seek saviors, people who can come in and work miracles in just a short time.

School boards across the country in urban settings have had modest success, at best, in governance. Invariably, the nation's students fare worst in big-city schools. By and large, school boards serving such districts have not fashioned successful policies to deal with learning in the midst of the concentrated deprivation that afflicts most such school systems. Perhaps better school boards could accomplish more for urban education, but the problems that afflict such districts may simply be too great for them to overcome. "It will be surprising if changing the governing structure alone solves the problems of urban education," said Joseph M. Cronin, the governor's secretary for education in Massachusetts in the mid-1970s.[13] The problems have only compounded since then.

Large urban school districts sometimes hire noneducators as superintendents. Presumably, the school boards that follow this course believe that a person familiar with leading a large organization of any sort can provide the expertise needed by a school system of unwieldy size. Other times the board may hope that it has found a charismatic noneducator whose personality will loom large, branding the school district positively and serving as an element to prod people to collaborate to solve problems. Perhaps school boards also look outside the education world to find someone willing to bang heads and take a hard-nosed approach of the sort that an education professional may find distasteful.

Michelle Rhee was one such urban superintendent, taking the reins in 2007 in Washington DC, where Mayor Adrian Fenty essentially conferred upon her the responsibility for both governing and managing the public schools when he named her chancellor. Rhee took a confrontational approach that won her enemies by the roomful. She sought to reform a system that had tolerated incompetence and corruption while student achievement lagged and per-student spending ranked among the highest in the country. Many of its schools did not measure up to the adequate yearly progress demanded by the No Child Left Behind Act. Extreme measures were needed, and Rhee took them, becoming a darling of the national media.

Rhee fired teachers, principals, and paraprofessionals whom she judged as inadequate. She closed about two dozen schools. She tried to make professional development more effective. And she picked a fight with the teacher union, which was accustomed to calling the shots and working closely with a political establishment that reputedly used the school system to dispense patronage. The union fought back and even sent its biggest gun, Randi Weingarten, president of the American Federation of Teachers, to exchange fire with Rhee.

It was not a stretch, relying on some of her statements, to imagine that Rhee would like to have eliminated tenure, but it was unlikely that she could achieve this goal. She talked about the need to swap tenure for higher salaries. She also wanted to be able to bypass the usual credentialing requirements and hire and retain as teachers those who gave most promise of performing well in the classroom. Ultimately, in exchange for whopping salary increases for teachers who would voluntarily agree to participate, Rhee and the union tentatively reached agreement in the spring of 2010 on a merit pay plan, a large portion of which private foundations agreed to finance.

## A Lack of Continuity

Turnover on school boards may leave superintendents in the lurch. The board majority that hired a superintendent and agreed with his or her plans may soon dissolve as another election alters the board and a different group of members attains power. This is the democratic way, but surely it has some weaknesses when it comes to the operations of school systems. What's a superintendent faced by such a school board to do? Within a year or two after signing a contract, a superintendent may no longer work for the group of board members that hired him or her. Buyouts of superintendents' contracts speak to a flaw created by the steady turnover in the composition of school boards. Democracy demands that members of elected boards regularly subject themselves to the voters, but the system has an inherent weakness in its impact on the board-superintendent relationship.

There is also the matter of the superintendent simply falling out of favor with the board. Alan Bersin, the San Diego superintendent from 1998 to 2005, lived through such a situation. He got into a running battle with some of the five board members and with the teacher union. He was accused of top-down leadership and of failing to get buy-in from the teachers for his initiatives.[14] Urban school districts tend to have many and fractionated constituencies. A superintendent courts disaster when he or she seeks to institute reforms without winning backing among the district's many constituencies. Michael D. Usdan wrote in an astute analysis of the San Diego situation that Bersin might have been more successful if he had involved the various groups in his efforts and if he had avoided personality clashes with his critics.[15] Easier said than done. In any event, according to Usdan, divisions in a school system, once created, are difficult to heal.

Ramon C. Cortines, the superintendent in Los Angeles, believed that it was up to the superintendent to let both board members and teachers know what he expected of them, a delicate role for a superintendent wanting to keep peace in a big-city district. "A lot of people like to rag on boards, but I think the superintendent has a responsibility to help a board and provide leadership as it relates to working together," he said in an interview with the *Los Angeles Times* in 2008. He also reflected on the observations he had made during visits to more than 40 of the system's schools during his first seven months on the job. Cortines said: "I find a wonderful teaching force; I find leadership. But I also find some mediocrity, and when I see it, I call out. I'm going to continue to put people on notice when I see they're not living up to what I believe students deserve." He prefaced his comments with the statement: "For too long, we have focused on the needs of adults and not the needs of students."[16]

School boards in large urban settings sometimes find it difficult to concentrate on the needs of students instead of those of the adults. Unionized employees of the school system can hardly be ignored. Racial and ethnic groups scrap for a fair share of whatever there is to divvy up. Taxpayers, when they pay attention to the public schools, moan about their pocketbooks. Government officials at all levels may not be able to restrain themselves from meddling. Many of these ingredients came together during the 2008 through 2009 school year in Los Angeles and Miami, and the school boards in those two cities did not emerge with the smell of roses upon them.

### The Lethal Mix of Politics and Education in Los Angeles

The troubles in Los Angeles began when the school board in 2007, concerned that the new mayor wanted to dictate the selection of a superintendent, raced to outdo him and sped down an unorthodox road to do so. The board—without a thorough search—chose David L. Brewer, a retired Navy vice admiral, to head the Los Angeles Unified Public Schools just as Mayor Antonio Villaraigosa was trying to persuade the state legislature to give him control over the system. Brewer probably knew a lot about ships and salt water, but apparently was much less familiar with lesson plans and formative evaluations. Any such appointment in a city in which the strains of diversity tug at the civic fabric is fraught with potential controversy. Brewer happens to be black and Latinos are ascendant in Los Angeles.

Nonetheless, Brewer looked like someone new and different, unstained by past associations and free of encumbrances. On the other hand, he turned out not to have the benefit of history and context within the Los Angeles Unified School District bureaucracy and, perhaps more importantly, lacked the political savvy to find his way through school board divisions and through a larger political structure in the city and the state.

Brewer got tangled early in a mess created by a school board that was trying to court the support of the teacher union by turning cafeteria workers into full-time employees to qualify them for health benefits. He objected to the move, saying it would cost $35 million a year to make such a change. Most of the board ignored the superintendent and lengthened the hours of the cafeteria workers, leading to an additional expense for a hard-pressed school system that within two years would find it necessary to send layoff notices to thousands of its teachers.

The school board's patience for Brewer to learn on the job waned, and his support weakened as candidates supported by the mayor gained control of the board. Brewer had no power base in the school system or in the city when whispers spread halfway through his four-year term that the board was moving toward buying out his contract. The fact that test scores were rising in the public schools and that Brewer had won voter approval for a $7-billion school construction bond issue did not seem sufficient to save his job. The board majority treaded gingerly, though, trying not to step on the sensibilities of the only black member, who had been a Brewer supporter. Finally, as Los Angeles was preparing for its annual snowless Christmas in 2008, five of the school board's seven members voted to pay Brewer some $517,500 to go away quietly.

The rise and fall of David Brewer illustrates the nature of the treacherous waters in which urban school superintendents must swim. The composition of the school board can change abruptly, dispatching the superintendent's supporters and leaving him reliant on successors not inclined to throw him a life preserver. The sharks, known as politicians, may circle the superintendent with ill intent. And the teacher union bides its time, knowing that, like the sea, it is a constant, outlasting any superintendent. An urban superintendency is no place for a naïf. This is not the beginner's pond. The post requires a powerful swimmer who can conquer deep waters, endure through many laps, and finesse a rebellious school board, if necessary.

### The Lethal Mix of Politics and Education in Miami

The story of Rudy Crew's superintendency in the Miami-Dade County Public Schools, the country's fourth-largest system, is different and yet somewhat the same as Brewer's. This time the superintendent was an adept veteran, his mettle having been tested as the schools chancellor in New York City, where he and the other Rudy, Mayor Guiliani, often seemed at odds. Confident and steely, Crew had the benefit of having played in the big show. But ethnicity, politics, and the shifting sands of school board composition illustrated that even experience does not guarantee success in the urban jungle with its many predators.

Miami had been proud to land Crew in 2004, when other school boards competed for his services. He was to be the magician who would turn around a school system that had had an inadequate commitment to boosting academics. The number of students taking Advanced Placement exams increased sharply on his watch. Academic improvement was modest, and he invested a great deal of his credibility in a $100-million school improvement zone that provided 39 schools with a special reading program, a longer school day, and a longer school year.

So much for superintendents whose boards expect them to pull rabbits out of hats. By the summer of 2008, with the school year looming, there was already talk of ousting Crew from a position that paid more than $300,000 a year. His take-charge style and his willingness to confront board members did not win him the support he needed, and a financial crisis engulfed the district. It was unclear whether the superintendent was responsible for a budget shortfall of tens of millions of dollars or simply the victim of forces beyond his control. Furthermore, the composition of the school board had shifted, and the margin of Crew's backing dwindled to a single vote even though the board had extended his contract to 2010.

One of his opponents on the board used a summer board meeting to read a manifesto calling for Crew's dismissal. This pronouncement stirred chaos on the podium and in the audience, a feat easily accomplished in Miami, a cauldron of volatile ethnic divisions where Cuban-Americans predominate and other groups contend for a modicum of recognition. Perhaps the position of an African-American superintendent in such a setting, especially one not keen on playing politics, was a controversy waiting to erupt. Crew called it a "high-tech lynching of my reputation."[17]

And so at the beginning of September, as the school year began, the board bought out Crew's contract and elevated one of his deputies to replace him without so much as a sham of a search. No matter that the American Association of School Administrators had named him superintendent of the year. The coup de grace came in 2009, when Crew was just a memory and a final report declared that his school improvement zone failed to deliver much improvement on the Florida Comprehensive Assessment tests.[18]

### Other Administrators

The team of top administrators that surrounds the superintendent does much to determine his or her success or failure. A school board, if possible, probably should defer to the superintendent's choices of people to fill these positions and give the superintendent the chance to choose the deputies upon whom his or her success depends. The two individuals who can do the most to bolster the superintendent are the business administrator and the associate or assistant superintendent, who occupies the number two position in the instructional hierarchy. Building principals are the most important administrators other than the superintendent. A school board should take a keen interest in these positions. The swiftest way to undermine a school is to appoint a bad principal or to allow a bad principal to continue in his or her position.

### Principals as Leaders

Since 2000, mainly at the instigation of the Wallace Foundation, the educational world has paid more attention than ever before to the importance of leadership among school principals. Wallace poured millions of dollars into research on leadership issues among principals. One such project, an extensive review of the research literature, concluded that "leadership is second only to classroom instruction among school-related factors that influence student outcomes."[19]

Yet until very recently programs to prepare principals—and superintendents, as well—did not focus on leadership. Some programs over the years have led to advanced degrees and certificates in "educational leadership," but this euphemistic label did not speak to the content or caliber of such programs, which mostly dealt with the same old management training. School board members should be looking for management skills in the principals whose appointments they approve, but that is not enough for the modern principal who ought to be able to lead instructional improvement.

Arthur Levine, president of the Woodrow Wilson National Fellowship Foundation, who wrote a major report on the preparation of school administrators, observed: "Principals are being called to lead in the redesign of their schools and school systems. In an outcome-based and accountability-driven era, administrators have to lead their schools in the rethinking of goals, priorities, finances, staffing, curriculum, pedagogies, learning resources, assessment methods, technology, and use of time and space."[20]

School boards should recognize that a weakness in the induction of new principals is the inadequate mentoring they receive. Boards may address such shortcomings by putting the right policies in place to provide mentors drawn from the ranks of experienced or retired principals who have demonstrated leadership in their own careers. No one should become a principal unless that person shows a deep understanding of the learning process and gives promise of applying this knowledge in a school setting.

This is not to say that school boards can rely on a precise formula to ensure that principals will be able to lead their schools. The demands on principals, particularly in the most troubled schools, call for leadership in situations that may appear beyond anyone's control. A full menu of difficulties seems to defy intervention. Some students return home each day to homes in which they may find little support for educational goals or where parents who want to reinforce schooling don't know how. Students' families may move frequently, disrupting educational continuity. The permeability of the schoolhouse may allow the intrusion of the effects of gang culture, poverty, lack of sleep, and homelessness. And yet, the principal is expected to lead the school to high academic achievement.

### School Board Members and the Administrators

Board members ought to get used to the idea that they preside over a large enterprise in which many of the employees see them as the bosses. While school boards do, in fact, approve the hiring—and infrequently the firing—of employees at the recommendation of the superintendent, it is nonetheless a stretch to portray them as bosses. The superintendent, as chief executive officer, works for the board and everyone else works for the superintendent. The amount of authority that the board has over the jobs of employees is defined essentially by the law: labor contracts that are the result of collective bargaining. Nonetheless, the misconception persists that school boards wield great authority over employees.

For all intents and purposes, the superintendent does all the hiring and the school board merely rubber stamps his or her selections to give them legal standing. Some school boards and some individual members act inappropriately, insinuating themselves into the process and influencing the choices the superintendent makes. Even in Massachusetts—where an ambiguous law seems to allow school boards to select not only the superintendent but also the associate superintendent, the special education director, and the business administrator—the school board generally acts in no more than an advise-and-consent capacity on these appointments.

"The CEO role insulates the staff from the board and the board from the staff," John Carver wrote of the superintendent.[21] The superintendent runs the school system, and the board of education, if it adheres to the letter of the law, must work through the superintendent to accomplish almost everything it wants to happen. It is not up to board members to give orders to district employees; board members should never speak to them critically about their performance. Board members should work through the superintendent on any matter involving the work of employees. I can't say this enough: The superintendent is the only employee who works for the board of education.

# Chapter 6

# Teachers

## The Heart of the Enterprise

When I ran for the school board, I spoke to a potential voter, who also happened to be a teacher in the school district, about the need to assure merit-based hiring, which means, of course, that jobs go to the most qualified, not to those best connected. Our slate was running on the slogan: "*Hiring should be based on what you know, not whom you know.*" This seems a reasonable enough proposition.

All the teacher-voter had to hear tumble from my mouth was the word "merit," a red-flag for many of the country's teachers. She immediately turned antagonistic. I quickly concluded that the word triggered notions of merit-based pay, which many teachers think means evaluating their performance and awarding higher salaries to those with the best records. I explained to her that I was talking only about the point at which teachers get hired. I was careful from that point forward to try to avoid the word "merit." I shifted my references to "hiring the best qualified."

Teachers figure mightily in the considerations of most school board candidates, especially in places with collective bargaining. The teacher union is the most potent force in many school board elections, and a candidate who runs without its backing or offends the union must struggle to get elected. The union often endorses candidates in contested elections, spends money and time in their behalf, and dispatches its members in force to vote for them. The union's campaign workers and donors are not only those who work and live in the district but teachers in neighboring districts who belong to the union and reside in the district where the voting takes place. Retired teachers are another bloc of potential campaign workers and voters, as well as members of other unions who are brothers and sisters in labor.

Terry M. Moe's study of the voting patterns of teachers in board elections in 70 California school districts showed that teachers vote at higher rates than other citizens, especially if they work in the same district where they live. Their occupational self-interest figures in their turnouts. Moe hypothesized that if teachers voted in school board elections simply out of public spirit and commitment to education they would cast their ballots at the same rate whether or not they lived in the district in which they worked. But he found that "teachers who live in a district but don't work there vote at lower rates than the teachers who both live and work there."[1]

## Power—But Not Necessarily to the People

The teacher union has almost unlimited resources to back its favored candidates and to push its agenda. A local teacher union can call on the state organization when it perceives a particularly strong threat to its influence. And where the stakes are especially high, one or the other of the national teacher groups—the National Education Association (NEA) or the American Federation of Teachers (AFT)—may get involved. Presumably, candidates whom the teacher union endorses for reelection have shown during their time on the school board that they vote in ways that the union approves, particularly when it comes to employment contracts and matters of salary and benefits. New candidates who win the union endorsement often have the blessing of the union's favorite incumbents and have indicated their sympathy with the union.

### The Union's Clout

I recall listening to a person who had spent several terms on a school board boast that he did not bother to raise money in behalf of his various campaigns for reelection. He said that even if some supporter sent him a check to help his campaign he would return the check, implying that he was above such matters. He didn't mention that he was a favorite of the teacher union and that the union endorsed his candidacy time and again. He didn't need to raise money and garner other forms of assistance because the union lavished support on him. Members of the union provided hundreds of hours of free labor—making phone calls, preparing mailings, erecting lawn signs, and doing anything else to promote his candidacy. For an upcoming campaign, the union had already asked teachers to contribute to a political action committee five months before the election, mentioning in its appeal, which remained confidential, that he would be one of the endorsees.

When I contended for a seat, I ran on a slate with two other candidates. Three seats were up for election on the nine-member board. The union endorsed the other slate, which consisted of two incumbents, both retired physical education teachers, and a new candidate whom they invited to run with them. Our slate decided early that we would run independent of the union and not seek its endorsement. The union invited all eight candidates—two men ran as independents, members of neither slate—to a meet-and-greet session at which the candidates mingled and chatted with teacher union activists. We also filled out and submitted forms that they had given us, requesting biographical information and answers to questions on our positions on some issues. I added a few sentences at the end respectfully declining the union's endorsement even if it chose to give it to me.

Democracy can be replete with contradictions. Such a special interest group as a teacher union has every right to endorse candidates. Yet democracy gives an edge to the wealthiest, the strongest, and the best organized. Thus, special interest groups, whether the issue involves elective politics or lobbying, tend to usurp the authority of the people. Office-holders and those seeking office—school board members or others—may defer to special interests to gain and retain their positions, which democracy also allows. The interests of the general public may coincide with those of special groups. The problem comes when this is not the case, when, for example, a more modest contract settlement with employees would better serve the taxpayers or make more money available for nonpersonnel purposes. Democracy is somewhat out of whack when it comes to school boards vs. teacher unions. The balance is uneven, like President Reagan's war against Grenada.

School board members who engage in collective bargaining are part-time amateurs lacking the experience and the expertise of the full-time professionals from the state organization whom the local union can bring to the table. Meanwhile, a typical school board may hold down expenses by using less-skilled bargainers. Curt Wary, director of labor relations for the New Jersey School Boards Association, reminded people that the teacher union's inclination to reject caps on taxes and on spending is "based on a deeply ingrained perception that no matter what happens elsewhere, the money will always magically float down from the heavens and into their pockets."[2]

An impasse between a school board and a union may end up in the hands of a mediator or a fact finder, but there is also the ultimate weapon in the arsenal of the teacher union: a strike or, at least, a slowdown. Strikes by teachers occur far less frequently than in former years, but they still loom as threats. Parents, as taxpayers, urge school boards to be firm with unions, but they don't want strikes. A strike interrupts a child's education, throws family schedules off kilter, and can fill a community with rancor.

Teacher unions in some districts can be relentless in waging campaigns in behalf of the contract settlement that they desire. They don't even have to strike to make their point. They may wear into their classrooms custom-made t-shirts carrying slogans that call for the contract to be finished. Like workers on a production line, teachers dissatisfied with the pace of negotiations may engage in a slowdown, adhering strictly to the letter of the existing contract and filing enough grievances to jam the system. Sometimes students become pawns in these efforts. For high school seniors, anxious about their college applications, it may mean the refusal of teachers to write letters of recommendation to admissions offices.

The union is a juggernaut against which candidates who challenge the union's favored candidates must compete. The state education department in New Jersey recognizes the influence of the teacher union and has a regulation disqualifying anyone who gets elected to a school board with union endorsement from joining collective-bargaining negotiations with teachers for a year after the election. Nonetheless, many candidates seek the union's backing, recognizing the difficulty of getting elected without it.

### Pressuring Board Members

Tales from two parts of the country illustrate what can happen when members of school boards lock horns with local teacher unions. Both were incumbents. One held onto his seat; the other lost her seat. In 2002, the first time Mike Treadway ran for and won a seat on the Blount County School Board in eastern Tennessee, there were two candidates for one position. The Blount County Education Association, the local union for the district's 750 teachers, coendorsed both and aided each of their campaigns. Treadway's father-in-law had been a principal in Blount County for 35 years and so the union looked favorably upon him.

It didn't take long for Treadway, vice president for operations at an architectural firm, to fall out of favor with the union. He discovered during his first year on the school board that teachers did not need to check in at the main office of their schools upon their arrival each morning. "It was a matter of respect," he told me in looking back on his unsuccessful attempt to change the provision. "You let the principal know that you're in the building so that someone will know whether to get on the phone and find a substitute and so a classroom is not left unattended."

The existing contract with the union did not require teachers to check in. Treadway was in a minority of two on a seven-member board. He wasn't about to get support from the other five members—four former teachers and the husband of a teacher, he said. From that point on, Treadway was not viewed as a friend of teachers. When he ran again three years later as an incumbent in line to become the board chair, the teacher union withheld its endorsement. Nevertheless, Treadway was reelected, but his relationship with the union did not improve.

During the 2008 through 2009 school year, when the economy turned sour, Treadway opposed a 2 percent raise for teachers that would come on top of previously agreed upon contractual increases scheduled for teachers on the steps of the contract. The local Alcoa plant had just laid off 400 more employees and home foreclosures in Blount County were rising. The school board embraced frugality in an effort to assure that it would not have to dismiss any teachers or even reduce their salaries. Treadway had a bitter exchange at a school board meeting with the president of the teacher union. "The president raked us over the coals for not granting the raise, and I told him that it was inappropriate when people were facing the kind of situation they were in our county," said Treadway, who felt disheartened and who at that point had one year remaining in his term on the board.

Johanne Presser got into a different sort of squabble with teachers in Suffield, Connecticut, a historic town of 13,500 in the north-central part of the state, near the Massachusetts border. The dispute cost Presser her seat after 12 years on the school board, just as she was about to become president of the statewide Connecticut Association of School Boards.

Presser raised the possibility of converting the high school to block scheduling. The math teachers especially disliked the idea, not wanting to change the way in which they organized the curriculum. Members of the teacher union and towns-people filled the auditorium when an effort was made to explain block scheduling. "I thought I'd get run out of town," Presser said in retrospect.

Tempers were still hot when the time came for the school board election. Some teachers pushed for Presser's defeat. She had further alienated the math teachers—and teachers in general—by intervening as a parent to try to focus attention on a teacher whom she and some other parents felt was doing a poor job teaching an honors math course to their children. It did not help in the election that Presser's name was last on the ballot listing eight candidates for five open seats. She lost her seat by nine votes.

### Playing for Keeps

Anyone who wonders whether teacher unions can play for keeps only has to look at the national political picture. Every four years, members of the NEA and the AFT make up the largest bloc of delegates at the Democratic National Convention. Any Democrat who does not curry favor with organized teachers does so at great risk. Jon Corzine, New Jersey's former Democratic governor, won a reputation for his sympathies for unions, perhaps the most vital source of his support. In 2008, he delayed signing a bill to put modest restrictions on pensions and benefits for teachers and other government employees. The state's largest newspaper said that he held back his signature at the behest of the president of the statewide teacher union. The delay beyond September meant that the change would not affect new teachers joining payrolls that fall, costing the taxpayers an estimated $1.4 million annually for the rest of the lives of those teachers.

Teacher unions involve themselves in statewide elections, spending money and mobilizing voters for and against various issues, as well as in candidates' races. In 2008, for instance, teacher organizations campaigned against California's Proposition Eight proposal to ban gay marriage; against South Dakota's Measure 10 proposal to prohibit governmental units and other groups from using tax money to campaign or lobby; against an Arizona proposal to make it more difficult to pass ballot items related to taxes and spending; and against elimination of the state income tax in Massachusetts.

The father of teacher power was Albert Shanker, who became president of the United Federation of Teachers (UFT) in New York City and, later, of the AFT, holding the two positions simultaneously for a while. In the 1960s and '70s he showed teachers that they could stand up to school boards and win—by striking, if necessary. I knew Shanker and wrote about him on many occasions. "Power is a good thing," he told me. "It's better than powerlessness."[3] Indeed!

Teachers, like other special interest groups, take for granted their right to be players in elective politics. When New York City's Department of Education asked principals to enforce a longstanding regulation banning school staff from promoting political candidates while on school property, the UFT sued for what the union claimed was a right protected by the First Amendment. A federal court ruled in 2008 that the city could prohibit school personnel from wearing political buttons in school but said that the teachers could place campaign materials in colleagues' school mailboxes and hang posters on bulletin boards maintained by the teachers union.[4]

Articles appear from time to time telling of the waning influence of organized labor. Often, those articles fail to note that this decline has occurred in the private sector—among autoworkers and steelworkers, for example. Meanwhile, unions remain powerful in government and employees covered by collective bargaining in the public sector, like teachers, hold many of society's most secure jobs, with the best health and retirement benefits available for workers of their income group. In 2009, for the first time in American history, most union members worked for the government, not in the private sector.[5]

It is easier for school boards to yield to teacher unions than to stand up to them on behalf of students and taxpayers. Writing about the leaders of America's car-making and steel-making corporations, which bestowed generous salaries and benefits on their employees rather than endure labor strife, the *New York Times* said of the two industries, "Both secured peace with their unions by vastly expanding benefits, a bargain that eventually hobbled them."[6] School boards may be permitting their employees to take the public sector in a similar direction.

### The Contract

The industrial model rather than the corporate model dictates compensation and benefits in school systems. Boards of education do little to change the situation. In practice this means that during the term of a labor contract, which ordinarily extends for about three years, the board obligates itself to pay a set amount to its educators and other employees and to provide prescribed benefits regardless of what happens to the economy and no matter how much tax revenues decline. Even if the board has to cut costs in response to the taxpayers rejecting a budget, the board usually does so only in noncontractual areas that affect students most directly—transportation, athletics, class trips, and textbooks, for instance. As a noncommercial enterprise the school system sometimes has no recourse but to mandate that parents pay fees for the aforementioned services.

Nothing is simple when it comes to the compensation of educators. When a contract contains a salary ladder, teachers may spend anywhere from five to 20 years ascending the rungs and getting specified increases along the way. Previous contractual agreements may raise pay within the salary guide no matter how outside fiscal conditions affect the district. School boards refer to these amounts as "old money" because they are the result of previous agreements. Employees move through the steps automatically, receiving pay increases at regular intervals—usually annually. The increase stemming from the latest negotiation is "new money," paid on top of the old money. When a school board negotiates a new contract with teachers, the percentage increase represented by the raise is almost always expressed in terms of what it means in new money at the lowest and highest points in the salary guide, not for the large number of teachers on the steps of the salary guide.

Thus, the taxpayers might think that a 3 percent settlement means, for instance, that the salaries of all the district's teachers will increase by 3 percent. But that may hardly be the case. The steps within the salary guide, called bumps, are seldom even, and at most points, a teacher may be in line for anything from a 5 percent to a whopping 15 percent raise in old money. The 3 percent figure would not begin to reflect the actual raises that some educators receive nor the full impact on the budget because these teachers get the latest increase in addition to the much larger increase set by the salary guide.

Reports on salary negotiations in the media and elsewhere concentrate on new money and seldom mention old money. An exception came in 2009, when *The Columbus Dispatch* carried an investigative article questioning why at a time when the salaries of some Ohioans were frozen, cut, or taken away altogether, teachers in almost every Franklin County district would average 5.9 to 8.8 percent raises.[7] Steps in the contracts, old money, were a large part of the reason.

### When School Boards Surrender Authority

The contract between a local teacher union and the board of education is a complicated document that may run dozens of pages. It not only sets salaries and other aspects of compensation, but also—depending on how willing the school board has been to bargain away its authority—the degree of control that teachers exert over working conditions and other aspects of instruction. "It is actually union contracts that have the greatest effect over what teachers can and cannot do,"[8] wrote Andrew J. Rotherham, an education policy analyst, in pointing out how the language in labor contracts may put straightjackets on schools.

Contracts with teachers may specify class size limits, hours of employment, how many hours a day and courses a year a teacher may be assigned to teach, and the conditions under which a supervisor may observe the teacher's instruction for purposes of evaluation. A contract may even elaborately set out the number of days that a teacher may take for bereavement without loss of pay. In my district, for instance, it was five days for the death of a parent, spouse, domestic partner, child, or sibling; four days for the death of a grandparent, grandchild, parent-in-law, grandparent-in-law, daughter-in-law, or son-in-law; three days for a sibling-in-law; and one day for a near relative—defined as an uncle, aunt, niece, nephew, or first cousin. No kidding!

And in areas of the contract that do not limit a school board's prerogatives, teachers may try to impose constraints unilaterally. The teacher union in Los Angeles called on its members in 2009 to boycott the periodic assessments that the district told them to administer to identify students' instructional needs while there was still time to prepare them for state-sponsored tests. The teacher union deemed the assessments costly and unproductive. The same year, elsewhere in California, the opposition of San Diego teachers to Superintendent Terry Grier's effort to use a value-added approach to identify the students who had the most effective teachers helped drive Grier out of his job after only two years.

Meanwhile, the union representing teachers in Florida's Pinellas County District filed a lawsuit in 2009 to stop the school board from instituting a seven-period day in the middle schools. The school system had lengthened the school day from six to seven periods before the beginning of the school year to obtain 14 more minutes of instructional time and to make more room for elective courses, a change that the school board said would save $2.2 million. The Florida teachers filed grievances, charging that the change added to their class loads and reduced their planning time without providing them with additional pay.

School boards retain dwindling control over the enterprise over which they preside. Boards have surrendered their authority to control costs and working conditions in successive bargaining agreements. Some experts maintain that these settlements impede the ability of school boards to improve education.

"Many common provisions of teacher contracts require school districts to spend substantial sums to implement policies, which research has shown have a weak or inconsistent relationship with student learning," stated a report from Education Sector, a nonpartisan policy organization in Washington. The report listed eight provisions that it said fall in this category and which account for 19 percent of expenditures even though they may not contribute to student learning: increases in teacher salaries based on years of experience; increases in teacher salaries based on education credentials; professional development days; the number of paid sick and personal days; class-size limitations; use of teachers' aides; lavish health insurance coverage; and generous retirement benefits.[9] The report did not necessarily call for spending less money but for spending it differently.

Various items in the typical contract create enough strings to tie the hands of most administrators. There are, for example, grievance procedures that drag on interminably for dealing with employee infractions and lavish provisions for leaves that complicate staffing. These are some of the last remaining contracts of the old industrial model, more appropriate for laborers in factories than for knowledge workers of the twenty-first century.

The authors of a report titled "A Better Bargain: Overhauling Teacher Collective Bargaining for the 21st Century" recommended that pay reflect the scarcity and value of teachers' skills in hard-to-staff subject areas, the difficulty of their assignments, the extent of their responsibilities, and the caliber of their work; that pension and health benefits resemble those offered by other organizations competing for college-educated professionals; that tenure be ended; that assignments to schools be made on the basis of educational need rather than seniority; that contracts have no work rules; and that contracts contain an explicit definition of managerial prerogatives.[10]

All in all, the message of this report means that school boards could better serve students if they dealt with teachers as individuals, not as fungibles to be treated the same and rewarded identically when their years' of experience and credentials are the same. It means that the level of pension and health benefits is unsustainable, and school boards should consider putting new employees into 401k plans. It means that due process laws adequately protect the employment rights of teachers and tenure is an unnecessary burden to school boards. Furthermore, it means that school officials should have the flexibility to make personnel assignments in the best interests of students and that provisions restricting working arrangements should revolve around what is best for maximizing learning opportunities for students, not what best serves adults.

### The Perquisites

School boards reward teachers by giving them permanent increases in salary for advanced studies. Usually, the contract specifies dollar amounts that teachers receive for academic credit hours and degrees earned beyond the bachelor's level. This is called differential pay, and it becomes a part of a teacher's salary base. Some boards are so generous that they pay the tuitions for teachers' graduate studies so that they may then qualify for the differential increase. It is unheard of for members of college and university faculties to receive added compensation of this sort for advanced studies, which is expected of them. School boards predicate these policies on the assumption that teachers who gain graduate degrees do a better job, but the underlying evidence is scanty.

At a time of growing fiscal pressures it would be good if school boards could revisit the policy of paying teachers more for graduate study. This practice costs school systems, collectively, $8.6 billion a year. California and New York State each spend more than $1 billion annually to compensate teachers for having master's degrees. The expense represents a per-student investment of more than $300 a year in New York State, Connecticut, Georgia, and Delaware.[11] Rather than not spending the money, spending it differently might lead to greater student learning.

Wait, there is more. The contract may specify a bonus for achieving tenure and many school boards provide longevity pay, too, adding bonuses for experienced teachers at different points of service. These sums become a permanent part of the person's salary. The tenure bonus, paid annually to teachers in my district once they have achieved tenure, added about $250,000 to our costs each year. Advocates of longevity pay insist it helps retain experienced teachers and rewards them for their loyalty. Critics say it keeps people from retiring and leaves less money for able newcomers.

Many contracts also specify the stipends that school boards pay to teachers for overseeing activities beyond regular assignments. A large portion of these stipends goes to coaches of athletic teams for both boys' and girls' teams. In my district, for instance, each of the two high schools had a seven-member coaching staff for its varsity football team at a total cost to taxpayers of $67,756 for coaching stipends. Most of the athletic coaches are physical education teachers, but teachers from the various academic departments may also coach.

It may come as a surprise to learn that physical education teachers get extra pay for coaching as one might assume that this is part of their regular assignments. But because teams practice and play their games during hours beyond the regular school day, a teacher can add thousands of dollars to his or her pay by coaching. Similarly, other teachers may receive stipends in elementary schools, middle schools, and high schools for overseeing debate teams, cheerleaders, literary and chess clubs, and a host of other after-school activities. The point is not that people shouldn't get extra pay for extra work, but that the salaries specified by the board in the labor contract are only a rough indicator of how individual teachers fare each year.

In addition, school boards may pay teachers stipends for teaching extra courses on top of their contractual load. In my district, this could mean $10,000 tacked onto a salary for accepting one extra course for the year. By contrast, adjunct instructors at many colleges and universities typically get no more than half this much for each course they teach. School boards justify this extra pay by explaining that spreading around the courses of a teacher on leave means not having to hire a new teacher with the commensurate benefits that the person would receive.

### The Springfield Solution

The concessions and failures of previous school boards sometimes hamstring the efforts of school boards that succeed them. Each school board is a link in a chain of events, subject to periodic elections or appointments, in which the cast of characters turns over with some regularity. Thus, a well-meaning school board may find itself, like a fly in a spider's web, caught in a trap. Boards negotiate every few years with each union whose members work for the school system. The concessions made by previous boards remain in force to haunt the latest board.

This was the case in Springfield, the second-largest city in Massachusetts, where the fiscal problems of the schools contributed to an economic collapse that caused the state to appoint a Finance Control Board in 2004 to assume oversight of local fiscal affairs. The control board superseded both the city government and the board of education. It assumed jurisdiction over a deteriorated industrial town typical of many such localities in the Northeast that saw their manufacturing base collapse and middle-income families flee.

When the time came midway through the first decade of the 2000s to negotiate with the teacher union, which hadn't been able to get its members a raise in four years, the control board—not the school board—went to the bargaining table. What occurred during that year-long negotiation is the stuff of legend, a story that shows how with enough gumption and grit a school system can clear the way to educational reform. "It's easier to achieve when a city is in crisis," said David M. Connelly, the Boston lawyer who led the bargaining team that represented the school system. On the team with him were Phil Puccia, executive director of the Finance Control Board, and Joseph Burke, the school superintendent. The process produced an agreement that provided these measures:

- linkage of student achievement data with teacher performance
- the right to assign the best teachers to the poorest-performing schools
- higher salaries for math, science, and special education teachers
- a longer school day
- merit pay for highly productive teachers
- elimination of annual step increases and longevity pay
- creation of teacher career ladders, allowing highly experienced and skilled teachers who have reached the top of the salary schedule to remain in the classroom rather than move to administrative jobs with higher pay
- a streamlined process for addressing ineffective teachers

The vehicle for a breakthrough was a process provided for by a state bargaining law enacted in 1973 that had seldom before been used in this manner. The impasse led to the intervention of a mediator, who after more than a dozen sessions decided he could not break the logjam. So the next step was a hearing before a fact-finder in a trial-like setting that lasted eight days, after which he issued a nonbinding, confidential report setting out provisions for a contract. The two sides could not reach agreement even with the report, and so after 10 days, its contents became public, as the law provided, and the fact-finder certified that the collective-bargaining process had concluded.

With the public now fully aware of the provisions that the Finance Control Board sought, the board said it was willing to reopen official negotiations but made it clear that the school system needed certain concessions if it were to contain costs and push forward a reform agenda. Even during the fact-finding the two sides had been meeting unofficially and the statewide teacher union had gotten

involved. At this point, the Finance Control Board had the legal right to implement its last-best offer and threatened to do so. The teacher union returned to the
table, where the fact-finder's report became the basis for an agreement that omit-
ted some issues to which the union had objected. The union president said, "They
basically had us in a corner with a gun to our head. We got the best deal that we
could for our teachers."[12]

The school board was essentially a bystander during this process because of the
special financial circumstances that allowed the control board to act in its stead.
Connolly maintained, though, that a school board anywhere in Massachusetts
could resort to this same process. "Teacher unions think and act for the long term,"
he said. "If someone comes along with an ambitious reform agenda they think all
they have to do is outlast him. At least now, people know there's a way to do it. Public sector collective bargaining laws in other states may have some comparability."

### Merit and Performance Pay

No one should doubt the ability of teachers to make a difference in a child's future.
The best teachers are dedicated professionals, who strive to promote students'
understanding of subject matter and to help each youngster succeed to the best of
his or her ability. John Dewey wrote of the "process of transmission" and its role in
continual renewal as being at the heart of society's existence. Teachers, along with
parents, are the chief transmitters of the culture. "This transmission occurs by
means of communication of habits of doing, thinking, and feeling from the older
to the younger," according to Dewey.[13]

Some teachers transmit better than others, a fact that collective bargaining seldom acknowledges. Ideally, each school board would hire, promote, and retain
the best teachers available, differentiating their salaries according to their performance and their specialties. School boards generally give in to teacher unions
and do not consider performance or specialties—teaching physics or calculus, for
example—in setting pay scales.

The notion of human capital development has only recently attracted attention
in the world of public education. A conference on the Strategic Management of
Human Capital took place in Washington at the end of 2008, one of the first gatherings of its kind directed at elementary and secondary education. Chances are
that few school boards took notice. "When you're in a school district, you realize
that people don't fundamentally acknowledge that things like recruiting, hiring,
placement, and training have got to be connected," said David Sigler of the Annenberg Institute for School Reform. "It's not that there haven't been lots of efforts, it's
just that most of them have been uncoordinated."[14]

The same group issued a report just months later urging the nation's governors to promote a better work force of educators by taking steps, among other
initiatives, to strengthen admissions standards for teacher-education programs, to

require programs to feature content-specific course work, to support performance pay and higher salaries in subject areas of teacher shortages, and to mandate evaluations annually and throughout the school year once teachers are on the job.[15]

*Helping Teachers Perform Meritoriously*

As it is, school districts rely on a series of unconnected acts to produce a teacher and to enhance his or her ability to perform. The future teacher is educated in a college or university program over which the board of education has no control. Then, school districts recruit and hire teachers as a sort of isolated act. Depending on the school system and the policies of the school board, principals may or may not have something to say about the placement of teachers in their schools and whether the school uses the teacher most suitably. The pretenure years may or may not contain an induction regimen and during the many years as a tenured teacher a person's continuing training may have no connection to students' most pronounced learning needs.

School districts should tie staff development more closely to instruction, but too often this does not happen. School boards are largely silent partners in this omission. A recent criticism of staff development, contained in one of the few comprehensive reports on the topic, said that most teachers in the country don't have access to programs that are ongoing, linked to practice, focused on the teaching and learning of specific academic content, and that build strong working relationships with other teachers.[16] Hayes Mizell, former director of student achievement at the Edna McConnell Clark Foundation, wrote that one way school boards could assert themselves even in the face of increasing incursions on their power would be to commit themselves to better staff development in their districts.[17]

Teachers, as professionals, should hone a set of skills and a body of knowledge and then—over the course of a career—revisit those skills and that knowledge continually to update and strengthen their ability to perform effectively. School boards should expedite this process. Ideally, education should be as much about the learning of teachers as about what students learn. Teachers at the Birney School in Philadelphia, for example, voluntarily tacked six minutes onto each working day and banked and accumulated the time. Then, students were dismissed early one day a month and the teachers used the time to advance their own learning. The teachers were part of the Annenberg Distributed Leadership Initiative, based at the University of Pennsylvania from 2006 to 2010.

The average school board appears to take for granted both the initial preparation of teachers and their on-going growth. School board members should ask more questions about professional development than most of them do. Professional development in any district should have a coherence driven by specific goals. Each teacher doing his or her own thing simply is not enough. Such a scattershot approach to development may not benefit the district as a whole and may not even accrue to the benefit of the individual teacher. School boards invest in professional development in several ways and do not think enough about getting value for that money.

First, school boards in many cases excuse students early or pay teachers to stay after student dismissal or to show up on scheduled off-days for professional development. Second, school boards authorize expenditures to pay experts to come to the district to lead sessions for teachers or reimburse teachers for fees they pay to attend such sessions out of district. Third, as I already pointed out, school boards add differentials to the salaries of teachers for taking graduate courses—which, in effect, are a form of professional development.

Ultimately, all of these steps ought to lead to the superior performance of teachers in the classroom. School boards, though, do not have enough knowledge of whether this happens. Unless individual board members hear occasional complaints from parents—or from their own children who happen to be enrolled in the district—board members tend to assume all is well in the world of instruction. Scores on state and national examinations become one of the few indicators by which board members measure outcomes. And usually, teachers get the credit when scores are high and students get the blame when scores are low.

### Singling Out Meritorious Teachers

Some observers would like to identify the most successful teachers and bestow higher salaries on them. The process of recognizing successful employees happens routinely with those who work in the for-profit sector, where few at such corporations as IBM or Procter & Gamble doubt that certain employees do their jobs better than others or that they should receive rewards for superior performance. Not so in public schools, where performance pay is anathema.

Unions generally object to singling out teachers for higher pay based on performance or subject area. School boards usually acquiesce to this opposition. Thus, gym teachers receive the same pay as chemistry teachers. Teachers who've been in the system 20 years get more than peers with five years' experience, regardless of performance. This approach is known as the single-salary schedule and it supposedly treats all teachers the same, giving consideration only to such factors as seniority when layoffs occur. Union leaders insist that there are no objective ways to identify higher performing teachers—certainly not on the basis of students' test scores, they assert—and, moreover, that it is unfair to pay some teachers more than others based on student outcomes.

When school boards make headway on this issue it tends to be because of a willingness to spread the merit pay among all the teachers in a building, not simply providing bonuses to those in classrooms that have made the most progress. New York City distributes bonuses based on meeting achievement targets, for example, as a pot of money from which the teachers in a particular school decide how to allot the funds, an approach approved by the UFT. Most often this apparently leads to the same-size bonus for each teacher in the building. New York City handed out $27 million in such payments for the 2008 through 2009 school year.

So school boards continue to base salaries largely on years of experience and the number of credits earned beyond the bachelor's degree, questionable criteria of excellence. "The available evidence suggests that the connection between credentials and teaching effectiveness, while substantial in the first few years in the classroom, attenuates over time. Though exact results vary from one study to the next, there is little doubt that credentials and additional years of experience (beyond the first few years) matter far less to teacher effectiveness than they do to teacher compensation as it is currently designed," said Jacob Vigdor, a professor of policy studies and economics at Duke University and a faculty research fellow at the National Bureau of Economic Research.[18]

What are school boards concerned about excellence in teaching to do? There are no straightforward answers. Tests administered to students represent only one measure of what a student and a teacher, together, have contributed to an outcome. Moreover, school boards and most experts on the subject know little about how merit pay affects the performance and attitudes of teachers—both those who receive recognition and those who don't. Research does not reveal either what the existence of a merit pay plan means to recruiting and retaining teachers. The debate over performance pay should at the very least impel school boards to consider more thoroughly the ways that their districts evaluate teachers and the goals that they have in mind for their teachers. They should link this conversation to questions about student outcomes.

It behooves a school board to discuss—at length and repeatedly—the hopes and dreams it has for its students. How do students feel about the studio and performing arts? How much should students know about the technology that will affect their lives? What are the indicators that one will become a responsible citizen? How important is it to prepare students to write coherently and persuasively? What does preparation for success in higher education mean? What does a school system owe a child who will not go on to postsecondary education? What can a school system do to produce students who will become happy and content adults? Finally, what implications do the answers to these questions have for teachers?

The performance of students on assessments is only a part of these outcomes. What about educational ends that do not lend themselves to examination? Teachers play a role in helping youngsters realize goals whether or not youngsters are tested, and how can the contribution of teachers be gauged? Ongoing evaluation of teachers is a messy, imprecise process, not a topic most school board members consider. Teacher evaluation is frequently perfunctory and sometimes it doesn't even happen. In Boston, where tenured teachers were supposedly evaluated every two years and nontenured teachers, every year, only half of all teachers were evaluated from 2007 to 2009. Moreover, one-quarter of the city's public schools did not turn in a single teacher evaluation.[19]

A report on teacher evaluation by Education Sector called it "a glaring and largely neglected problem in public education, one with consequences that extend far beyond the performance pay debate." It went on to say that evaluation is "a potentially powerful lever of teacher and school improvement."[20] The report's description of a typical evaluation is devastating: "a single, fleeting classroom visit by a principal or other building administrator untrained in evaluation wielding a checklist of classroom conditions and teacher behaviors that often don't even focus directly on the quality of teacher instruction."[21]

This is an area ripe for school board intervention. Effective instruction should be the aim of every school board. Surely, boards can adopt policies and negotiate contract provisions to improve evaluation and to help bolster the practice of teachers—both tenured and untenured—who show deficiencies. Any worthwhile system of teacher evaluation should provide feedback and point in the direction of appropriate interventions. Such states as Connecticut, Georgia, and Idaho have moved toward formulating better evaluation procedures. Such organizations as the National Board for Professional Teaching Standards and the Teacher Incentive Fund offer models with appealing features.

# Chapter 7

# The Mirage of Local Control

The powers of local school boards have eroded as the state and federal governments have assumed increasing authority over school districts. The state role grew as states took on a greater portion of the funding for public schools. Federal influence far exceeds the modest level of backing, 8.3 percent, that the U.S. Census Bureau reported in 2009. The federal government sought to enlarge its role by setting out under President Obama to allocate, over a two-year period, more than $115 billion in stimulus funds for elementary, secondary, and higher education. The administration appeared poised to use money as a lever to produce changes out of all proportion to the small share of federal support.

The judicial system, too, has become involved in the public schools to an extent that few people could have anticipated before the 1950s. Judges sometimes intervene to determine, among other matters, who may be hired or fired, the circumstances under which students may be suspended, which students the district must send to private schools at public expense, and even whether schools may require students to recite the pledge of allegiance. Boards of education have had to yield to the courts on matters as seemingly insignificant as, for instance, the propriety of the message on a student's T-shirt or the suitability of articles in a student newspaper.

Mandates emerge from above, ordering school boards to offer this program or that program, to provide this or that service to students. The mandates, often unfunded by the state or federal governments or by the court that dictated them, are a sort of final indignity for school boards, further undoing their ability to determine their own destiny and forcing them to pay for programs and services that they did not freely choose to offer. Legislators and interest groups push pet projects on the public schools.

Sometimes, teacher unions, with their abundant influence, are the source of these mandates. They may persuade legislators to dictate that school employees must possess unnecessary credentials as a way to create or protect jobs or that certain classroom conditions must exist, infringing on the prerogatives of school boards. In 2009, the New Jersey Education Association—much to the chagrin of the state's school boards—pushed the legislature to adopt bills to require school boards to hire only union journeymen electricians, to prevent school boards from subcontracting for noninstructional services, and to require arbitration upon the nonrenewal of nontenured teachers. These bills, defeated in that session, would have intruded on the authority of schools boards and driven up costs.

Such initiatives have fostered a top-down approach in public education. Laws, rules, and regulations are piped in from above, and members of school boards must dance to a tune not of their own making. Some would say that this outcome is appropriate as school boards are not adept at making good decisions, but there is no mistaking that local control has been seriously reduced. Some would deem this a desirable result, short of abolishing local school boards altogether. On the other hand, if there is advantage in having the voice of the community figure in the governance of the schools, that voice—like a trumpet with a mute in its bell—has been muffled. In some places, outside interventions have carved a schism between the community and its schools. This is hardly the democratic approach that supporters of school boards envision.

Thus, local control is something of a mirage, an oasis in the minds of taxpayers who would like to think that they and their representatives on the board have the authority to affect what happens in the community's schools. William Hayes, who estimated that he attended more than 600 school board meetings, first as a principal and later as a superintendent, found that almost all board members were surprised by the limits that the state and federal governments put on their power.[1] Fifty-one percent of school board presidents surveyed in the late 1980s said that their state departments of education had "great influence" on their decision making and 24 percent said that federal authorities had "great influence" on their decisions.[2] No doubt state and federal officials have even more authority today over school boards and their presidents.

A major threat to the control retained by local school boards and states revolves around the prospect of national standards for learning. The states are responsible for adopting standards, but momentum has gathered since the 1990s for the creation of a common set of standards in all states. Several major organizations, including the National Governors Association and the Council of Chief State School Officers, endorsed the call for national standards, and representatives of almost every state embraced this effort. Presumably, grade-by-grade standards would enable students to reach a culminating point at the end of high school.

Many states appeared ready to adopt the academic standards that the panel formed by the governors and the state superintendents put forward in 2010. There were already commonalities among some states. An analysis of standards for English in 12 states and mathematics in 16 states found that the states shared a common, though not identical, core.[3] All the states involved in the study were part of the American Diploma Project, an activity to promote rigorous common standards. By 2010, signs emerged that the Obama administration wanted to devise ways to make the allocation of federal education funds to states contingent on their acceptance of national standards.

The diminishing authority of school boards tends to make them spectators to a parade of reforms that the states and the federal government march past them. Seldom are board members the drum majors at the head of the pack. The emphasis has been on bypassing school boards, leaving them mired in the status quo. The failure to consult school boards impairs efforts to change education as implementation of plans dictated from above can be thwarted by school boards. It may be that the need to believe that democracy prevails in the operations of public schools makes people reluctant to admit the extent to which authority has ebbed away from local officials. It was more than a joke when some delegates to the annual convention of the New Jersey School Boards Association in 2008 in Atlantic City wore buttons on their jackets and sweaters proclaiming: "We're Not Irrelevant."

## The Expansion of State Influence

A school board is a hybrid, an agent of the state and, simultaneously, a local entity. State laws and regulations provide the parameters within which local school boards operate. Governors, legislatures, state departments of education, state boards of education, chief state school officers, and education secretaries who sit in some governors' cabinets all try to dictate to school boards. The powers of these various bodies and individuals are consolidated in such groups as the National Governors Association and the National Conference of State Legislatures—both of which have extensive educational arms—as well as the National Association of State Boards of Education and the Council of Chief State School Officers. There is also the Education Commission of the States to provide research and support to those who seek to influence local school boards from the state level.

The state's authority over elementary and secondary education owes much to the omission of any mention of education in the U.S. Constitution, thereby ceding this role to the states. Thus, the constitution of virtually every state lists education as a responsibility and, in effect, sets the stage for state jurisdiction over local school boards. For most of the country's existence, the states largely abdicated this role, though the states generally made it clear that the local boards operated under their aegis. The states reserved the right to impose laws and statutes and to countermand decisions by local school boards.

Lines of authority between the state and local school boards vary from state to state. Chief state school officers and members of state school boards are elected in some states and appointed in others. The state board in 40 percent of the states appoints the chief. Some state constitutions established state boards of education and chiefs and other states rely on statutes. The relationship between the state board of education and the state department of education is not the same from state to state. In some ways, these arrangements provide checks and balances. In other ways, there is merely a lot of confusion as to roles. Governors, like potentates trying to consolidate power, increasingly have tried to wrest power away from other players at the state level. Whatever happens at the state level, life generally becomes more difficult for school board members.

Though "board of education" is part of each of their names, the state board has no particular affinity for the local boards, which generally view the state board as just one more entity trying to control them. State boards generally make no special effort to represent the interests of local boards. That is a function of the state level organization of local school boards that attempts to lobby the state board of education and the other agencies with authority over local education. State education departments were once toothless organizations that did little to assert themselves. They grew teeth after becoming conduits for federal aid to local school systems that began flowing with the passage of the Elementary and Secondary Education Act in 1965. After that, state governments assumed more of the financial burden for public schools and, in turn, carved out greater authority.

### Dictating and Mandating

The states—not local school boards—dictate, to varying degrees, what students must study in each grade and how thoroughly they must learn their subjects. The states set the basic criteria for becoming a teacher, principal, or central administrator. Many states require that the curriculum in each local school district include certain add-on topics whether or not local school boards want to spend the money and the states require that districts make available time in the curriculum for someone to teach those topics.

State history, for instance, is a mandated subject in the elementary schools in many states. But directives can get even more esoteric. Rhode Island required all middle schools and high schools to teach students about dating violence as part of the health curriculum after a 23-year-old was killed by her abusive boyfriend. Ohio followed the same path in 2009, when the legislature passed an act named for a 19-year-old, already in college, who was murdered by her former boyfriend. New Jersey mandated a unit about the Holocaust to memorialize the victims of that horror. Texas required the teaching of "religious literature," including the Old and New Testaments.

States intrude on school boards not only to order the teaching of courses and curriculum units, but also to tell those at the local level how to operate their schools. Legislators in Connecticut, for instance, grew concerned about the number of pupils—some only kindergarteners—that schools were suspending and sending home. So lawmakers enacted a statute that took effect in 2009 under which public schools had to use only in-school suspensions except in cases in which administrators determined that a student posed a danger to others or would disrupt the educational process.

In another action in 2009 that almost took effect, legislators in Connecticut framed a law in response to those who wanted to ban animal dissection from science courses. The bill, titled "An Act Concerning a Policy Regarding Dissection in Classrooms," would have ordered the State Department of Education to consult with the Institute for Humane Education, the Humane Society of the United States, the American Society for the Prevention of Cruelty to Animals, and other animal welfare organizations to develop a curriculum delving into the humane treatment of animals and promotion of compassion, empathy, and respect for animals.

School board members in Connecticut shouldn't have been surprised by their legislature's tendency to meddle in the public schools. Back in 1984, certainly a symbolic year for big brother, lawmakers decided that teachers sent too much work home with students and proposed a bill to regulate homework. Cooler heads prevailed after educators and school board members asked the legislature to simply say that every local board should frame a policy on homework, leaving it to individual boards to determine the content of that policy.

Local school boards, like Gulliver tangled in knots, have had their freedom of movement restricted as states have tightened their controls, generally in ways that state officials insist will redound to the benefit of students. In 2009 alone, for example, Kentucky imposed a series of tests benchmarked to international standards, New Mexico increased the number of credit hours of math that future teachers must take in college, and New Jersey ordered that students receive a half-year of instruction in economics and financial literacy.

*Governors Get Involved*

The extent to which some governors try to reach into local affairs was seen in the summer of 2009, when Nebraska's Dave Heineman put pressure on school boards across the state to raise teachers' salaries. In a letter forwarded by the Nebraska State Education Association to leaders of its local unions, Governor Heineman wrote of his desire that much of the Nebraska's $234 million in federal stimulus money for the schools be spent on teacher salaries. "I've grown increasingly concerned that the substantial increases in state aid have not been reflected in teacher pay," he stated.

Nebraska's average teacher salary of $42,044 from 2006 through 2007 exceeded that of only eight other states, according to the U.S. Department of Education, and advocates of higher pay have statistics on their side in this argument. Nevertheless, school boards in the state intended to use this extra aid in ways of their own choosing. Moreover, some local school board members worried that the governor's support of higher teacher salaries would figuratively put him at the bargaining table in negotiations of teacher contracts.

Critics of Governor Heineman's position pointed out that stimulus funds from Washington were a one-time fiscal infusion and that school boards that directed the money toward higher salaries would then have to find other sources to support the raises in future years. The most cynical of the governor's detractors cited the fact that he would be up for reelection the following year and that the state education association could be a powerful backer of his candidacy.

Another governor, this one in Oklahoma, also got involved in public education in 2009 in a way that indicated the extent to which governors have become part of the standoff between states and localities. It happened after legislators passed a bill in 2009 to allow school districts to opt out of some of the mandates that the state had imposed on them over the years. The Oklahoma State School Boards Association favored the bill, which dealt with what boards considered burdensome and unfunded demands that the state placed on them. The Oklahoma Education Association (the teachers) opposed it as a threat to teachers and to education quality.

"We have been inundated over the years with mandate after mandate and no way to fund them," Jeff B. Mills, executive director of the school boards group, told me. "Now, more than ever, school boards and communities need the flexibility to make decisions locally that most impact the district, much like charter schools."

The bill, the School District Empowerment Program, proposed to allow districts to not comply with the state mandates they considered most onerous. In its wording, the legislation said that its purpose was to empower locally elected school boards to govern school districts and make decisions based on the needs of their students and prevailing circumstances. The bill specifically stated that school boards would still have to adhere to such state provisions as those regarding the minimum salary schedule for teachers, the provision of health insurance to employees, participation in the Teachers Retirement System, and employment of certified or licensed employees

A major dispute revolved around the potential impact of the legislation. The president of the state teacher organization said it would wipe out requirements for counselors, library services, and class sizes, though many of the state's school systems were already exempt from class size requirements because of their bonded indebtedness.[4] Mills said, in referring to the issue of counselors and librarians, that "local schools should have the flexibility when placing staff to best meet the needs of their students." Much of the disagreement centered on the potential loss of the collective-bargaining process (which existed in about 20 percent of Oklahoma's schools) and a change in the teacher dismissal process.

Originally, the bill called for a pilot project to free ten Oklahoma school districts from certain mandates so that observers could see and gauge the effect of the change. Some enthusiastic supporters, though, expanded the bill to cover all the state's school districts from the start. That was the bill that Governor Brad Henry, who faced considerable pressure from school boards on one side and teachers on the other, vetoed, citing what he considered the need for rigorous state standards.

## Widening Influence by the States

Across the country, the regulatory power of state education departments often rankles members of school boards and local administrators. Massachusetts is perhaps one of the states in which the face-off has grown most intense. Members of local school committees (the Massachusetts name for boards) looked with disdain on the state's Department of Elementary and Secondary Education (DESE), to which they referred derisively as "Dizzy." They felt that the regulatory climate for public schools was overly complex and punitive. Some local critics maintained that this milieu diminished interest in running for seats on local boards.

A state's strongest tool for controlling local school boards may be the power of the purse. As I pointed out in the chapter on school finance, every state provides some of the funding for school systems, though some individual districts may get next to nothing from the state. There are usually regulations to which school boards must adhere in exchange for infusions of funds, evaluations to carry out, and reports to file. Frequently, boards must spend the money for specific purposes. Accountability has increasingly meant that state and federal governments can shape the curriculum, require courses, and even set standards for teachers and principals. An example of the state's intrusion is the trend since the 1980s for states to prescribe minimum requirements for a high school diploma. Some states have adopted exit examinations that students must pass and other states have created end-of-course tests. Half the states, containing 74 percent of the nation's students will have such a requirement in effect by 2012.[5]

The attacks of September 11, 2001 had an impact on boards of education around the country that most Americans do not realize. State by state, considerations of homeland security have led to mandated standards for the construction of new school buildings to make them less vulnerable to potential attacks by terrorists. Schools are known in security lingo as soft targets—minimally defended and inviting to those who want to wreak havoc. A result has been the adoption of regulations that make referendums for school construction more expensive than they would otherwise be. Regulations for building a new educational structure in New Jersey, for instance, affect the configuration of sites, safety provisions on perimeters, access to buildings, outside lighting, the positioning of rooms to minimize intrusions, and interior emergency systems. School boards will almost certainly be under mounting pressure in coming years as states and the federal government burrow ever deeper into local turf.

### The Federal Role

Federal involvement in the public schools during the last half-century can be viewed through four major phases that, cumulatively, stress the limits of authority of local school boards. First, after more than 150 years of remaining largely detached from school districts, Washington forever altered the relationship in 1965 by passing the Elementary and Secondary Education Act, with Title I as its centerpiece. Then, in 1975, Congress enacted the Education of All Handicapped Children Act, making millions of students eligible for support that local school boards are compelled to provide. The Federal government intruded more extensively than ever into the process of teaching and learning with the No Child Left Behind Act in 2002, setting up a process by which Washington could intervene in school districts in which students did not make adequate progress. Finally, the American Recovery and Reinvestment Act, the economic stimulus response to the nation's financial collapse, and other Obama initiatives pumped billions in federal aid into schools—with commensurate requirements. This happened in the last years of the first decade of the twenty-first century, setting the stage for the administration to prescribe specific reforms for dealing with failure.

### Early Federal Interest in Education

The newly born United States hardly had the capacity to support a system of education, though there were early attempts in this direction. The Continental Congress touched on the topic in the 1780s by passing the Northwest Ordinances. This legislation, never fully implemented, required each new town to set aside land for schooling in that "religion, morality and knowledge, being necessary to good government and the happiness of mankind, schools and the means of education shall forever be encouraged." Thus, the preservation of democracy was closely linked to schooling.

After the nation adopted the fourteenth Amendment with its equal protection clause to promote the well-being of freed slaves, Congress sought to guarantee the process of citizenship through the provision of educational opportunity. Congress created a Department of Education in 1867, tacit recognition of some responsibility to the nation's schools. In 1870, Rep. George Hoar of Massachusetts introduced a bill to establish a national system of elementary schools that the government would monitor. The ill-fated act would have authorized Washington to intervene in delinquent states, possibly to assess school taxes against residents, as well as to build schools and prescribe textbooks.

President Ulysses S. Grant, a staunch supporter of federal action in education, even proposed amending the Constitution to firm up Washington's undefined role. In 1879, Sen. Ambrose Burnside moved to sell some federal lands to raise funds for public schools, as well as for the new land-grant colleges. Neither Grant nor Burnside prevailed, but there is no question of the intent they and others had of enlarging the federal role.

Sen. Henry Blair of New Hampshire introduced a bill repeatedly during the 1880s to grant federal appropriations to the states according to their illiteracy rates. It even included a provision for equal per-pupil amounts to both black and white public schools, a startling notion at the time. Sen. Joseph Brown of Georgia argued in behalf of Blair's unsuccessful act that "if Congress has power to protect the voter in the free exercise of the use of the ballot, it must have power to aid in preparing him for its intelligent use."[6]

### New Initiatives in the Twentieth Century

Passage of the Smith-Hughes Act in 1917 to promote vocational education marked one of the few federal forays into elementary and secondary education during the first half of the twentieth century. It took a verdict by the U.S. Supreme Court in 1954 to sound a thunderclap that left no doubt about whether the federal government would play a role in public education. The directive in *Brown v. Board of Education* to desegregate the public schools "with all deliberate speed" reverberated through the nation like thousands of cannon firing in unison. The federal judiciary, especially with the Brown decision, became a major influence on education, and the executive branch took a part in enforcing Brown and the civil rights activities that it spawned.

The Servicemen's Readjustment Act of 1944, inspired by President Franklin D. Roosevelt in anticipation of the surge of military veterans who would return to the civilian world after World War II, was one of the most influential forays by the federal government into education, though at the postsecondary level. Called the G.I. Bill, it provided the financial wherewithal for millions of Americans to pursue education beyond high school and forever changed their lives and the role of higher education in America, democratizing the country as never before. Another Roosevelt inspiration, the creation of the National Science Foundation, eventually cemented that relationship by giving Washington a role in supporting research at colleges and universities and, eventually, curriculum development in elementary and secondary schools.

In the next decade, Congress enacted the National Defense Education Act, the beginning of large-scale federal aid for students in higher education. This 1958 legislation won passage when the nation sought to bolster learning, especially in math and science, after the Russians launched the Sputnik satellite. It was the harbinger of an extensive network of federally supported grants and loans for college students that developed in ensuing years. Finally, the federal government wiped away forever any doubts about its role in education with passage of the Elementary and Secondary Education Act (ESEA), the subject of fierce debate among those who favored and opposed such a role. In the various renewals of this bill through the decades, under different names and containing new and reshaped sections, Congress moved far beyond any earlier reservations about its involvement in education.

The pursuit of equity has been a hallmark of federal involvement in the schools since the adoption of Project Head Start and ESEA. Through a succession of bills, regulations, and court verdicts, Washington has focused its efforts in education on students who are disadvantaged, English language learners, and those in need of special education. This is not to say that other pupils have not benefited from federal largesse, but the government's emphasis has been on those in greatest need. One could draw a straight line from ESEA—with its Title I—to the No Child Left Behind Act (NCLB) of the current century. NCLB, the successor act to ESEA, sought to raise not only the achievement of all elementary and secondary students but, in particular, targeted youngsters who have fared worst historically.

The federal government's role in elementary and secondary schools deepened in other ways as well. One of the most prominent features of Washington's involvement was the creation and expansion of the National Assessment of Education Progress (NAEP), which administered its first tests in 1969. While some lawmakers and others have continued to resist the imposition of federal standards, NAEP results became a proxy for such standards. NAEP offered a measuring stick against which to view scores on the many different tests that individual states used to see if their schools had made adequate yearly progress in meeting requirements under No Child Left Behind.

### An Outpouring from the Obama Administration

President Obama took a giant step toward enlarging federal involvement in the public schools, a move with broad implications for school boards across the country. The administration not only boosted Washington's level of support but began attaching more requirements than previously existed to force elementary and secondary schools to follow certain paths. As pointed out in the beginning of this chapter, the administration earmarked about $115 billion of the $787 billion in the American Recovery and Reinvestment Act for education at all levels, with at least half the funds destined for public schools.

School boards used the largest portion to avoid layoffs during the 2009 through 2010 school year. Federal government figures showed that 325,000 jobs, more than half of those said to be created or saved by stimulus money, were in elementary and secondary schools. Like the rest of the money that Congress doled out under the Recovery Act, the funds arrived at a time when states suffered from declines in tax revenues due to the sagging economy and its effects on jobs and commerce.

A portion of the aid was set aside for grants in a program called the Race to the Top for which states had to apply. The competitive aspect of this program and the criteria that the federal government set for judging applications were indicative of the Obama administration's emerging philosophy for public education. Four specific goals guided the allocations: strengthening standards and assessments; improving the effectiveness of educators; using achievement data to guide year-to-year decisions; and developing strategies to turn around low-performing schools—including dismissing teachers, closing unsuccessful schools, and creating more charter schools for students to attend. There was even an attempt to persuade states to rescind policies that barred the use of student test scores as a factor in awarding tenure.

These objectives characterized the new, aggressive Obama approach, even if certain sectors of the education establishment objected and deemed some of the remedies as unproven. He clearly sought to change the balance so that Washington would exert greater influence over public schools, a move that would inevitably lessen the power of local and state authorities in this zero-sum game. Sixteen states were declared finalists in the first round of Race to the Top. Only two, Delaware and Tennessee, ultimately got grants in that round, stirring consternation among officials in other states that had expended time, energy, and money filling out elaborate application documents.

President Obama affirmed the high priority he put on education when he proposed in 2010 to hike federal spending for the U.S. Department of Education at a time when some other budgetary areas faced reductions or no increases. He set out to tie more strings to education aid than any previous administration. The administration also began describing its goals for reauthorizing the principal act for funding elementary and secondary education. The president wanted to replace No Child Left Behind with a law that retained the assessment of students and the accountability of schools but that focused more closely on the 5,000 or so schools suffering chronic failure. The administration wanted teachers and principals to take greater responsibility for student performance, a proposal destined to arouse opposition. The Obama plan also sought to advance the move by the states toward common academic standards.

Interestingly, the ambitious agenda that the U.S. Department of Education promoted for elementary and education was of concern not only to school board members, but to state legislators, who thought the federal administration was playing the role of schoolyard bully. The National Conference of State Legislators issued a report stating: "The effects of federal policy are now grossly disproportionate to its contribution to the K-12 endeavor. If we continue on our current policy path, federal resources, which now account for slightly more than 7 percent of the enterprise, will drag the entire system into the rabbi-hole world where compliance with federal dictums masquerades as reform."[7]

A tug-of-war was shaping up with state governments at one end of the rope and an increasingly muscular federal government at the other end. The prize was the chance to dictate policy to hapless local school boards, which seemed to be excluded from the contest but would have to do the bidding of one side or the other. Local control, in other words, was a concept fading almost as quickly as a name inscribed by a wet finger on a steamy window. It remained to be seen in 2010 if school boards, like gentle giants that don't know their own strength, would assert themselves.

## The Power of the Courts

The ruling in *Brown v. Board of Education* was a watershed moment for elementary and secondary education. It showed that the judicial system could fill a powerful role in education, laying down a principle that no school board has been able to ignore in the more than half a century since the U.S. Supreme Court rendered that verdict. Courts at the federal, state, and local levels continued to intervene in education in ways that have both gratified and disappointed school boards across the country. Brown's legacy, above all, has underscored the part that the federal courts can play in assuring fair treatment for all students. Brown spawned federal court intervention in school districts across the land—from Boston to Charlotte to Cleveland to Louisville to Kansas City to Galveston. While court involvement in school desegregation has ebbed, it established once and for all that membership on a school board requires one to be ever aware of the possibilities of litigation. Actions by Congress in such areas as special education and bilingual education opened other battlefields on which lawyers for school boards and for plaintiffs squared off over issues of equity.

While school boards have been more attune to the possibility of court intervention since Brown, the courts, even before 1954, had already made it clear—especially in regard to religious liberty—that they had a role to play. Democracy was at issue for both sides in the landmark case of *Pierce v. Society of the Sisters of the Holy Name of Jesus*. On one side, the State of Oregon maintained that propagation of democracy depended on where the children of immigrants got their education. The state enacted legislation to compel all students to attend public schools. The Society of Sisters defended the democratic right of parents to choose the place for educating their children—so long as these schools met state standards—and, in effect, the right of Catholic schools to exist. The U.S. Supreme Court in 1925 struck down the Oregon law.

Thereafter, in the 1930s and 1940s, a series of cases brought by members of the Jehovah's Witnesses also revolved around democratic principles, testing freedom of religion in the public schools. The culmination came in two cases. First, in 1943, the U.S. Supreme Court decided in *West Virginia Board of Education v. Barnette* that school officials could not compel a student to salute the American flag if such practice violated his religious beliefs. Another U.S. Supreme Court verdict, in the 1947 case of *Everson v. Board of Education*, established the right, even the duty, of school boards to provide services to students attending nonpublic schools.

All the ways that school boards have lost authority have not involved Congress or the courts. In the past, school boards could choose from among many publishers of textbooks and tests when they spent their money. If they didn't like one company's product, many others were available. This is no longer the case. Only a handful of major publishers of textbooks and tests remain after a succession of buyouts. Limited selection means limited authority for school boards. Power is worth much less when there is a Hobson's choice.

# Chapter 8

# The Special Burden
# of Special Education

Like a powerful hurricane that alters the landscape forever, the Education of All Handicapped Children Act that Congress passed in 1975 ensured that nothing remained the same for local school boards. A little history. School boards traditionally ignored and failed to serve the needs of disabled children. Blind and deaf youngsters were largely barred from attending neighborhood public schools. Those confined to wheelchairs and having other physical disabilities were unable even to enter school buildings that made no accommodations for them. Those with learning disabilities remained unidentified and were treated as simply dumb or lazy until the time came for them to drop out of secondary school. Children with mental developmental difficulties, with few exceptions, had no hope of attending public schools.

The time was ripe for change. Lobbyists representing the Council for Exceptional Children and other advocacy groups labored to improve the situation. What they wrought with passage of the 1975 legislation produced deeper and more far reaching change than almost anyone could have imagined. I wrote a front-page article for *The New York Times* about the pending legislation just three months before it was enacted, and it was the first time that many Americans heard that the act was wending its way through Congress.

Today, every school board in the land is keenly aware of the fiscal impact of IDEA, the Individuals with Disabilities Act that succeeded the original legislation. The law forces each school board to divert a disproportionate share of its budget to disabled students. Fully 13 percent of the nation's schoolchildren, almost 7 million, are classified as handicapped. The federal government requires school systems to spend whatever it takes to educate them even if this means less money for other students.

The New Jersey school district in which I served spent about 20 percent of its budget on just more than 11 percent of its students, disabled youngsters. Transportation costs for disabled students consumed half of the expenditures for busing. Many of these students, unlike those who were not handicapped, received door-to-door services in passenger vans. Few Americans realize the financial strain that special education puts on school budgets. Few critics want the notoriety that comes with questioning these added expenses. Policymakers talk often about reining in expenditures for the elderly—Social Security and Medicare, for example—but seldom mention putting a cap on expenses for disabled students.

"Special education is a runaway train," said John A. DeFlaminis, a former school superintendent now on the faculty at the University of Pennsylvania. At one time, Pennsylvania reimbursed school districts for the excess costs they incurred for special education students—above and beyond the cost of educating regular students. Then, the state withdrew that support and for the last nine years of his superintendency DeFlaminis traced the cost to his district of not getting reimbursed. He calculated the cumulative expense to his suburban district of 3,600 students at $14 million.

Americans like to root for the underdog. One of the features of Sarah Palin's campaign for vice president in 2008 that attracted attention were her repeated promises to help the families of disabled children to get as much extra financial support from Washington as possible. A *New York Times* reporter described one such suggestion by Palin as "a controversial and potentially costly proposal likely to be welcomed by many parents and bitterly opposed by many school districts."[1]

### 3 to 21

Unlike other young people in the United States, the disabled are entitled to educational services at public expense under IDEA from the time they are three years old until they turn 21. Experts see the years before kindergarten as crucial to their development. Interventions at this point would benefit many nonhandicapped youngsters, as well, but they enjoy no such federal entitlement. Washington's regulations even require "Child Find" procedures, obligating each state to search for children eligible for special education and related services. School systems send trained personnel to the homes of disabled children, as required by federal law, before their third birthdays. Experts evaluate the children and refer them for early intervention. Districts offer prekindergarten classes to the children they classify as disabled. The federal government underscored its commitment to preschool-age disabled children in 2009 by earmarking part of the $12.2 billion in stimulus funds for special education to a portion of the program that specifically serves infants and toddlers.

Public schools usually wash their hands of young people once they reach the age of 18, but they may not do so with those classified as disabled. Schools devote increasing attention to ensuring that such students will have plans for advancing into the workplace or into postsecondary education. Handicapped students in high school are entitled before graduation to receive summaries of their strengths, weaknesses, and skills. Theoretically, this document serves as the first step for a student and his or her family to build a road map to college or into a job. The transition from high school can be especially difficult for disabled students who during their elementary and secondary education grow accustomed to the benefits of a support structure that the law requires schools to assemble for them. Moreover, particularly if they leave home for college or a job, they lose the network of relatives and others who have sustained and nurtured them.

The lengthy obligation that public schools have to disabled students also may extend through the summers, when other students are on vacation. Many expenses for school boards cease or at least diminish during the summer, but through June, July, and August some disabled students receive an extended school year. The costs continue year-around. If a the student has been in an out-of-district placement the school system will probably continue to pay for tuition and transportation to that site during the summer even though the sending district has empty classrooms on the theory that to do otherwise would disrupt the continuity of the child's experience.

For decades, even after handicapped students gained access to public schools, educators tended to ignore questions regarding their scholastic achievement, figuring it was a concession just to admit them and that schools should not expect too much of them. A change that began with passage of the No Child Left Behind Act, though, forced schools to pay closer attention to the achievement of disabled students once they reached the third grade and became subject to the provisions of the law. Districts had to record their test scores and show that they made what NCLB called adequate yearly progress. Otherwise, the schools faced sanctions.

An entire school might be judged by the federal government as "in need of improvement" if its disabled students did not make acceptable academic progress. It happened to one of our high schools even though students made adequate yearly progress in 40 of 41 other categories. Some of the expectations for achievement by disabled students under NCLB were clearly unrealistic and unfair both to school systems and to the children involved.

## Handicapping Conditions

The millions of students classified as disabled have a wide range of handicapping conditions, from some so mild that the youngsters participate fully in the general education program to those so severe that they must be institutionalized—at the district's expense. Occupying the vast area in between are many students who divide their time between general education classrooms and settings in which they get special attention individually or in small groups.

One disabled student may join general education peers only for physical education and such subjects as art and music. Another may spend his or her entire time in general education except for a daily trip to a resource room for tutoring. Yet another may be accompanied to general education classes by an aide who sits in the class with the student and offers personalized assistance. School boards must pay teachers, consultants, psychologists, paraprofessionals, aides, and private providers to deliver what amounts to a "free and appropriate public education" to all these children, as federal law mandates.

Some of the most obvious and indisputable disabilities that lead to classification for special education are visual, hearing, and orthopedic impairments; traumatic brain injury; and mental retardation. Most children become eligible for special education, however, for reasons that are less apparent to the untrained eye. These include attention-deficit/hyperactivity disorder (ADHD) and a whole range of specific learning disabilities that affect listening, thinking, speaking, reading, writing, spelling, and calculating.

One way to gauge these disabilities in terms of qualifying for special education has been to look for discrepancies between the youngster's achievement level and his or her age and ability. Students also receive special education because of emotional and behavioral disorders and speech disorders. Federal regulations have a category even for "other" health impairments having to do with "limited strength, vitality or alertness, including a heightened alertness to environmental stimuli."

In other words, public schools—if they had the money, inclination, and personnel—could probably find ways to classify many more students as in need of special education. Eligibility could be as elastic as the school board chose to make it. Few of us at any age are perfect physical specimens and could benefit from extra attention to overcome our weaknesses, our shortcomings, and our personal deficits. Learning is difficult work that requires focus and diligence that even the most dedicated students cannot always summon on demand. School boards might find themselves with so many students with special needs that they could double, triple, and quadruple demands on taxpayers if they followed the law to its logical conclusion.

As it is, some aggressive parents deliberately seek short-term special education placements for their children who would not ordinarily be assigned to such programs. The parents want them to get additional help for a year or two. Some states once limited the percentage of students that a district could classify as handicapped, but those caps were largely eliminated. In New Jersey, for example, a school system that deemed more than 12 percent of its students as disabled could lose state aid, but the cap was lifted in the mid-1980s and the number of classifications soared in some places.

Some school systems get a reputation for doing a better job than others in meeting the needs of disabled students, particularly for a certain kind of handicap as, say, autism. These school systems may also be more liberal in their willingness to provide services. As a result, families with such youngsters are more apt to move into those districts, thereby accelerating costs to the taxpayers and complicating the plight of school board members who must wrestle with budgets.

Increasingly, diagnoses of autism, especially, have driven up expenses for educating disabled students. This condition generally manifests itself in a child's social interaction, communication, and behavior. Concern about autism, which disproportionately affects boys, has grown so prevalent that the typical Barnes & Noble store has two shelves of books devoted to the topic. Estimates of the incidence of autism among American children range from one in 110 to one in 150. Educators apply the term "spectrum disorder" to autism, an indication that the affliction can range from mild to severe. It is a personal tragedy for every child so diagnosed and the bane of many a school board because of the implications to the bottom line. Children with the worst cases are among the most expensive to educate.

The needs of these children challenge educators, whether they attend general education classes or separate schools that enroll only special education students. They need classrooms in which they find the order and structure that comfort them. They require a minimum of stress, an absence of distractions, and a calm environment. Consistency is important in trying to educate students with autism. Often, they require extensive modifications in the instructional program and a carefully tailored curriculum free of ambiguity and as concrete as possible. Some families have even fought to get public schools to allow dogs into classrooms to accompany their autistic children on the premise that the trained animals calm their children.

*The New York Times*, trying to get a handle on the cost to the city's public school system, found that the number of students diagnosed with autism increased from 3,278 in 2001 to 6,877 in 2008. As of the 2008 through 2009 school year in New York City, 4,200 of the autistic students attended special education classes with a small student-to-teacher ratio, 285 were taught in a program alongside general education students, 28 attended a charter school with a one-to-one ratio of students to teachers, and the rest were sent to private schools, with their annual tuitions—in a usual range of $30,800 to $48,100 covered by the taxpayers.[2]

No one should doubt the difficulties that families face when children suffer with autism and other maladies, but where does the responsibility of the public schools end? Where is the line beyond which public health services should intervene and assume the expenses? It is simply inequitable for nonhandicapped students to receive a dwindling portion of school revenues as has been the case for more than a generation.

### An Individualized Education Plan

The key to the provisions that local school boards must make for the disabled is the Individualized Educational Plan (IEP) that the law requires for each student. Unlike other students, those deemed to have handicaps are entitled to specific learning plans addressed to their personal needs. The IEP not only prescribes details of the instructional program for the disabled student, but additionally spells out expected outcomes. It also dictates the extra assistance that the school system must provide—as, for example, audio devices, the administering of prescriptions, and a special aide to assist the youngster.

It goes without saying that school systems hire special education teachers—by the dozens, hundreds, or thousands, depending on the district's enrollment. But this is not the full extent of the expenses for personnel that school boards have absorbed under the law. Child study teams, a class of educators that did not exist before passage of the law, now figure into the payrolls for which school boards are responsible. Members of these teams—and a district may have a number of such teams—examine the cases of students, decide which ones to classify as disabled, and confer with parents, teachers, psychologists, social workers, and outside consultants to devise an Individualized Education Plan for each child so classified.

It is up to the school system to provide services mandated by the IEP in the most inclusive way, allowing the disabled student to be educated in the mainstream with nondisabled students to the greatest extent possible. A school district that lacks facilities, personnel, or both, to accommodate the most seriously disabled youngsters and cannot fulfill the provisions of the IEP places the disabled student in a public school in another system or in a private school. In addition, 45 states have publicly operated regional programs that serve groups of districts, usually at a lower cost than that charged by private schools. Whatever sort of placement it selects, the school board bears the expense, including the transportation and an aide on each vehicle, a cost that in total can reach tens of thousands of dollars per child.

An IEP may call for such technological devices as text readers for the sight-impaired and broadcasting devices in the classroom for the hearing-impaired. An IEP may state that studies should be adapted and modified to meet the needs of some students or mandate a particular kind of differentiated instruction. Some school systems have become veritable Scrooges, quietly and privately trying to spend as little extra money on disabled students as possible. School boards may tacitly countenance such an approach as a method to hold down expenses and free money for other uses, but this practice is not acknowledged publicly as it could invite the scrutiny of federal officials.

One of the more notable examples of a school system allegedly withholding services to reduce costs occurred in Baltimore, where a lawsuit filed in 1984 accused the district of denying disabled students their legally mandated rights. Apparently, students did not receive speech and language therapy or occupational and physical therapy, as well as transportation, to which they were entitled. The legal conflict lasted until 2010, when a U.S. District Court gave preliminary approval to a settlement that would finally end court oversight of the school system's special education program.[3]

Depending on the handicapping condition and the Individualized Education Plan, regulations in some states may require that a district place the student in a classroom that has no more than, say, seven, eight, or nine students. A visitor wandering down the corridors of a school may do a double-take when he or she sees so few students in some classrooms built to accommodate 25 or so students. This policy may not make much difference in school systems with falling enrollments, but in those with growing enrollments and no extra space, it could mean the expense of a bond issue to construct additions to schools or at least the cost of sending out-of-district disabled children for whom there is no more room.

*Least Restrictive Environment*

Laws and regulations require educators to design each Individualized Education Plan so as to allow the most possible interaction between disabled students and nondisabled students. School systems are supposed to assign such students to special classes and special schools only when their handicaps prevent them from attending regular schools and classes. Disabled students have an implied legal right to be included in general education settings, the so-called "least restrictive environment." That's where the challenge begins for school boards.

Teachers of general education classes—where the vast majority of students are not disabled—receive special training to deal with disabled students assigned to their rooms. The schools may provide aides and supplementary services to enable disabled students to function in general classes. Given the needs and number of special education students in a regular classroom, it is sometimes possible to see as many as three or four adults—each assigned to provide one-on-one help to a specific child—besides the teacher in the room. The procedures that school systems follow in conforming with requirements are the product not only of laws enacted by Congress and additional state requirements, but also of a succession of federal court decisions rendered over the decades. These verdicts were handed down in response to cases brought by families dissatisfied with the ways in which school officials implemented the law.

Educators must weigh the benefits of each possible choice, deciding which setting (possibly including aides and supplementary services) will have the best effect on the disabled child. They may also consider the impact on general education students who might have their education disrupted or even be physically threatened by a particular disabled student. Some disabled students have problems that end up taking a disproportionate time from teachers and interfering with the schooling of classmates. Referring to classrooms in which he has tried to teach reading to special education students with learning disabilities, Randy Ariey of Bakersfield, California, said, "I struggle very hard to reach my kids, many of whom have so many problems that learning is sometimes not all that important."[4]

The benefits for a disabled student might not be strictly academic. If educators judge that the child would gain socially from being in a general education classroom that might be reason enough for the placement. In a case decided in a U.S.

Court of Appeals in Texas, the judge ruled that social interaction with nondisabled peers justified a placement and that it did not depend on the ability of the disabled student to learn the same material that his peers learned.[5]

The restrictions that the physical environment places on some disabled students are also of concern to Washington. The Rehabilitation Act of 1973 was already in place when Congress enacted the legislation in behalf of handicapped pupils. Congress adopted Section 504 of the Rehabilitation Act to extend protection from discrimination to qualified individuals with disabilities in school settings. Thus, the federal government became able to apply the provisions of the Civil Rights Act of 1964 to the handicapped along with those who might suffer discrimination because of race, religion, sex, and national origin.

Disabled students suddenly had a legal right to gain access to school buildings and to the facilities within. Students in school buildings across the country now take for granted the ramps, enlarged stalls in restrooms, wider corridors, and lower lab benches in science classrooms that even a youngster in a wheelchair can reach. The Americans with Disabilities Act tightened requirements in 1990 and legislative changes in 2009 brought additional changes.

### Sending Children to Out-of-District Schools

School systems that lack the space or expertise to serve some of their special needs students place them in schools out of the district, often in private schools to which buses deliver them each day. The cost of tuitions at such schools and the expense of transporting students are budget-breakers for schools boards. The most severely disabled youngsters attend residential private schools at public expense. The cost to a school board of an out-of-district placement may vary according to the seriousness of a child's disability. For example, it may cost 50 to 100 percent more for the tuition of an autistic child than a child with another sort of handicap.

More than one fifth of the spending on special education in Massachusetts, $436 million, went to pay for the private schools, that educated just 7 percent of the state's disabled students. On top of this amount, transportation consumed another $43 million.[6] The cost of out-of-district tuitions and the legal expenses incurred in responding to parents who sought such placements tripled in New York City in the three years leading up to the 2009 through 2010 school year, according to the *Wall Street Journal*. In New Jersey, public schools allocated 39 percent of their special education funds for tuitions and transportation to send students to out-of-district schools.[7] It is not unusual for a public school system to spend anywhere from $35,000 to $65,000 per student on tuition to place a disabled student in a school outside the district. At one point, the board on which I served was spending $11,058,998 on tuitions for 208 students it had placed in out-of-district settings. In addition, it cost us $4,520,000 to transport these students to the schools outside the district.

For the vast majority of handicapped youngsters attending day schools to which they are transported back and forth each day, the bus—with its driver and required attendant—can be as expensive to the school board as the tuition. If more than one child rides the minivan, the cost per student drops. I remember the November meeting in 2009 when we approved a per diem cost of $336.60 for a bus (including an aide) to carry one student each day to a school outside the district. This would be $1,683 per week, enough for someone to commute each week from New York to a job in London, and $60,588 for the school year, enough to buy a comfortable condominium studio apartment in some cities.

## The Courts

The Education of All Handicapped Children Act was untested and somewhat vague at the start. It took a series of decisions by the federal judiciary, right up to the U.S. Supreme Court, to amplify and clarify the law's intent. Gradually, most of these rulings turned the screws a bit tighter on the nation's school boards, which had largely to bear the costs for legislation that Congress passed eagerly but funded reluctantly and insufficiently. Boards of education, as the governors of school districts, have frequently been defendants in suits—often filed by parents—or at least figured prominently in the cases. Several landmark cases helped bring the law into sharper focus, leading to verdicts that defined the conditions under which public schools operate today.

### Among the Notable Cases

Among the first notable cases reaching the U.S. Supreme Court was *Hendrick Hudson School District v. Rowley*, decided in 1982, almost seven years after the enactment of the handicapped law. It involved Amy Rowley, a deaf kindergartener in Peekskill, New York, whose parents brought a legal challenge that produced a definition of the free and appropriate education mentioned in the act. Little Amy, despite her disability, was an able student in a regular classroom. She received a minimum of extra help through her IEP and the school board argued that, given her achievement level, she had adequate support. Her parents disagreed and wanted her to get more attention, including the services of an interpreter.

The U.S. Supreme Court ruled that free and appropriate public education, despite the "cryptic" nature of the law, meant special education and related services at public expense. Furthermore, it said that the law's provision of due process required that a student have access to the judicial system to determine whether a specific IEP enables him or her to receive educational benefit from the plan. On the matter of just how much assistance the law obligates a school district to provide, the dissent from the verdict by three of the justices highlighted the question of whether the law intended for each child to receive minimum—as the majority of the justices held—or maximum opportunity.[8]

*Burlington School Committee v. Massachusetts Department of Education* held that placement in a private school—now the most costly part of special education to school boards—is acceptable if it is the best way to provide a free and appropriate education not available in the public schools. Moreover, the case determined that a child has the right to remain in an appropriate private school at public expense until the issue is resolved.

In this case, decided by the U.S. Supreme Court in 1985, the parents of a third grader argued that his difficulties in school stemmed from neurological problems while school officials insisted that the problem was emotional. The parents rejected a proposed IEP and enrolled the child in a private school. Later, a hearing officer for the state's Department of Education backed the family and ordered the school board to reimburse the family for its tuition payments to the private school. The U.S. Supreme Court ultimately supported this decision and stated that, under the circumstances, placement in the private school at public expense constituted a free and appropriate education of the child.[9]

Building upon and enlarging the Burlington decision, the U.S. Supreme Court ruled years later, in 2009, that parents of a disabled student may receive reimbursement for private school tuition even if the public school district never provided the child with special education services in the first place. The court, in *Forest Grove School District v. T. A.*, cited a 1997 amendment to the Individuals with Disabilities Education Act to declare that after the public schools failed to identify a child with disabilities the parents acted reasonably in having him evaluated by a private school that classified him as handicapped and enrolled him.[10]

Another case, *Honig v. Doe*, led to a decision in 1988 by the U.S. Supreme Court regarding the sort of discipline that a school system may inflict on a student with an Individualized Education Plan. Even in the face of violent and disruptive conduct, public school officials may not suspend a disabled student indefinitely as they did in San Francisco. Such a student, declared the courts, may remain in his or her existing placement pending a review and a suspension may not exceed 10 days. The court rendered this verdict in accord with the law's "stay-put" provision that prohibits excluding a handicapped student from the classroom for behavior related to the child's disability.[11] The verdict set the tone for how school systems today handle disruptive or violent disabled students. The court was satisfied that the public schools have sufficient tools for dealing with such students without long-term expulsion and that the ten-day limit was enough time to seek appropriate legal relief.

Decisions in a pair of cases that reached the U.S. Supreme Court, first in 1984 and then in 1999, underscored for school boards the lengths to which they must go—and the commensurate expense—to comply with the law affecting the education of disabled students. The earlier case in Texas, *Irvington Independent School*

*District v. Tatro*, ended with the court deciding that a public school must offer clean intermittent catheterization for a child suffering various impairments including a neurogenic bladder.[12] Then, 15 years later, the court affirmed this interpretation of the law in *Cedar Rapids Community School District v. Garret F.*, under which a public school system had to accept financial responsibility for providing a ventilator to a student entirely dependent on the apparatus.[13] These verdicts appear to deal with medical services, which the law does not obligate public schools to provide, but the courts declared that they were health services that properly fall under an IEP and enabled the recipients to participate in the educational program. They were, in other words, legally acceptable related services. The key, as indicated in the Cedar Rapids case, was that these were not services that required a physician.

So after some 35 years of court verdicts, there is a system in place that assures disabled students of a free and appropriate public education; a right to due process to ensure that guarantee; placement in a private school at public expense if the public school cannot meet a disabled child's needs; entitlement to reimbursement with tax dollars under certain circumstances to parents who unilaterally choose a private school; limits on the ability of public schools to discipline children classified for special education; and the provision of quasi-medically related services if dictated by an IEP.

Collectively, the financial implications for school boards are enormous. Associate Justice David H. Souter, who dissented from the U.S. Supreme Court's decision in the Forest Grove case that called for reimbursement of parents who unilaterally place children in private schools, warned, "Special education can be immensely expensive, amounting to tens of billions of dollars annually and as much as 20 percent of public schools' general operating budgets. Given the burden of private school placement, it makes good sense to require parents to try to devise a satisfactory alternative within the public schools."[14]

### A School Board's Losing Fight

A single case in Chattanooga, Tennessee, encapsulates the implications of the special education law for school boards. In this instance, the local school board spent at least $2.3 million on expenses to resist a family that objected to provisions of the Individualized Education Plan implemented for their child. A court also ordered the school board to pay $241,300 of the family's legal expenses. The case dates to 1997, when the Hamilton County Public Schools developed its first IEP for Zachary Deal, an autistic child then 3 years old. Differences between the family and the school board led to a hearing before an administrative law judge in 2000, followed by various appearances in the U.S. District Court and in the U.S. Court of Appeals for the Sixth Circuit.[15] The case did not conclude until 2009, when an entry of findings by a court clerk was not appealed.

The case speaks to the questions involving the extent to which a school system can dictate a specific educational approach for a child, the right of parents in an IEP meeting, the obligation to provide a disabled student with a program that extends through the summer, and the right of parents to reimbursement for educational expenses they incur when the school system does not provide the program they desire.

Zachary's parents wanted the Hamilton County Schools to provide Zachary with applied behavior analysis (ABA), an intensive, painstaking approach that involves a great deal of one-on-one interaction. A teacher finds out what motivates a child and uses reinforcement in structured and natural environments to help the student learn skills. The teacher breaks down the work into small, measurable units and systematically presents it, preferably through enjoyable experiences. The school system had purchased a different program for autistic children and preferred to offer it to Zachary instead of ABA. His parents, Phillip and Maureen Deal, felt they were not permitted adequate input in their meetings with the school representatives about the child's IEP and on at least one occasion they were apparently told they could ask no questions. Moreover, the IEP did not call for interventions that the Deals thought would be appropriate throughout the year.

At the heart of the case is the finding that the school system did not meet the intent of Congress to give Zachary Deal a program providing a meaningful education benefit toward the goal of self-sufficiency. The school board maintained throughout the case that it did not put credence in applied behavior analysis— a rather expensive approach—and that it had its own program for dealing with autism. The Court of Appeals stated, "The obvious objection to the meaningful benefit standards is the expense involved."

The case was a triumph for families with autistic children at a time when public schools are enrolling increasing numbers of such students. The decision serves as a sobering reminder to school boards across the country that mounting costs for special education cannot be readily contained. An article on the case in the *Tennessee School Law Quarterly* cautioned board members and education officials that their school systems "must go into IEP meetings with an open mind. If you don't seriously consider every available option, which could provide the child FAPE [a free and appropriate public education], then you risk the possibility of a judicial determination that you have substantively violated the provisions of IDEA."[16]

## What Special Education Means to the Budget

In difficult financial times, such as districts began experiencing in 2008, school boards trying to hold expenses in check had to exact savings from every other part of the budget. Disabled students were spared cutbacks because federal and state laws dictate provisions for them and school boards have scant leeway for making programs for the disabled absorb a fair share of the fiscal burden. Moreover, on top of Washington's requirements, individual states have added their own mandates. New Jersey, for example, has 78 such specific mandates pertaining to special education.

Mark J. Finkelstein spent almost his entire career in special education. He is now superintendent of the Middlesex Regional Educational Services Commission, a public entity providing services to school districts in central New Jersey. From his vantage, he said he has seen a history of overregulation by the state, which has introduced one onerous requirement after another. He stated,

> This started with the strong voices of special interest groups. [It] resulted in the pendulum swinging from one end of the spectrum to the other, seemingly overnight . . . The result was a state code that exceeded the federal code, a greater number of classifications to place students within [special education] and a greater number of approved private schools for the handicapped. An increased number of classified students for special education proved to be the end result . . . It must further be noted that while concerted efforts in New Jersey are now being made to decrease the number of students placed within special education, history will show that this has not always been the case.

New Jersey spends $3.3 billion a year on special education, according to a 2007 report from the state's school board association, which said that public schools spent an average of 1.6 percent more on each disabled student than on other students. Altogether, in New Jersey, local taxes paid for 57 percent of the cost of special education, 34 percent of the amount came from the state, and 9 percent from the federal government.

I saw the portion of the budget devoted to special education in my district balloon by 12.7 percent in a single year, one of the largest annual increases in any one category. Meanwhile, the growth in the number of teachers remained relatively static in general education. School boards around the country that balk at the extra spending are subject to the intervention of federal courts. Parents dissatisfied with the decisions of school boards regarding the treatment of their disabled children may readily turn to the courts and the law mandates that school boards pay for both the legal costs to the parents and for the expenses incurred by the school system.

Massachusetts is one of the three top-spending states, along with California and New Jersey, when it comes to special education even though it has a smaller population than many other states that spend less. Massachusetts was early to the game, having adopted its own ambitious special education law, Chapter 766, even before passage of the federal legislation. Moreover, the wording in its law, which the state still follows, obligates Massachusetts to strive toward maximizing its services for disabled students. As a result, the state spends about $2 billion annually on special education.

There is not only the cost of the out-of-district tuitions and busing that I have already mentioned, but even for children who remain in the district's schools, there are smaller class sizes and paraprofessional aides. There is the expense of child study team members and the consultants and therapists who get involved in classifying students and in serving their needs once they are in the program. A separate staff of secretaries may assist the various personnel working in special education. School nurses and health services may serve all students, but the needs of disabled students may take up a disproportionate amount of their time.

On the other hand, school systems have perfectly legal ways to try to head off some of the need for special education placements. Students with learning difficulties that schools can address early may require less special education or none at all. One antidote to special education—at least for some children—may be prekindergarten, which federal law mandates for disabled children but doesn't require for others. A good prekindergarten can help youngsters narrow gaps and better prepare them for kindergarten.

Another approach, Response to Intervention (RTI), is a teaching technique meant to help students who lag in their grades or in their courses. It is a safety net designed to catch students before they fall too far behind. At first, they receive intensive instruction in small groups. Teachers carefully monitor their response to the lessons, called "interventions." Students may receive small-group instruction and if that proves unsuccessful, individual tutoring. Those who make sufficient progress may altogether avoid placement in special education. If they continue to lag despite such continued intervention, however, they may be referred for evaluation for special education.

While the general public has little understanding of the huge financial burden that special education puts on school districts, members of school boards are keenly aware of these pressures. Ninety-three percent of board members in districts of 5,000 enrollment and larger place special education high on their list of concerns, ahead of such issues as teacher quality, parental support, regulation, drug use, and discipline, according to the National School Boards Association. One reason that the cost of special education receives so little attention from the public has to do with the reluctance of school boards to discuss this burden.

Aid from the states and from Washington is simply not enough to relieve the burden on school districts. Originally, Congress authorized the federal government to underwrite more than 40 percent of the cost of special education, but in none of the 35 years since then has the portion covered by Washington exceeded much more than 15 percent. President Gerald R. Ford turned out to be prescient when he signed the bill on December 2, 1975 and stated, "Unfortunately, this bill promises more than the federal government can deliver . . . Despite my strong support for full educational opportunities for our handicapped children, the funding levels proposed in this bill will simply not be possible if federal expenditures are to be brought under control."

It is not surprising given the enormous bite that special education takes from the budget of the average school district that school boards sometimes countenance efforts by administrators to find ways to meet the requirements of the law in the least expensive manner, possibly skirting legal requirements. The process of holding down special education costs starts with the identification of students for special services. Some students whose disabilities are marginal may not be classified as eligible for programs.

Once so classified, the issue becomes just how much service the Individual Education Plan prescribes for the youngster. Does the child really need so many extra services? Is it necessary for a paraprofessional aide to attend regular classes with the child? Possible contention can arise, for instance, over the use of applied behavioral analysis, the one-on-one teaching method I mentioned earlier for youngsters with autism. If, say, the IEP calls for a specialist to visit the home to instruct parents in how to use the method with their children, it could well be that the parents would prefer that the specialist keep coming to the home so that they don't have to teach the lessons themselves. A school system, on the other hand, can save money by keeping the specialist's visits to a minimum and expecting parents to take over the teaching.

A Congress that created a financially privileged class of students did not deliver on its promise to cushion the fiscal impact on nondisabled students. There was little appreciation of the effect that the bill would have. Members of Congress held hearings around the country when they began considering possible legislation to assist students in need of special education. U.S. Sen. Walter F. Mondale opened one such hearing in 1973 in St. Paul, Minnesota, with a statement that, while attesting to the value of passing such a law, also showed how poorly he and his colleagues anticipated the potential fiscal impact. Mondale said, "One of the main barriers to providing quality education for all handicapped children has been the cost. There is no question that it is more expensive to meet the educational needs of a child who is blind or deaf or mentally retarded or who has learning problems than to meet the needs of a child without those problems. A recent study shows that the extra cost per child ranges from at least $400 to $800 annually."[17] It turned out that the extra costs may run about 100 times those amounts.

# Chapter 9

# The Inner Workings
# of School Boards

A bove all, a school board exists to ensure that students in a given district get
the best possible education. Board members address issues that extend over
a wide horizon, but they should never lose sight of their main responsibility for
doing all they can to facilitate learning for each child. This is so obvious as to leave
readers wondering why I even mention it. Yet all too often school boards get so
tangled in thickets of minutiae that they neglect to walk the straight course that
they should follow in the pursuit of solid education. And the underpinnings of
democracy are weakened when students receive anything less. Such failure dimin-
ishes their life prospects. There should be no alternative to governing well.

School boards are destined to wallow in ineffectiveness when they lack the skills of
governance. "The sad fact is that many school boards are not capable of the kind
of high-impact governing work that will make a real difference in their districts,"
said Doug Eadie, a consultant to school boards. "They fall so short of their governing potential that, in my professional opinion, school boards, along with other
public and nonprofit boards, might very well be America's most underdeveloped
and underexploited precious asset. The dismal situation is clearly not the result of
an inadequate pool of people who are bright and committed enough to govern at
a high level. Rather, it reflects inadequate attention to developing and managing
our school boards as governing organizations."[1]

## Who Serves

School boards draw their members from the general public. A small number of
men and women launch political careers and go on to higher office after gaining
seats on the school board, but this is not typical. About the only political experience that Ben Bernanke had when he arrived in Washington in 2002 to assume the
chairmanship of the Federal Reserve was a two-term stint on the school board in
Montgomery Township, New Jersey, where he was best known as a member of the
economics faculty at nearby Princeton University. Most members of school boards

are ordinary citizens who never seek higher office. They are neighbors from all walks of life.

When I joined a school board in central New Jersey, I found the other eight seats occupied by a truck driver, a retired physical education teacher, the woman in charge of the floral department at the A&P, a chemistry teacher working at an adjoining school district, a lawyer, an English teacher at the local community college, a stay-at-home mom, and a deputy police chief in our town. I remember the night when I sat next to the police official, who wore a pressed dress shirt and tie and had removed his suit jacket. Strapped to his hip, on the side closest to me, was his holstered pistol. I did a double-take and asked him about it. He told me that regulations required him to carry his weapon virtually all the time.

On average, 44.6 percent of school board members identify themselves as having a professional or business background and the next largest group, 26.2 percent, are homemakers or retirees. Thirteen percent work in educational fields. By and large, school board members are more affluent than the general public that they represent, 60 percent having annual incomes of more than $75,000. They are also more educated than the average American, two-thirds holding college or graduate degrees. Six of every 10 are men and three-quarters are between the ages of 40 and 59. Only 5.4 percent are under 40, making most of them older than many of the parents whose children they serve.[2]

Many districts have another sort of gap between their school boards and the students. The complexion of the nation is changing faster than that of most school boards. One has only to examine demographic statistics to understand and appreciate this phenomenon. One in four American counties has passed or is approaching the point at which black, Latino, and Asian youngsters make up a majority of the under-20 population. Members of the nation's school boards, though, as a whole are 85.5 percent white, 7.8 percent black, and 3.8 percent Latino.[3]

### Changing Constituencies, Changing Boards

The population of Bethlehem, Pennsylvania, shifted throughout the 1990s and during the first decade of the 2000s, but the composition of the school board did not. The resignation of a member from the all-white school board in 2008 and the tussle over a replacement exemplifies the slow pace of change on some school boards. Some in the community urged the appointment to the vacancy of a man who was a lawyer and executive director of the Council of Spanish-Speaking Organizations of the Lehigh Valley. Yet the school board rejected this candidate, who in addition to his other attributes was a trained practitioner of conflict resolution, and instead named to the post another qualified candidate who happened to be white.

Even as the school board resisted change, the town it served was no longer the same. The remains of blast furnaces and empty mills lent ghostly testimony to the former existence of Bethlehem Steel. The company had supplied the structural skeletons for some of the nation's iconic structures—the George Washington and Golden Gate bridges, the Hoover Dam, the Chrysler Building, and the Merchandise Mart, not to mention the armor plate and ordnance to fight World War II. The legacy of the Moravians who founded the town in 1741 lives on primarily in the name of the college they also founded. And a gleaming casino—with an industrial motif—opened in 2009 on one corner of the 1,600-acre abandoned steel-making site.

Bethlehem was Pennsylvania's fastest-growing city in the early 2000s. An influx of Hispanics made up some 20 percent of the population and at least 30 percent of the public school enrollment before the end of the decade. An all-white school board no longer reflected the demography. And so it was that a federal civil rights suit was filed over the lack of diversity on the board that governed the Bethlehem Area Free School District. The settlement approved by a U.S. District Court called for establishing three geographic districts from which members of the school board would be elected, leaving the other six members to be elected at-large.

Under the agreement, one of the geographic districts would be an area with a concentration of Hispanics. Residents of this new district elected Aurea Ortiz to the school board in 2009. She had grown up in Puerto Rico and New York City and had moved to Bethlehem in 1997. Ortiz, reflecting on her victory and the circumstances that brought it about, told me, "People have to see that they have a responsibility to be fair and to treat everyone in the city equally. It is shameful that in our country we say we are free, but we have to go to court to be represented on a school board. I still believe in democracy. We have a wonderful democracy. Some people try to put a barrier to that democracy."

Good education is good education, regardless of the color or ethnicity of the students or the members of the school board, but sensibilities demand that school boards position themselves to respond to the needs and interests of the families that use the public schools. This should probably mean something other than an entirely Caucasian school board when the majority of the students, or at least a large portion of them, are no longer Caucasian. I was elected to a board serving a system in which Asian-Americans made up half the enrollment, but no such members sat on the board. It is to the benefit of a school board when it draws its members from all walks of its community.

Responses to diversity are just one aspect of a board member's responsibility. Too many board members know little about schools except what they learned as students and parents. Such knowledge is certainly helpful to a board member, but it hardly equips one to make major decisions about a school system. Ideally, board members will know how to interpret assessment data and recognize the implications for the instructional program. School board members also will be aware of teaching philosophies and strategies. They will recognize impediments to learning and have ideas about how the school system might address them and know more about finance than simply how to balance a checkbook. I am not saying that school board members should be education experts. They set the policies and the staff implements those policies. The point here is that too many people gain seats on school boards having only the foggiest notions about education and never bothering to learn much more.

## Gaining a Seat on a School Board

It was like one of those televised lottery drawings. Eight slips of paper, each containing the name of a candidate, were put in a receptacle and pulled out, one by one, for ballot position. The name of the candidate was announced as the paper was drawn. I was delighted when my name came out first, giving me the top position on the ballot. What a fortunate piece of luck. I was as lucky as a jockey who gets the rail position in the Kentucky Derby. The names of candidates are often unknown or barely familiar to voters in school board elections and so for those who mark ballots arbitrarily from top to bottom my name would appear first.

### A Taste of Partisan Politics

School boards in most states are supposedly nonpartisan and—unlike those who contend for other offices—candidates run without party designation. They are identified by their political affiliation in just 10 percent of school board elections, according to a survey by the National School Boards Association. In Connecticut, one of the exceptions, Democrats and Republicans field candidates to run under their banners for seats on local school boards. Furthermore, school board elections in Connecticut are held in November, at the time when the two parties conduct their usual battles.

Sometimes political parties get involved in school board elections even when party identifications do not appear officially on the ballot. This happened in Cincinnati, where the election for the supposedly nonpartisan school board in November 2009 might as well have been a traditional test of party strength. The Democrats—allied with organized labor and with the Cincinnati Federation of Teachers—fielded a slate of candidates for the board that included only one of the three incumbents seeking reelection.

The Democratic Party made it clear that the other two incumbents, both of whom happened to be Democrats, had been disloyal in not supporting a push by the party for "prevailing wages," a measure to require higher pay and benefits for workers on school construction projects. The slate, consisting of three newcomers and the one incumbent, had the benefit of the publicity and the pre-election machine that the party mobilized in behalf of its endorsees for all the offices contested in the November election.

This was not the end of the story. The Cincinnati Charter Committee, an independent group with the standing of a third party that offers endorsements without regard for whom the major parties back, supported the two incumbents the Democrats shunned. This group added to its ticket a third candidate without elective experience. The charter committee did not bother backing anyone for the fourth spot, feeling no one else merited its support.

The 85-year-old committee had no money for the campaign, but gave its endorsees use of its nonprofit mailing privileges and the prestige that comes with support from one of the country's oldest good-government organizations. *The Cincinnati Enquirer* backed the committee slate in an editorial. It was a race with 12 candidates for the four contested seats. In the end, the only Democratic Party endorsee who won was the incumbent. The other two incumbents and the newcomer backed by the charter committee captured the three remaining seats.

Like it or not, members of boards of education almost everywhere operate in a political arena of sorts, even the 90 percent who don't run with party designation. It may not be party politics, but partisan-like forces may come into play. Thus, contending for a school board position can mean carrying out a campaign very much like a candidate for a partisan office. This was especially true of our slate of three candidates in 2008. We handed out and mailed printed campaign materials, erected lawn signs, and used lists of registered voters who had gone to the polls in previous school elections to select the homes that we approached. On first thought, a voter list may seem unnecessary, but candidates use time best by visiting the homes of those most likely to vote when knocking on doors in a town of 100,000 residents.

### Campaigning for a Position on the Board

Campaign materials were important to us as we tried to overcome opponents who had the advantage of incumbency and the endorsement of the teacher union. Given the demography of our town, we sent some mailings in Hindi and in Mandarin. We made it our business to speak at school board meetings, to write letters to the editor, and even to hold a few news conferences. Articles in daily and weekly newspapers proved invaluable in helping us reach potential voters. Hitting the streets and walking door to door provides fresh insight into one's town. In my case, in Edison, New Jersey, it revealed to me that not all homes have address numbers posted or even doorbells. I was surprised to see how many people, women and men, answered the door in various states of undress. I encountered people in underwear, pajamas, and robes who thought nothing of engaging in a full-blown conversation about the public schools at the open door in their skimpy attire.

Our campaign for the school board was an anomaly. More than half of school board members reported in a survey by the National School Boards Association that their elections were only "occasionally competitive" or "not competitive" at all. Just 15.5 percent of school board elections were "very competitive," like ours. One characteristic of the electoral process is the power of incumbency. Sitting school board members may lose elections more frequently than incumbent candidates of the U.S. Congress, who seldom lose, but a challenger nonetheless faces an uphill battle in unseating an opponent who runs to retain his or her seat on the school board.

Term limits might be a good idea for school boards. Incumbency and the name-recognition that it confers on those seeking to hold their positions are high hurdles for challengers to overcome. In almost half of all school board elections incumbents do not lose and in another 27.9 percent of school board elections only one incumbent loses. Thus, in three-quarters of the cases, no more than one incumbent loses. Three-quarters of school board candidates spend less than $1,000, mostly out of their own pockets, on their election.[4]

Some districts have no more candidates for the school board than there are seats available. These races are noncompetitive, causing me to wonder whether this is the result of the voters' contentment or their lethargy. What does it mean for democracy when citizens lack interest in serving on school boards, when so many members of the public don't learn about the issues involved, and when so few bother to vote?

Just as in partisan politics, it helps in the world of school board elections to have a burning issue on which to focus a campaign. In our case, the incumbents generously handed us an issue. Five months before the election, the board ousted the superintendent and replaced her with another administrator already working in the central administration. They could not actually fire the superintendent as she had a contract. So they directed her to not show up at work and called her successor "acting" superintendent as there was already a superintendent, though rendered inactive.

The ousting came just a little more than a year after the board had extended the superintendent's contract and she had more than two and a half years remaining on it. This meant that the taxpayers would spend more than a half million dollars on her salary and benefits to keep her at home, not to mention an almost equal amount for the acting superintendent. The taxpayers were irate. It was a gold-plated issue and proved instrumental in helping two of the three members on our slate of newcomers to win.

People did not understand why the board had taken this action, the reasons for which were kept confidential as a personnel matter. The episode contributed to the failure of a construction referendum that spring, when I ran for the board. The community wondered about the relationship between the board and the ousted superintendent: Why had she been hired in the first place without a search? Why was her contract extended? What outrageous acts had she committed to cause her removal? Why hadn't there been intervention to prevent relations from reaching this nadir? Buyouts of superintendents' contracts by school boards are all too common, and the public should be outraged by such squandering of their precious money.

## School Boards Should Be Goal-Oriented

America's school boards are too easily diverted from larger purposes. They may get bogged down in issues better left to staff. Some school board members want to meddle and they get more involved in administrative matters than they should. They sometimes invest precious hours in matters of little consequence. In other words, school boards too readily waste time and effort.

The school board should specify objectives and then leave it largely to the professionals to decide which programs and what use of human resources will attain those ends. A timetable can help set parameters for judging the school system's progress toward goals: What should the district achieve by what dates? This means that a school board can be spare and succinct in its actions. By operating this way, the board has a yardstick for measuring and evaluating its superintendent, who really is the only person that the school board can hold directly accountable for achieving results.

Are the means that the administration uses in reaching the desired ends beyond the scope of the school board's concerns? Of course, not. The methods should be fair and ethical. They should be affordable. They should be gauged against the best interests of students, taxpayers, and staff. A school board that turns its back on questionable practices that lead to desired results is derelict in its duty.

Ends do not justify means. An example of such a failure, drawn from higher education, was seen in the behavior of the board at Rutgers University in New Jersey after some members decided that they wanted Rutgers to become a big-time football power. They looked away as the athletic department spent millions of dollars without their authorization and paid the coach out of hidden accounts. The university abolished several minor varsity sports to enrich the football budget. Finally, the situation grew so egregious that the board and the university president were called to task for, in effect, allowing Rutgers's football fortunes to soar regardless of cost or ethics.

### A Need to Plan

Planning can help a school board operate more effectively. I joined a board that had a strategic plan that had been created at least two years before I arrived and which extended five years into the future from the time I became a member. During the first half of my term on the board, I never once heard my board colleagues or anyone else refer to that strategic plan—the product of an elaborate process. The strategic plan might as well have been placed in a bottle and thrown into the nearby Atlantic.

I'm sure that the leaders of any organization can devote too much attention to planning and end up neglecting more immediate tasks. On the other hand, given the arc of time and the nature of formal education, which unfolds as a result of actions taken over a period of years, an educational enterprise and the students in its classrooms can benefit from conscientious planning by those responsible for the outcomes. A good plan for acquiring and using technology as an adjunct to learning, for instance, offsets the dangers of piecemeal adoption of technology. A mathematics curriculum designed to reflect in secondary schools the impact of foundation-building in the primary grades has a better chance of succeeding than a math curriculum that fails to give sufficient attention to students' year-by-year accumulation of knowledge.

Citizens ought to ask about the beliefs and values of their school board members. Such inquiries do not happen enough, and the few members of the public who ordinarily seek such information from their boards are viewed as gadflies. Democracy should demand more of school boards. There is no use having a board of education if it does little more than go through the motions of governance.

My district had neglected to plan for an expanding enrollment. Most of the system's 11 elementary schools by 2009 had gyms too small for serious physical activities. Many of the schools had to convert their art and music rooms into regular classrooms, and art and music teachers, like itinerant peddlers, wheeled carts full of supplies from room to room to teach the subjects. In some schools, children had to eat lunch at their desks, and in another school, the only space available for preparing meals had previously been a large closet. School libraries had been partitioned into teaching spaces, and special education students had their pull-out sessions in what had been small windowless storage rooms. There were not enough labs at the high schools to offer all the Advanced Placement science courses for which students clamored.

A lack of foresight and inadequate planning in my district had resulted in the construction of no new schools in almost 40 years, a failure to acquire land parcels for prospective schools, and the disposal of four perfectly good school buildings on the notion that the district wouldn't need them in the future. Admittedly, no school board has a crystal ball, but proper planning can lead to better results than a district like mine had. Flinchbaugh wrote, "Educational leaders do not feel the need to engage in planning because it does not seem like a viable use of their time."[5]

The instructional programs of school districts across the country suffer from compromises forced on them by school boards that have inadequately planned. I referred earlier to the fact that I served on a board that presided over a system in which students on one side of town achieved to a greater extent than those on the other side of town. The portion of youngsters scoring at advanced proficiency levels, for example, was much greater at some schools than in others. Any attempt to deal with such disparities requires planning, but I seldom heard discussions of this phenomenon among board members or among central administrators during most of my term on the board.

Some provisions had been made to try to address the problem, but there were few discussions among board members about fine-tuning the efforts to make them more productive. As a matter of fact, during a candidates' debate, when I ran for the board, I raised the issue only to have an incumbent candidate chide me for not considering demographics. Such excuses can be barriers to improvement. Donald R. McAdams, president of the Center for Reform of School Systems, did not want to let school boards off the hook in instances such as these. "When a school district fails to improve," he wrote, "it is not the district's workforce that fails; it is the board that fails."[6]

I return to the idea that a democratic approach should lead citizens to elicit information, first from board candidates, and then from board members, about their beliefs and values. Another consideration here is that the board's beliefs and values, as translated into its plans and policies, may not reflect the positions of all the individual members. Those who have the votes to control the board may make their beliefs and values those of the board's, regardless of how dissenters may feel.

Nonetheless, there is supposed to be a level of decorum and at least an outward show of civility at school board meetings that one may not find so readily in partisan bodies. School board members, for example, are not meant to play games of "gotcha," trying to catch fellow members or administrators with unexpected inquiries at public sessions. The unwritten rule is that the object of a query will know in advance that questions or statements are coming so that they may prepare for them. This is not the British Parliament with the well, in which the prime minister stands to receive the arrows of the back bench opposition. Does this mean that all school board meetings are necessarily lovefests, places where everyone respects each other, and seldom is heard a discouraging word? Hardly.

### The Process

Sunshine laws and pressures for openness in most states compel school boards and public entities of all kinds to conduct their business in open sessions. Such laws usually block a majority of school board members from gathering privately, lest they talk about board business. The law requires that binding action generally be the result of regularly scheduled public meetings. This doesn't mean that members don't discuss business except at scheduled meetings. They may circumvent the law by gatherings in twos and threes so long as the number does not constitute a quorum. Members may also be in touch by phone and by email, though caution dictates that telephone and video conferencing as well as communication via the Internet involving a majority of members may not be acceptable. But chances are that one way or another at least some members have discussed some issues before they gather in public.

Members also have committee meetings. Committees consider many of the items before they appear on the agenda for a vote in public. The full school board signs off on recommendations that originate in committees. The typical school board has about five committees, the most common ones being budget/finance, facilities, and policy.[7] Some school boards, particularly smaller ones, choose to operate without standing committees, considering all issues as a committee of the whole.

While the committee structure makes sense for carrying out many tasks, there is an inherent downside to the process. Committees must resist the temptation of usurping the role of paid staff. There is a thin line between being privy to decisions involving personnel or curriculum or facilities, for instance, and directing the actions of those who work in these areas. Board members have to remember that recommendations to the board ultimately should emanate from the superintendent, not from board committees. The full board has the authority and the responsibility to give thumbs up or thumbs down to those recommendations.

The closed or privileged sessions at which school boards are authorized to consider personnel, legal matters, and other issues entitled to confidentiality are perhaps most intriguing of all, or at least I have found them so. The conversation is most frank and opinions are expressed most vehemently. Normally, the only people present other than board members are the superintendent and perhaps some top administrators and legal counsel. Sometimes the board may invite a person involved in a particular action to state his or her case. It is a serious violation to reveal what occurs in a closed session, which is not to say it does not happen. Two kinds of issues tend to receive the most attention in the closed session, matters involving personnel and those involving special education students. Big bucks may be on the line in either instance.

Personnel matters take several directions. The closed session is where the board hears about and discusses employees whom the superintendent proposes to discipline or dismiss and possible legal suits that have resulted. Teachers and other school personnel have many safeguards, including contractual language, to protect their employment and are entitled to due process. It is common in closed sessions for someone to bring board members up to date on actions of employees who have sued the board on the basis of alleged contractual violations, discrimination, harassment, or ill treatment of one sort or another. These cases may be protracted affairs, dragging on interminably, appearing on the list of continuing legal actions at the closed sessions for months and even years.

Various kinds of complaints may arise concerning students, but usually nothing involving them commands the attention of school boards more than actions brought by families of children in special education. Federal law empowers these families, unlike those of nondisabled students, to sue over any and all aspects of their instruction. The most common suits involve placement and services that the family seeks and the school board opposes.

*Student Safety: Small Margin for Error*

One area in which getting it right or getting it wrong leaves little margin for error is the responsibility that every school board has for adopting policies to keep students safe and secure. Enormous challenges face school boards in the post-Columbine, post-9/11 world. Who could have imagined in the days when Archie and Veronica attended Riverdale High that any school board in the country would have to consider such matters? Where once readily accessible school buildings symbolized the openness of democracy, many now are sealed citadels.

Older Americans remember a time when school grounds went unprotected, the doors to the building remained unlocked, and no one bothered to check on strangers in the hallways. Then, by the 1960s, circumstances changed, first in urban schools, where security became a concern. During the 1970s, more and more schools began to have guards, locked their doors from the outside, placed weapon-detectors just inside the front entrance, and required outsiders to check in and get passes at the front office.

School boards today tend to regard security with utmost seriousness. The Columbine massacre and assorted attacks on students and on educators have demonstrated that violence knows no geographic boundaries. The terror at the World Trade Center and the Pentagon underscored the vulnerability of school buildings. In some schools, identification badges now dangle like jewelry around the necks of students and staff. Security cameras scan the environs. School boards in many locales approve and periodically reapprove plans for biosecurity, crisis management, and pandemics. It's not quite like adopting policies for curriculum and instruction, but some school boards approve detailed procedures for dealing with potential shooters inside school buildings and have principals schedule lockdowns as drills to be ready for the worst.

Nonetheless, precautions are not universally employed. One-third of the country's schools reported in a survey that exterior doors are occasionally or often propped open when they are supposed to be closed and almost 60 percent of school buildings have no panic exit devices at strategic locations.[8] On the other hand, officials at some schools are too zealous in trying to get it right. The trustees in a north Texas district allowed teachers in 2008 to carry guns so that they might fight off possible intruders. Also, overly ambitious school personnel can get it wrong as those searching a 13-year-old middle school girl did in Arizona when they stripped her to her bra and underpants and pulled back those garments in a search for drugs. The U.S. Supreme Court ruled in 2009 that this search was unconstitutional.

Chapter 10

# The Good, the Bad, and the Ugly in the Work of School Boards

Reconciling and satisfying the various constituencies in a school district is a juggling act that a school board ignores at its peril. Far more than many other kinds of nonprofit boards, those that oversee public schools operate in a fishbowl, taking on issues that may ignite public passions. Democratic principles seem to demand that school boards respond to public wishes, but this is not always possible—especially when the public is divided or makes demands that are not in the best interests of the school system. People who've paid no attention to the local school board seem to get it in their sights quickly when a board wants to, say, rezone attendance areas feeding into particular schools or change busing policies.

### A Full Measure of Controversy

The rapidity with which an issue can heat up was illustrated by a decision that our board made less than three months after I became a member. We scheduled a vote on a construction referendum to build a new elementary school and to add classrooms to three existing elementary schools. We were restricted to scheduling the vote on one of three dates that the state previously authorized for such balloting. Only two such dates remained in the calendar year—one in September and one in December. We chose the earlier date as that would open the possibility of completing the additions before the next school year began.

The date we selected, September 30, was the first day of Rosh Hashanah, the Jewish New Year and one of the holiest days on the calendar of that faith. Anyone who objected to going to the polls on that day had the option of casting an absentee ballot. Little did we realize that we were fueling a firestorm. The school system once had a sizable enrollment of Jewish students but their numbers had dwindled, a fact that made no difference to our critics.

Protests filled the letters columns of local newspapers. Board members and top administrators were besieged by email objecting to the date of the referendum. Critics accused the school board of every objectionable practice, including anti-Semitism. Finally, we changed the date for balloting to December 9 even though we knew that it would probably mean delaying the start of construction if the referendum passed. There was such tumult that the state legislature got into the picture afterward by unanimously enacting a bill to outlaw elections that coincide with major religious observances. Edison is an unusually diverse school district with many residents of East Asian and South Asian ancestry, along with the usual assortment of Caucasians and others. I wondered when we would next blunder into an offense against Buddhists, Hindus, or Muslims.

Consider controversies around the country during the first decade of the twenty-first century, most of which began innocently. The school board in San Francisco put itself in a no-win situation by wondering whether Junior Reserve Officers' Training Corps belonged in its schools. In Hillsborough County, Florida, the board weighed a plan to make the school calendar secular rather than decide which religious holidays to observe, a sure-fire way to excite the public. The question of how and where students should recite the pledge of allegiance faced the school committee in Woodbury, Vermont. The school board in Fairfax County, Virginia, at the last minute scrapped a plan to rearrange bus routes for a later start so that high school students could sleep later—parents objected to the impact the change would have on the lives of the adults. In San Diego, the school board apologized to 90-year-old folk singer Pete Seeger almost a half-century after a previous school board had demanded that he sign a pledge promising not to promote Communism in a concert he was about to give.

### When School Boards Get It Right

A school board should exercise good judgment and make decisions that move the school system forward in the best possible manner. Members of such boards sort out the issues, have short and long range goals, and keep tabs on how the district progresses, calling for adjustments in areas where the district falls short.

A board may take many actions that seem tangential to its central mission of supporting teaching and learning. For example, a school system needs its board to provide and maintain facilities, furnish transportation, and cause an annual audit of the district's accounts and financial transactions. Are these duties as important as hiring a superintendent, providing a curriculum, and approving textbooks? Not really, but unless a school board diligently carries out its more mundane responsibilities it can weaken the rest of its mission.

Much of the business that comes before a board of education bears on its policies and, ultimately, on teaching and learning. Sometimes, the impact can be more clearly discerned than at other times, but observers would do well to ask in regard to almost any action that a board takes: What does this mean for education in our school system? Doug Eadie, the consultant quoted earlier, observed that school boards that have a positive impact tend to follow four golden rules:

- They play a role in shaping the policies by which they govern rather than merely reviewing finished work by the staff.
- The board, along with senior administrators, engages in intensive dialogue before making complex, high-stakes decisions.
- They regularly review and update the governing process, including strategic planning and the budget.
- They govern through a collaborative process that involves all board members, the superintendent, and senior administrators.[1]

Each school board operates within a cultural context. It may be positive; it may be negative. It may be supportive; it may be destructive. It may become the culture of the entire school system. Educators feel valued or they feel violated. Parents and taxpayers trust the board of education and the schools or they view the board and the system with suspicion. This culture shapes the district's values, influences the morale of educators, and may affect even student achievement.

Robert W. Flinchbaugh wrote that prevailing culture does not readily change, even when new members join the school board. New members may have every intention of changing board culture, but Flinchbaugh pointed out, they may be excluded from the power source, or they may simply capitulate to the status quo.[2] It is difficult, in other words, to alter board culture and, in turn, to change the prevailing tone of the district. The inspired visions of new administrators, new principals, and new teachers may be dashed by much the same phenomenon.

Interestingly, Flinchbaugh saw democracy as a lever for improving culture. "If a board finds itself with a preponderance of members who believe they should operate more democratically and equitably," he wrote, "it can begin to practice these values internally in the school district."[3] In other words, a school board may promote democracy by conducting its own work in a democratic manner.

### When School Boards Get It Wrong: Clayton County, Georgia

The Clayton County School Board in Georgia, just south of Atlanta, exemplified a school board gone wrong. The Southern Association of Colleges and Schools (SACS) in 2008 asked the district to show cause as to why its accreditation should not be revoked. SACS deemed the district of 53,000 students in violation of five of the association's seven standards. In many places across the country, public schools and school systems do not seek accreditation but it became widespread in Georgia as a requirement for students to qualify for the state's Hope Scholarships.

Seven of the board members interviewed by an accrediting team said their board was dysfunctional. The team found inappropriate influence on the school board by outsiders, ethics violations by board members, many allegations by board members regarding the financial fidelity of the school district, doubts about whether all the board members resided in the district, and faulty student attendance records—stirring questions about chronic absenteeism, legal issues tied to attendance, and state aid based on daily attendance. All in all, the team reported that the board and the administration operated in a state of chaos. There were even racial overtones in a district in which most of the population had shifted from white to black.

Almost everything that could go amiss seemed to have happened by the time that the governor stepped in to remove four of the school board's nine members for ethics violations. Some other board members had already resigned under pressure. The board had also appeared before a judge for an administrative hearing. The school system—with its motto of "World-Class Education for All Children"—verged on becoming one of the few in the country to lose its accreditation. The board had violated open meetings laws, ethics requirements, and provisions against micromanagement. "There was a complete breakdown of the relationship between the community and the school district," said Mark Elgart, president of the Southern Association of Colleges and Schools. "There was no evidence that the school system had improved student achievement over the last five years."

The conduct of some members of the Clayton County Board of Education was so egregious that the Georgia legislature moved to adopt new laws for school boards throughout the state. Certain board members had apparently threatened parents and employees and had tried to insinuate themselves into hiring and curricular decisions. The board even included as a member the executive director of a local teacher union. Elgart said that Georgia needed new laws because the state code minimally addressed the role of school boards. The act was drafted, in light of the Clayton County experience, to specify that it "shall not be the role of the local board of education or individual members of such board to micromanage the superintendent."

The bill, passed by the legislature in the spring of 2010,[4] dealt with such details as expense reimbursements to board members, provisions relating to the board secretary, conflicts of interest among board members, and even the size of school boards, limiting membership in most instances to seven individuals. Research conducted in conjunction with drafting the legislation indicated that 90 percent of the state's school boards had no more than seven members and that having more members introduced a greater probability of conflict. Some school boards around Georgia were concerned that the legislation represented an overreaction to serious wrongdoing in just one place.

Clayton County Public Schools regained probationary accreditation in 2009 with a mandate to meet specific requirements and expectations. As one of the first efforts to bring about change, the board was reconstituted and it hired a new superintendent from California, a person with no apparent ties to the district. Board members also relinquished the office space they had occupied in the central administrative complex, a step seen as reducing opportunities for board members to meddle in administrative functions and in daily operations. During its probation, the board was to initiate a community-based process to review and revise its vision, mission, and values; implement strategic planning with input from all major stakeholders; conduct a review of the system's organizational structure including job descriptions; and establish an action plan defining the chain of command with an emphasis on having staff and board members commit to a process for solving problems and conflicts.

### When School Boards Get It Wrong: Marysville, Washington

Strains between school boards and teachers are inevitable, but seldom does the rancor rise to the level that it did in Marysville, Washington, a small city on Puget Sound, where the annual Strawberry Festival reminds people of the community's agricultural origins. The conflict built during the early 2000s as some of the five school board members made it clear that they did not like collective bargaining and that they thought the district's teachers should be willing to work more than the requisite 180 school days without additional compensation. The strife reached the point that the Marysville Education Association went on strike at the opening of the school year on September 2, 2003.

Day after day the tension rose as the positions of both sides hardened and the schools that served the system's more than 11,000 students remained closed. Several weeks into the strike a parents' group called Tired of the Strike sued both the teacher union and the district to open the schools. Finally, 49 days after the school year was to begin, a judge responded to the suit by issuing a back-to-work order. The teachers, weary and facing fines if they failed to heed the court directive, returned to their classrooms the next day. It turned out to be the longest teacher strike in Washington State history.

The strike garnered so much attention across the state that Gov. Gary Locke appointed two special masters to examine the issues that provoked the strike. Their report, issued just days before the end of the strike, declared "enough is enough," recommending binding arbitration if the union and the school board could not settle their differences. It called teacher salaries in Marysville "among the highest paid in the state" and student performance "compared with districts with similar student demographics, a legitimate concern." On the other hand, it labeled the school board "too ambitious" in its efforts to regain control over the salary schedule.[5]

Clearly, the public did not approve of the way that the school board had handled the dispute and hundreds of families reportedly moved out of the district or transferred their children to private schools. Normally, folks in Marysville did not provide the kind of sustained interest in school board matters that the report by the special masters indicated was appropriate. The school system serves both rural and suburban families, who live close enough to Seattle to commute to jobs there.

It draws students from families on a naval base and on an Indian reservation. It has recent immigrants of Hispanic and Russian background.

The three board members who stood for reelection after the strike were voted out of office and, gaining control of the board, the new majority removed the superintendent that the old board had installed, paying her $340,000 to leave with two years remaining on her contract. The new majority hired a consultant to find an interim superintendent and to conduct a search for a new permanent superintendent. "The board had tried to break the union," John Fotheringham, the consultant and the former executive director of the Washington Association of School Administrators, said to me in looking back on the events.

Some citizens initiated a recall petition against the two remaining members of the old board whose terms had not yet expired, not wanting to wait until the next election to see them removed from office. The Superior Court in Snohomish County certified the charges in the petition and said the recall effort could proceed. The two board members appealed that decision all the way to the Washington Supreme Court, which affirmed the ruling to allow the recall to go forward. The two members refused to resign from the board, but finally avoided possible recall by not seeking reelection.

A. Michael Kundu, who became president of the reconstituted board, was satisfied that he and the two newly elected members "patched up" the board's relations with the teacher union within a few months after being elected. They also hired a superintendent, Larry Nyland, who by 2007 was Washington State's superintendent of the year. What did Kundu learn from the experience in Marysville? He said, "The public needs to pay more attention to the groups they put at the helm and the direction in which they are going. A lot of parents just don't give a damn. Only when something dramatic happens do they pay attention to personalities, agendas, special interests, and the intelligence level of the board. The system is broken. There should be credentials to seek a board of education position."

## Are School Boards Rubber Stamps?

There is the recurring question of whether a school board shapes its actions or simply applies a rubber stamp to proposals originating with the superintendent and his or her top aides. There is nothing wrong with ideas coming from the staff. A school board, after all, hires a superintendent to administer the schools. The board, though, should in one way or another take ownership over the actions that it approves. Otherwise, a board is merely going through the motions and meeting legal obligations. John Carver, who has written extensively on governance, suggested that boards examine their proposed actions by asking themselves, "What good shall we accomplish, for which people or needs, and at what cost?"[6]

Ownership of policies implies that members of the school board understand completely every action upon which they vote. This is the democratic way. This is the reason for the existence of the school board. School boards should not be window dressing. To take this proposition to its logical conclusion means expecting a great deal of school board members—who usually serve in part-time positions without compensation or staff. Carrying out one's responsibilities as a member may involve enormous sacrifice. The amount of material that passes before a conscientious board member each month and the meetings and school visits require hours upon hours of commitment.

Board members spend, on average, 25 hours a month on board business, about one-third of this time consumed by meetings. Commitments vary, though, and 10 percent of members give more than 12 hours a week to board business and almost 70 percent spend fewer than seven hours a week on such work. School board members in larger districts tend to devote more time to the activity than those in smaller districts, apparently reflecting the volume of the work. In fact, it is not uncommon for some members in larger districts to commit more time to board work than state legislators do to their activities.[7] So the success of school boards depends on members freeing up the time from the rest of their schedules to do the work expected of them.

This clearly is one of the flaws in the process. Even dedicated board members trying to perform their tasks to the fullest measure can be overwhelmed. On the other hand, those who invest little time or effort in their board service—and there are such board members—fail their constituents and betray their hard-working fellow board members.

The board may feel somewhat impotent even as it votes. All the necessary information may not have been available to school board members. Limits imposed by courts and by government at the state and national levels may tie the hands of board members. Time and deadlines force boards to take actions that they cannot delay, however uncomfortable they may feel about acting prematurely. Yet there is reason to believe that members of public school boards even with the limitations imposed upon them may be ahead of their counterparts—the trustees on college and university boards—when it comes to being informed and asserting their prerogatives.

Trustees of institutions of higher education probably are apt to defer to college and university presidents more often than school board members yield to superintendents. Some college presidents, in effect, imply to the trustees that they should know their place in the pecking order. This can mean ceding to the presidents, not only the right to administer, but to govern, as well. This, at least, is what the Association of Governing Boards, the umbrella group of higher education trustees, found in a survey. The report revealed that only 64 percent of private institutions inform all members of the board of trustees of the president's total compensation package, for instance, a practice that would be unacceptable to almost all members of school boards.[8]

One difference between boards in higher education and those in school districts is the pivotal role that a college or university president plays, especially at private institutions, in identifying and recruiting potential board members. Then, these very same people are charged with overseeing the work and performance of the person to whom they largely owe their place on the board. By comparison, the route to membership on an elected public school board looks like the epitome of the democracy process.

When I spent 11 years as a senior fellow at the Carnegie Foundation for the Advancement of Teaching, a private think tank in Princeton with a very ample endowment of its own, I had a box seat from which to view this phenomenon. The president of the foundation—which operated along the lines of a private college—handpicked the members of his board and then had the board rubber stamp his choices. Those selected were distinguished individuals who in many cases ran organizations of their own. Yet once ensconced on the foundation board where they were treated royally, they seldom challenged the foundation president and apparently scrutinized few of his expenditures. So in judging public school boards perhaps a question to ask is, "As compared with what?"

*The Perils of Micromanagement*

Everyone has to understand that it is the job of the board of education neither to run the schools nor to impart the instruction. Democracy does not mean that the people's representatives—the school board—take over and operate the schools any more than it means that the board members of a symphony play the violins. School boards exist to govern school districts and they let down the public when they do not bring to governance the kinds of skills that good superintendents bring to organizational management. The public should not have to put up with members of the school board micromanaging the schools—individually or collectively. Everything should flow through the superintendent. The school board should maintain some distance from the action once it has determined a desired course.

Sometimes, school boards get in the habit of micromanaging the schools and no one has the courage and clout to intervene so as to tell board members that they have overstepped their boundaries. Micromanagement was endemic among school board members in Atlanta when Beverly Hall arrived in 1999 as the fifth superintendent in ten years. "Administrative staff expected direction from the board, they were nervous about offending the board, they felt their jobs depended on whether or not certain members of the board liked them,"[9] Hall recalled ten years later, after putting a stop to the bad behavior and settling in for a long superintendency.

A classic case of micromanagement occurred in New York City's million-student system during the early 1970s, with the beginning of school decentralization. The system was broken into 31—eventually 32—community school districts, with a centrally based chancellor presiding over the entire enterprise. A series of weak chancellors yielded to the dictates of the school board, which first had five members, appointed by each of the borough presidents and then, seven members, including two additional people appointed by the mayor. Each board member was, in effect, backed by a politician and the board named a chancellor, who had no political base of his own, to administer the system.

Adding to the precariousness of the chancellor's position was a decentralization law that allowed for each board member to have an office and staff at the school headquarters, the legendary 110 Livingston Street, in downtown Brooklyn, a former clubhouse and hotel for the Benevolent and Protective Order of Elks. Each board member also had a car and driver, an expense account, and an annual salary of some $30,000. It was officially a part-time position, and most members of the board had other sources of income. The chancellor's office was on the eighth floor of the building and the offices of the board members were on the eleventh floor, emphasizing both literally and figuratively who was in charge.

After a succession of lackluster chancellors who played a deferential role, the board in 1978 appointed Frank J. Macchiarola to the position. They might have had an inkling of what they were getting into with Macchiarola, a lawyer and college professor with a PhD. The vote was 4 to 3, with the powerful Albert Shanker, president of the teacher union, lobbying with all his might against Macchiarola. Shanker, the greatest labor leader in the history of American education, confided afterward that this was one of the only times under decentralization up to that point that he didn't get his way with the board of education.

Macchiarola, an amiable but firm individual, wasted little time asserting himself. He had barely moved into an empty office and not officially taken up his duties when an aide came to him with two calendars for the next school year and said that the school board would be deciding which one he was to follow. Macchiarola, though he wasn't asked for his opinion, chose one of them and directed the aide to "let the board tell me if they don't want it." The days of micromanagement were numbered. It had been the board's custom to select the top central administrators of the system and have the chancellor rubber stamp their choices. Macchiarola asked all such appointees to submit their resignations, and he decided who would have the positions.

And so it continued until 1983, when the school board—no longer in the role of micromanagers—clashed with Schools Chancellor Macchiarola over whether some eighth-graders would be permitted to attend ninth-grade at a high school rather than at a junior high. This time the central board of education had the support of the organization of community school boards and the teacher union. Macchiarola quit, but he had established that it was the chancellor, not the school board, that was supposed to administer the system.

*Anything But a Rubber Stamp*

School boards in Louisiana are in a class by themselves. So much so that the State Superintendent of Elementary and Secondary Education tried in 2009 to get the legislature to enact a package of bills to reform school boards. He argued that Louisiana's low standing in education could not improve until board members conducted themselves in a more ethical and more responsible manner. Examinations administered by the National Assessment of Educational Progress in 2007 placed the state's eighth graders forty-fifth in reading and forty-sixth in math among the 50 states.

The bills that the state superintendent backed imposed term limits on school board members, made them ineligible for compensation, put limits on hiring relatives, created a minimum requirement of a high school diploma to serve on a board, required a supermajority to terminate a superintendent, strengthened professional development requirements for board members, and authorized superintendents to make appointments and terminations without board approval.

"There was interference with what superintendents were trying to do," the state superintendent, Paul Pastorek, told me. "And as I explored more deeply I discovered that building principals, too, lose control and integrity over their operations because of interference by school board members. They were becoming de facto members of the school administration. This is more than a coincidental, occasional event. At first I thought it was isolated . . . but it's more and more apparent that it's widespread and culturally ingrained in the system."

Legislative supporters organized the provisions into four separate bills, hoping that lawmakers would pick and choose and pass at least some of the measures. Representative Steve Carter, the main sponsor, told me, "Many superintendents felt the pay and benefits school board members received was a reason they got involved in hiring because it would enable them to hire people that would, in turn, assist them in getting reelected."

Two major statewide business groups backed the legislation, as did the Republican governor and the Democratic senator. Nevertheless, three of the bills never emerged from committee and the one that reached the floor lost. The State Senate never even got involved. Legislators' offices were flooded by hundreds of email messages, letters, and phone calls opposing the bills, most of them, according to Carter, from school board members and their friends and relatives. The Louisiana School Board Association launched a withering attack on all four bills and the two statewide teacher organizations added their lobbying efforts to the opposition, apparently preferring the devils they knew to the possibility of having reformers join school boards. Teachers charged that giving superintendents unilateral power to dismiss employees and removing board members from the equation could impede the grievance process and eliminate due process.

Opponents portrayed Pastorek's support of the bills as an attack on democracy, an effort by Pastorek, a former official of the National Aeronautic and Space Administration, to deny the elected representatives of the people their rightful place in the education hierarchy. Never mind that school board members in Louisiana got paid $800 a month ($900 for the president) or that many of them included themselves in their districts' health care coverage. Never mind that some boards in the state routinely micromanaged and fired superintendents who objected to their intrusions. Never mind that the state has a history of board members putting relatives on the payroll or that board membership could easily turn into a lifetime sinecure. And forget about the fact that members of some of Louisiana's school boards apparently never completed high school.

## Sources of Friction

Sometimes, shouting matches among board members grab the attention of the community, but far more often school boards try to adhere to exemplary standards of behavior and are no more rowdy than city councils, state legislatures, or the houses of Congress. Court rulings, state regulations, and codes of conduct set forth by state school board associations serve to remind board members that they are in the public eye and appropriate decorum is expected of them.

One situation that draws scrutiny to school boards involves dissension in the ranks. This makes good fodder for the media and provides lively theater for the public, but boards on which members cannot work together effectively probably will not accomplish as much as boards that are able to achieve consensus.

### Dealing with Differences

Differences among individuals on a board of education may derive from clashes of personalities, philosophies, political alignments in the community, or pressures from special interest groups among other possibilities. Every member of a board has the power that the law and regulations confer, but individual power is insufficient for getting much accomplished. A board member's position will not lead to the result that he or she wants unless that member can win a majority on a particular issue.

This is not to say that differences should be hidden. School systems benefit from a thrashing out of views among board members. Democracy allows for differences of opinion and even expects people to part on some issues. Let's say that a school system is about to adopt a new reading program for the primary grades, and board members differ over two proposed programs, one of which, some board members argue, does not sufficiently emphasize phonics. A thorough discussion by board members can bring up various points about competing reading programs and, one hopes, lead to a reasoned decision.

A school board on which members seldom disagree probably does not give enough attention to a range of options. Those who dissent may have valuable opinions to offer. A member who tries to force colleagues on the board to review the numbers one more time may help a board avert a terrible mistake. Spending the public's money and educating other people's children make it imperative that school boards not rush to judgment. Everyone gains if a school board meeting is a forum for healthy debate. The seven members of the Grosse Ile Township Board of Education in Michigan agreed in a public statement that they were guided by the proposition that "the board will govern in an atmosphere that encourages and respects free expression of opinions and ideas, whether in the minority or majority."[10]

The world of school boards, though, ordinarily expects that once a board determines a course of action, the members, regardless of their positions before the decision, will unite and act as a single body to support the majority opinion. Once all opinions have been heard and the vote has been taken, the outcome becomes the board's position, regardless of how individual members cast their votes. Consensus should be the order of the day in governing schools, according to some experts. This does not always happen, and boards may carry their differences into subsequent areas of decision-making. Such a split can undermine a board's effectiveness and spill over into the instructional program, much to the disadvantage of students.

*The President: Reconciler or Autocrat?*

When the majority on a split school board agrees on a course of action before the board as a whole meets, excluding the minority from the decision-making process, they do damage to the cause of democracy. The result is much the same when the president decides matters unilaterally and has a loyal following that rubber stamps his or her position, in effect disenfranchising other board members. An autocratic board president can stifle discussion among members and limit community input into some of the school system's most important decisions. Thus, he or she can surely add flaws to the democratic process so far as the board's activities are concerned. There may be a fine line between a president whose leadership style brings others along and a president who plays the dictator.

The president is pivotal. He or she has greater influence on board culture than anyone else does. The president does much to determine the degree to which the rule of democracy will prevail within the board. The president usually has a special relationship with the superintendent, carries legal authority not vested in other members, determines the agenda of meetings along with the superintendent, and can limit the information that other board members receive.

School board presidents, like other members, may spend great amounts of time on board activities or may keep their service to the minimum. As unpaid public servants, board presidents have considerable leeway in the time they devote to leadership tasks. One survey of board presidents found that 30 percent of them felt that they gave what they considered "too much time" to matters related to labor relations. More than 40 percent of them felt that they gave "too little time" to interacting with other local governing bodies and selecting and adopting school curricula.[11] No single member, not even the president, has the legal right to take action as an individual on behalf of the board unless so authorized by the board in a duly constituted meeting.

All members may contribute to the board's decisions. The staff and, certainly, the superintendent have input. Members of the general public may serve on committees that the school board creates. No one other than a board member, however, has the legal authority to sign off on final actions. Individual members of a school board—except for the president and certain duties conferred on him or her—have no corporate authority other than that which is vested in the whole board. The board exists and acts as an organism apart from any of its individual members. This may seem like a small and legalistic point, but people should bear it in mind when they hear a member of their local school board spouting off on one topic or another. Whatever that person says is his or her opinion and may or may not represent the position of the board.

### The Board as Conduit to the Public

A main obstacle to the democratic process by which school boards are supposed to operate is their lack of information. Few school boards have staffs that serve board members exclusively, leaving boards largely dependent on the superintendent and his staff for information about almost everything. The superintendent generally is the gatekeeper for the information that filters through to the board. A superintendent who is not candid and open with board members can keep information from them.

Ideally, the board—in collaboration with the superintendent—should be a conduit to the public, revealing to the community as much about the inner workings of the school system as is legally possible. This means baring all the numbers that impinge upon the budget, the cumulative results of student assessments, details (without specific names) pertaining to student progress, changes in policies, and the actions taken by the school board in formal sessions. Some school systems are a lot better about this than others. The school board ought to be something of an ombudsman for the public whose interests it should represent. But if the members of the board of education are themselves in the dark they are unlikely to be able to shed light on matters of great concern.

Ostensibly, a democracy thrives on transparency and candor, though this proposition has been seriously tested at all levels of government. One should consider the public, as well as the board, in this context. Even a public that does not clamor for information about the schools is nonetheless entitled—within the bounds of legality—to know what is happening. Unfortunately, not enough people, even parents of the schoolchildren, care about this information. This is not a reason to abandon the practice of openness, but these flaws on the part of the public—just as their unwillingness to turn out in large numbers for school elections—should be taken as challenges to the board to seek and win the support of the larger community.

There is a dilemma here, a weakness in the governance system of school boards. The people at the top, the board members, are supposed to maintain a proper distance from staff, who, after all, work for the superintendent. This means that board members who cultivate their own sources of information within the system may violate accepted protocol, not to mention putting those staff members on the spot. But not to do so may mean not possessing information essential to decision-making. Thus, a school board, one way or another, ought to develop a system—ideally through the superintendent—that provides a steady flow of information essential to the good decision-making.

In this day and age, a board that is forthcoming with information tries to maintain a website that provides a full array of information about the system and about individual schools. Such a school system may also publish a newsletter (perhaps electronically) and ensures that it is more than a propaganda sheet that simply extols the virtues of the district without delving into challenges and difficulties. The board makes available on its website agendas in advance of meetings. The board holds hearings throughout the district whenever a budget or referendum item is scheduled to appear on a ballot.

Increasingly, school boards will have to assume more of the responsibility for obtaining and dispensing information. Daily newspapers have been a diligent ally of the public in efforts to assure accountability in all ranks of government. But the daily newspaper industry is in a state of collapse, and reporters who used to cover school board meetings and investigative reporters who looked into wrongdoing have lost their jobs as revenues have shrunk.

Jim Willse, who retired in 2009 as editor of *The Star-Ledger*, New Jersey's largest newspaper, said that "the threat of stories," as much as actual articles, formerly held corruption in check.[12] Forty percent of the more than 300 journalists on his staff accepted a buy-out on December 31, 2008, and Willse and everyone else in New Jersey saw the threat of stories diminish. There is little hope of national media making up for the deficiencies. Less than 1.5 percent of stories on television, newspapers, websites, and radio in 2007, 2008, and 2009 dealt with national coverage of education.[13] One would hope that school board members, like all public officials, will discharge their duties honorably and responsibly, but human nature is human nature.

# Chapter 11

# Accepting Responsibility

Accountability doesn't begin and end with the board of education. Educators should be accountable for providing high-quality instruction. Students should be accountable for putting forth the effort to perform to the best of their ability. Parents should be accountable for reinforcing education in the home. Taxpayers should be accountable for giving schools the fiscal capacity to do their work. School board members should interact with all these constituencies, spending money wisely and effectively, and doing all within their means to promote the best possible teaching and learning. The school board should never neglect outcomes. It should not lose sight of the ends that it has in mind. Members of school boards should set goals and return continually to the same question, asking of themselves, "How are we doing?"

Let's say, for instance, that a school system has been remiss in making instructional technology available in its classrooms. Progress can be readily determined if the board sets goals in this regard. Another such area might deal with offering more Advanced Placement courses and boosting enrollments of students in the courses. This goal is readily measurable. Clarity of this sort on the part of the school board puts a district's entire staff on notice that the board values certain aims and outcomes and that these objectives merit the attention of teachers and administrators. Those who work for the school system deserve to know the parameters against which the board will measure progress. There should be little room at the end of the day for the superintendent or anyone else to say, "I didn't know that it was so important to the school board."

David Mathews, president of the Charles F. Kettering Foundation, maintained that accountability is essential to restoring public confidence in the schools. He worried that democracy itself is in jeopardy when the public schools lose their connection to the public. Openness and candor, what Mathews called a full account of what happens in classrooms, are central to the schools' accountability to the citizenry.[1] It turns out, though, that in most cases only students are held accountable. This should be no surprise. They have the least power of any group in the schools. Most others—parents, taxpayers, educators, lawmakers, and school board members—pretty much resist accountability. This evasion of responsibility represents a breakdown in the democratic system. Despite its virtues, democracy does not always operate in the interests of its weakest members—who in the case of schools are the students.

Accountability arises from a milieu that encourages and supports people by asking challenging questions about their institutions. Shane Osborn, the state treasurer in Nebraska, said that his state is special in that "we have an inquiring public that demands to know how tax dollars are spent. That's called accountability."[2] School boards should take the same tack, opening to public scrutiny everything that legally can be so exposed. I like the way that Donald R. McAdams linked accountability to empowerment and capacity. It is not simply a matter of asking people to take responsibility for outcomes, but doing so after empowering them with some control over the circumstances for which they will be held accountable, and giving them the capacity to carry out the task. Capacity may involve skills, knowledge, tools, and resources.[3]

### Holding Educators Accountable

The apparent lack of accountability of their children's teachers troubles some parents. They know from reputation and from the experiences of their children that some teachers are better than others. Yet it seems to parents that school boards do nothing to deal with this uneven situation. "You would be dismayed to discover that not only can no one tell you which teachers are most effective, they also cannot say which are least effective," stated a report on the failure to acknowledge differences in teacher effectiveness and the tendency of school boards and district officials to act as if effectiveness is the same in every classroom.[4]

Parents would like to have mechanisms by which to rate teachers and to share their opinions of teachers so that they would know which teachers their children should avoid. The Internet would be a perfect vehicle for gathering and disseminating such information. It is routine at colleges and universities for students to rank their professors and for those rankings to be available for public perusal. Some institutions of higher education even include student rankings in their evaluations of faculty members for promotion and tenure.

Such practices scarcely exist in elementary and secondary schools. Boards of education want to avoid conflicts with teachers, who almost certainly would object to ratings by parents. Isn't it interesting that one may go online and visit sites rating physicians, dentists, and lawyers, but such sites are virtually nonexistent so far as elementary and secondary school teaching is concerned. "The schools say the law requires them to stay mum, but some experts disagree," said Jay Mathews, education columnist for *The Washington Post*, referring to an earlier column in which he wrote of the "public schools' routine refusal to share information about bad teaching with parents of affected children."[5]

Teachers form the most important link in the chain of learning, but—especially once they gain tenure—they are largely unaccountable for their performance. They resist the idea that they should in any way be measured by student outcomes. Boards of education have little jurisdiction over the performance of teachers so long as teachers carry out their duties and do not violate the law, however poorly their students may fare. State laws, statutes, regulations and provisions of labor contracts protect teachers. It is true that school boards negotiate those contracts with teacher representatives, but the boards are inclined to back off from demanding contract language that would acknowledge that some teachers carry out their duties in a manner far more exemplary than others.

## NCLB as a Tool for Accountability

Teachers are held accountable indirectly when the schools in which they work face accountability. This collective responsibility was at the heart of the No Child Left Behind (NCLB) Act that congressional lawmakers on both sides of the aisle rallied to support when President George W. Bush asked them to pass it early in his administration. The law proposed to bring all the nation's students to proficiency by 2014. Student testing underpinned the legislation, and it contained various sanctions for individual schools—but not for teachers—that did not improve the scores of students.

Many educators grumbled about NCLB and its onerous sanctions, but to a certain extent educators and school boards brought the law upon themselves by taking the low test scores of certain students for granted, as if divinely ordained. Too many students, especially the neediest ones, have been unsuccessful in school for all too long. Moreover, school boards over the years did not provide ways to hold schools accountable for the progress of such students. Voila! The No Child Left Behind Act. School boards had little ability to escape the bright light that the law shined on them.

The most distinguishing feature of NCLB was its requirement that school systems examine separately the test scores of minority groups, special education students, and English language learners. Few school boards previously approached student progress in this manner. Rather, they tended to look at over all scores, more or less burying statistics of traditionally low-achieving groups within the total results. NCLB compelled school officials to disaggregate data. Discussions about achievement gaps will not go away so long as the law rubs educators' faces in test scores in this way.

The nation's two largest school systems, New York City and Los Angeles, both had procedures for rating their schools. Though it collected data on individual schools throughout the 2000s, the Los Angeles Unified School District did not package those data for parents and provide school report cards that went beyond minimum state requirements until 2009. New York began giving letter grades to schools after they came under mayoral control in the first decade of the 2000s. It cost the city's education department $130 million a year to carry out the process of grading schools, which the department regarded as part of its effort to be more accountable.[6]

Holding teachers accountable for student outcomes is not so straight-forward a process as some may imagine, though. It may prod some teachers to do a better job, but there may be unintended risks to applying this kind of pressure. The resulting anxiety of teachers may make them less effective, particularly when they think they do not have enough time to impart the desired instruction and insufficient support from parents. One research study of the response of elementary teachers to policies expecting them to be more accountable for student test results found they suffered more stress and even burnout. As a result, teachers can become less engaged in their work, emotionally exhausted, and prone to leave the profession.[7]

What began as a love fest among supporters of No Child Left Behind devolved into divisiveness when school districts complained of the law's inflexibility. Schools were deemed as "in need of improvement" when a small subgroup of students did not make adequate yearly progress even if the vast majority of students achieved the expected results. Almost 30 percent of the nation's schools failed to make adequate yearly progress during the 2007 through 2008 school year,[8] stirring concern among critics about the reasonableness of the law.

Imposition of the law also brought up complaints that have long bubbled beneath the surface about standardized testing. A one-time score is but a snapshot in time of learning that evolves over an entire school year. Multiple-choice assessments lend themselves to manipulation. Test preparation can squeeze out other kinds of teaching. When Margaret Spellings succeeded Rod Paige as the federal government's Secretary of Education she tried to give states and school districts a little more flexibility in applying NCLB requirements. Criticism of the law continued into the Obama administration, which sought ways to file down the sharp edges of the law.

### Accountability of Principals and Superintendents

Whatever one may think of NCLB, the law underscores the responsibility of school board members to dedicate themselves to the success of all students, not just those who have the most advantages. "It rightfully put before us the issues of the achievement gap,"[9] Spellings said of the law in her waning weeks as Secretary of Education. This attention to pupils ought to lead to closer scrutiny of principals, who ostensibly lead the effort in each building to maximize student achievement. Once they approve the appointments of principals, though, school boards tend to pay them little heed, acting as if schools run on automatic pilot. School boards should not take the leadership of principals for granted.

Schools with high-achieving students and good teachers can usually survive poor principals, but school boards should give greater attention to the work of principals in schools with disproportionate numbers of low-achieving students. Public Agenda found in a study of low-performing districts that principals could be classified as "copers," who do just enough to get by, and "transformers," who seek to change student performance in their schools. Principals in both groups spoke of "instructional leadership," but transformers devoted most of their efforts to evaluating, coaching, and supporting their teachers, while copers didn't seem to do much of it.[10]

Ultimately, the superintendent is responsible for overseeing principals, who, in turn, supervise the teachers. Clifford B. Janey was asked after his first year as school superintendent in Newark whether observers should gauge his success by students' scores. He said that scores would be a partial measure, but that his success, in effect, was dependent on others and that he should be measured by whether "we have put the district in a position to win—ensuring that we have teachers who want to be teachers,"[11] for instance.

A school superintendent is accountable for everything. If a school bus driver forgets to drop off a child, the school board may hold the superintendent accountable. If a teacher has a sexual relationship with a student, the school board may hold the superintendent accountable. If the district's students reach college unable to pass introductory math courses, the school board may hold the superintendent accountable. That's the way democracy works: The buck has to stop somewhere. Someone has to take charge and the superintendent, as the chief presiding office, must accept the blame.

"From the board's point of view, the important lesson is that the board's relationship with the CEO be formed by the accountability of the CEO position, not its responsibility," wrote John Carver.[12] In other words, the board should be most concerned with outcomes for which it holds the CEO accountable, which, essentially, is everything that happens in the school system. Only the conduct of the board itself is not under his aegis.

## Holding Students Accountable

It is difficult to separate the performance of students from the work of their teachers. The test scores that students attain generally have some connection to the prowess of their teachers. Good teachers tend to get the most out of their students and poor teachers tend to stultify the growth of students. The links in this chain of cause and effect are not always sturdy. Some able students do well in spite of their less-than-able teachers and some ostensibly gifted teachers can't motivate certain students. All kinds of intervening factors affect test scores and many critics have made persuasive arguments that assessments are faulty indicators of outcomes—for either students or teachers. Yet for want of better yardsticks, test scores of students remain one of the few measures available for gauging student progress.

Whatever the worth of test scores, however, it is abundantly clear that it remains incumbent upon students to do the work expected of them. For this, they should be accountable. Students have control over the amount of effort they put forth in behalf of their studies. Self-discipline and good work habits help them achieve. When President Barack Obama addressed the nation's students on television at the opening of the school year in 2009 he acknowledged that it is not easy to do well in school. He said, "At the end of the day, we can have the most dedicated teachers, the most supportive parents, and the best schools in the world and none of it will matter unless all of you fulfill your responsibilities. Unless you show up to those schools, pay attention to those teachers, listen to your parents, grandparents, and other adults, and put in the hard work it takes to succeed."[13]

One of the greatest gifts that schools can confer on students is to imbue them with such qualities as perseverance and resiliency. They can be more accountable for their work if they learn to stick with it and to overcome setbacks. So while it falls to each child to strive to the best of his or her ability—and to be accountable for doing so—schools have not been very good at conveying such traits. Thus, I have less to say here about the accountability of students than about the accountability of the adults—educators, parents, taxpayers, and school board members—who do so much to shape opportunities for young people.

### Holding Parents Accountable

Where does one draw the line between the responsibility of the school board and the responsibility of parents? The board of education can provide clean, orderly classrooms that are staffed by qualified teachers, who have the equipment and materials they need to do their job. And, still, some children do not learn. Is this the fault of the school board?

One feature of a democracy is the leeway that parents have for raising their children as they see fit. Some youngsters show up for the first day of kindergarten already knowing their letters, numbers, and colors. They have parents who have read to them and engaged them in steadily more complex conversations. Others appear for kindergarten with few of these attributes, as if they had been dropped into the school buildings from Mars.

#### *When Parents Are Irresponsible*

Then, the school year starts and only some parents respond to notices sent home by the school and to invitations to meet with teachers to discuss the progress of their children. Others behave in ways counter to the interests of their children. They do not even bother to determine how their youngsters are faring in school.

Let's face it: Some parents do not do a very good job when it comes to giving their children a foundation for learning and reinforcing the goals of schooling.

What is a school board to do? There are philosophical differences among educational policymakers. Some maintain that, as a prelude to teaching and learning, society must address poverty and the deficiencies that make some families dysfunctional and hinder the education of their children. Others say that the school should take youngsters as they are—not being overly concerned with factors over which schools have little or no control—and provide effective education regardless of what happens outside schools.

Society understands that parents bear primary responsibility for their children. Nevertheless, the state will intervene at certain points as, for example, when parents neglect or abuse their children. All 50 states appear to have statutes pertaining to parental responsibility if minor children steal items from stores, vandalize property, injure playmates, or otherwise willfully act in ways that violate the public interest. During colonial times, parents were responsible for educating their children and for finding ways to train them for gainful employment. Eventually, public schools assumed these tasks, but it wasn't until many decades passed that parents were obligated to make sure that their children attended school.

If parents don't fulfill their responsibilities, then school systems must prod them. It shouldn't be that way, but society owes it to youngsters to hold their parents accountable for acting in their behalf. The school board in Springfield, Missouri, recognized this necessity and adopted policies to enable the district to step up efforts to improve attendance. The various initiatives culminated in the 2008 through 2009 school year with the best attendance rates that the Springfield Public School District had in 20 years. Springfield, in southwest Missouri, just an hour from the Arkansas border, bills itself as the Queen City of the Ozarks and benefits from the tourists who pass through the region on trips to nearby Branson, a mecca for country music fans.

An attempt to make the entire community aware of the need to promote better attendance was launched with a federal grant of some $250,000 under the Safe Schools/Healthy Students program. Banners looking like huge license plates appeared throughout town, paid for by the grant and supported by the businesses that hung the banners with the message "BN Schl." The district used most of the funds to hire social workers to help promote attendance at individual schools. The district's six-member attendance coordinating staff led efforts for several years to ensure that more of its 24,000 students went to school regularly. The campaign was helped by a goal that the state set for improving attendance in every district in conjunction with meeting federal requirements for adequate yearly progress under the No Child Left Behind Act.

District representatives telephoned homes to inquire into absences. The schools even made wake-up calls and distributed alarm clocks. Attendance officers drove to homes to pick up students who missed their buses. District officials sent letters to about 200 homes a year when attendance lagged, reminding parents that state law mandated daily attendance and that failure to comply could result in sanctions. If there was still no improvement, the district asked the county attorney to send a follow-up letter, stressing the legal requirement of parents. Finally, the five or so most recalcitrant families received summons. "We tried to put in place the things we could do as a school district to assist parents," Becky Morgan, the school system's attendance coordinator, told me. "We don't want to hear a lot of excuses."

*What Can Be Done?*

When it comes to student achievement, it is usually not enough for parents to comply with compulsory attendance laws. That's where their legal responsibility ends, but success for most students depends on parents doing much more. There is little doubt that what happens in the home and under the guidance of the family can greatly affect outcomes in school. Some parents, starting very early in the development of their children, surround them with the accouterments of literacy. They converse with them and provide more than one-word answers in response to their children's questions. They read to them and make books part of their environment. Then, once the children attend school these parents reinforce the lessons of the classroom in the home. They give children quiet, comfortable places to do homework and discuss their assignments with them. They take them to zoos and circuses and expose them to music and art. They take them on stimulating family outings. They show through word and deed that they value learning and encourage their children to strive to master their schoolwork.

Can a board of education and the educators it employs compel any of this? Not readily. The education sociologist James S. Coleman wrote in the 1980s that families at all levels were becoming ill-equipped to engender the kind of support that complements and augments the schools in preparing children for a productive and fulfilling future.[14] The dysfunction of families has grown only worse, burdening school boards that want to address questions of achievement. Some districts try to attack the problem of insufficient parental responsibility by setting requirements for parents. The examples are legion. School districts withhold students' report cards until a family member comes to school to confer with someone about the youngster's performance. Teachers ask parents to sign their children's completed homework assignments. Some schools try to require every family to find a time slot during the school day when one or another caregiver can serve in the classroom as a volunteer.

School systems can help parents be more responsible, but often this requires school boards to spend more money. In some districts, particularly with large numbers of poor or immigrant families, programs offer parents opportunities to learn how to help children with homework and how to interact with the schools in ways that promote their children's learning. Boston had such a program in the

1990s, but allowed it to expire in the early 2000s. The school system revived the program in 2009 as Parent University, beginning with an all-day session at the University of Massachusetts at Boston and followed by other sessions during the school year. Elsewhere there are such programs as Parents as Teachers, the Nurse-Family Partnership, and the Parent-Child Home Program that send personnel into homes to instruct young parents.

Are such measures sufficient? Can school boards explore other ways to extract more accountability from parents? When I pointed out that the school district in which I was a board member had an achievement gap between schools in one part of town and those in another part of town, one of my board colleagues said this was not the fault of the school board. She said that in some of the lower performing schools the No Child Left Behind guidelines that made those students eligible for free tutoring had been ignored by parents, who, by and large, did not take advantage of the offer. There is, in fact, just so much that school boards can do to adopt policies and to urge their superintendents to prod parents to take responsibility for educational outcomes. Yet I suspect that schools have not come close to exhausting the possibilities. This matter merits the reflection of every school board member.

### Holding Taxpayers Accountable

Earlier, I mentioned the growing portion of households without children attending public schools. In many districts no more than one of every five homes uses the public schools. This change in the character of the country affects the ability of school boards to carry out their work. More and more Americans feel no connection to the public schools and believe that they have no stake in them. Hard-pressed senior citizens, especially, squirm under the pressure of rising school taxes from which they think they derive no benefit. They watch taxes increase while their incomes remain fixed. Meanwhile, many households with children in public school have seen the value of their homes fall and their savings degraded. School boards in some locales are not able to make a compelling case to the taxpayers in behalf of support for the public schools.

Local taxes for schools are perhaps the most democratically imposed of all taxes—essentially, the only tax over which people have a direct vote. Most school boards put an annual budget on the ballot for the citizens' approval. This procedure puts school boards in a position that Congress, state legislatures, and town councils do not face. On the other hand, what many members of the public do not realize is that even when voters reject an annual budget the cuts that the school board makes in response come mostly at the expense of students, not employees. Ongoing employment contracts remain in force and salaries and benefits are almost never reduced when a budget fails. School boards make reductions in such areas as transportation, textbooks, after-school programs, supplies, team sports, and purchases of instructional technology—almost all of which fall most heavily on students.

The truth is that there is no good rationale for giving the taxpayers the chance to vote on the school budget. They have no direct say over contract negotiations for salaries and benefits, which account for as much as 80 percent of the expenditures. A state might just as well limit annual increases in the school budget and end the practice of voting on the budget, as New Jersey proposed to do.

The relationship between school boards and taxpayers should be reciprocal. School board members face constant challenges in deciding between the needs of taxpayers and the needs of students. School boards have every right to expect taxpayers to support reasonable budgets and to vote for capital improvements that will provide buildings, additions, and renovations that students need. Schools require the financial capacity to provide each child with a proper education.

In turn, taxpayers should expect school taxes to remain at affordable levels. They don't want increases to employees for salaries and benefits to climb at unsustainable rates. "School district finances are organized around the assumption that revenues will increase more or less steadily, and at a rate higher than inflation," warned policy analysts Marguerite Roza and Raegen Miller. "Recent shifts in the underlying economic conditions of the country, however, suggest that it would be foolhardy to continue operating under this assumption. Many school districts will face stagnant or declining revenues for some time to come."[15]

New York State recognized the reciprocal responsibility of government and taxpayers in establishing the office of taxpayer accountability in 2009. In announcing the creation of the office, Governor David A. Paterson said its mission would be to save taxpayers money by lowering costs, sharing services, eliminating duplication, improving service delivery, limiting unnecessary and unfunded mandates, and attacking waste, fraud, and abuse. These goals are obviously laudable and to the extent that New York State government achieves them the citizens may feel that accountability is not a one-way street for taxpayers. There could be lessons here for other states.

### Holding the School Board Accountable

School boards are seldom held accountable for student learning. How often have you heard of a local school board election being determined by perceptions of whether students have been learning? A review of the few studies of the extent to which voters hold school board members accountable in school board elections for students' test scores led to mixed conclusions.

Looking at elections in 46 counties in South Carolina, researchers found a relationship in 2000 between student test scores and voting patterns, but none in 2002 or 2004. They hypothesized that widespread media coverage of test results preceding school board elections in 2000—the first to follow passage of the state's accountability system—was a factor in voter behavior but that test scores did not influence incumbents' electoral fortunes in the next two rounds of balloting, when media coverage shifted to other issues.[16]

The evidence from South Carolina suggests, according to the researchers, that voters do sometimes hold school board candidates accountable on the basis of learning outcomes. Usually, though, school board elections attract scant attention and people, generally uninformed about test scores, do not focus on scores in deciding which candidates to elect to boards. This result suggests, too, that transparency and the promulgation of information—which ought to be inherent in a democracy—can promote accountability.

An experience in Metuchen, New Jersey, a small, commuter town with a station on the main route of Amtrak's Northeast Corridor between New York City and Washington, illustrates how, once informed and aroused, an otherwise quiescent community may demand accountability of its school board for student achievement. Following the publication in *New Jersey Monthly* magazine in 2008 of rankings of high schools around the state, residents of the community wanted their school board to explain why Metuchen High School did not rank in the top 75.

Ten years earlier, the school placed at number 27 and, at number 56 in 2006. People voiced concerns that a downgrading of the high school would have an adverse effect on the town and its school system. Residents began pressing the school board for explanations. Citizens for Quality Education (CQE), a local independent, nonpartisan group that monitors the Metuchen Public Schools, posted an entry at its website stating, "Coming in at #86 among more than 300 schools is not so bad. Moving up 30 spots would set us going in the right direction. Moving down 30 spots will knock us out of the top third."

The school board's initial reaction was to push back and question whether the rankings were meaningful and whether the community should care about them. People continued to care. They came to board meetings, watched broadcasts of the meetings, and exchanged electronic messages registering their dissatisfaction with the school board. "It seems those who have been on the board the longest are the ones who get most defensive when you mention areas that need to be improved," Jim Jaques, president of CQE, told me in retrospect. Finally, after critics of the board insisted that the categories used in the rankings were not arbitrary and that the statistics were objective, the board and the administration scheduled a pair of seminars about the school system and its high schools with presentations, after which participants broke into discussion groups.

The school board had been yanked into the limelight by the magazine's rankings, by the position statements on the CQE website, and by the network of email messages that flowed in the article's wake. The dissatisfaction snowballed for several months as residents focused their criticism over the Internet, a process indicative of the new ways that citizens have for holding school boards accountable. The traditional town square is disappearing, being replaced by a virtual gathering place built on websites, email, and tweets. Democracy sometimes finds a way to express itself even in the absence of old-style New England town meetings.

### The Hard Road to Board Accountability

School boards may not find it as easy in the future as they did in the past to evade accountability for student achievement. They, after all, select the superintendent and approve all hiring by the superintendent. They vote yea or nay for every curriculum guide and textbook used in the system and sign off on the professional development for educators. All the expenditures fall, one way or another, under the school board's purview. People with such power should presumably be able to generate a substantial effort in behalf of teaching and learning.

A board cannot simply blame others for its failures. One former superintendent, describing the role of school boards, said they should be accountable for providing an effective and efficient governing structure. To this end, he saw five main functions for the board: selecting and evaluating the superintendent; developing, evaluating, and monitoring school policies; monitoring student learning; monitoring the collective-bargaining process; and preparing, adopting, and monitoring the district budget.[17] Shortcomings in any of these areas may indicate a lack of accountability by the board.

The business community may be well positioned to hold school boards accountable, though this group has been reluctant to flex its muscles in this regard. Business pays a large portion of the property taxes, depends on the schools for employable workers, and looks to the schools to make the community desirable. After the tawdry episode with the school board in Clayton County, Georgia that I described earlier, the state board of education asked four organizations including the Georgia Chamber of Commerce and the Metro Atlanta Chamber of Commerce to assemble an advisory panel on school governance. The panel was instrumental in helping get a bill through the state legislature to reform school boards.

Self-assessment, too, can be part of a school board's effort to hold itself accountable. In the 1980s, the Institute for Educational Leadership worked with several state school board associations to develop measures to let school boards evaluate their own performance. The assessment included a rating scale by which to examine such factors as procedures for oversight and review of policies and programs, indicators to assess progress toward objectives, indicators to look at student achievement, and whether ongoing expenditures are in line with the budget. There are, of course, other variables that figure into school board performance, but the point is that boards that do not regularly take their own temperature may not recognize when their work is subpar.

Those wishing to hold a school board accountable should inquire into the factors that go into the board's decision making. Why did the school board decide to close this school and not another? Why did the school board adopt this particular reading program? How does the school board know that the money it spends for computers in classrooms increases learning among students? School boards should be pushed to evaluate and act upon the results of the decisions they make.

A school board, like a human being, may find self-assessment distasteful. Implicit in the process, after all, is the assumption that board members will admit to failures. They must be ready to see themselves as lacking in some areas. But board members, like most people, may get defensive when asked to account for their shortcomings. It is easier for boards to critique the performance of their main employee, the superintendent.

It is up to the board to monitor the superintendent and, in turn, to be sure that the superintendent keeps close tabs on those who work in the system. The board has itself to blame, though, if the superintendent consistently fails to perform acceptably. The superintendent, as the only direct employee of the school board, should be properly monitored. Perhaps it sounds like a cockeyed notion, but one of the best sources, in turn, for holding the board of education accountable is the superintendent, who like a satellite looking down from above, is positioned to observe the board's actions. The problem may be the reluctance of superintendents to speak frankly about their bosses. It would be worth exploring ways in which superintendents could offer candid observations of their boards without suffering penalties for doing so.

*How Citizens in Two Districts Tried to Hold Their Boards Accountable*

As the influence of daily newspapers fades, the Internet will probably figure more prominently in attempts to induce the accountability of school boards and educators. The activities of Parents Coalition in Montgomery County, Maryland, illustrated the strength that the Internet can generate for those dissatisfied with the transparency that a school board and its system provide. Parents Coalition functioned as a kind of electronic irritant to school officials, reaching its audience through a listserv, a website, and a blog.

The county-wide school system of 144,000 students is one of the better large districts in the country, but the several dozen activists who were the moving force behind Parents Coalition began their efforts in 2002 because they thought the school board was not sufficiently responsive to the populace. "As we envisioned when we started, we are the resource to help other folks advocate," said Rosanne Hurwitz, one of the organizers, looking back on the first meeting in Ellen Paul's house. "We serve as the oversight for the county educational system because the board of education simply refuses to act."

It was unlikely that the school board would have agreed with the need for activism by Parents Coalition—which operated under the heading "Dedicated to Improving Responsiveness and Performance." Entries on the group's blog sounded a drumbeat of grievances. At one point in late 2009, for instance, there were items concerning the "devastation" of state cuts to special education, the testing and placement of kindergarteners, alleged "inattention" to the gifted, and the performance of the superintendent. Among the features on the website were copies of audits of the activity accounts that principals oversee at individual schools, a daily diary of the peregrinations of Superintendent Jerry Weast and other district representatives who traveled widely for conferences and various events, and reports accounting for expenses on the 1,400 school system credit cards carried by ranking district employees.

An ongoing disagreement between the Coalition and school officials dealt with the district's practice of charging students' families for some of the books and supplies that are free in other school systems. The Coalition encouraged families to refuse to pay the so-called curricular fees and was at loggerheads with the district over the practice. "Virtually everything we've brought up has elicited a response, but not to us as an organization," Janis Sartucci, a Coalition stalwart, told me. "The school board doesn't acknowledge that we exist."

Another citizens' group, this one in Pittsburgh, was more successful in winning the school board's grudging acceptance of its role. A+ Schools, which called itself a community alliance for public education, created Board Watch as an arm to improve the city's public schools by making the school board more effective and more accountable. Trained volunteers attended school board meetings and rated the board along five dimensions—focus and mission, transparency, conduct, role clarity, and competency. A+ Schools hoped that the information and ratings that the volunteer watchers produced would keep the public more informed and engaged.

During the period from March to May 2009, feedback from the volunteers resulted in an overall B– score for the school board, an improvement over the C+ during the period from November 2008 through February 2009. Board Watch, examining the specifics of the five dimensions, gave the school board a C+ in both periods, for instance, based on the way the board managed its time at the meetings and the degree to which it focused on its goals and on student achievement. The score for transparency improved, based on whether the volunteers felt welcome at the meeting and their ability to obtain the agenda and related items.

The score for conduct dropped to a C+, reflecting the way the board handled differences of opinion and whether comments of members at meetings were solution-oriented, sarcastic, or accusatory. The score also fell for role clarity as volunteers rated the extent to which the board exercised its role in planning for the implementation of policies and strategies to achieve the district's goals. The board maintained a C+ rating for competency, based on the volunteers' ratings of the preparation that board members exhibited at meetings and whether they acted on facts, research, and effective practices.

In summing up its rating of the board during the March to May 2009 period, Board Watch acknowledged the many tasks that the law requires the school board to perform, but made some pointed overall recommendations. The group called on the board to raise the level of its conversation to focus on planning to meet achievement goals rather than devote so much discussion to routine administrative details. They also asked the board to designate specific time in its agenda for discussions of strategy and follow-up.

*School Boards as Captives*

In the end, those attempting to hold school boards accountable, as in Montgomery County and Pittsburgh, must recognize that these bodies do not fully control their fate. I have pointed out the degree to which state and federal pressures limit the autonomy of school boards. At what point do boards become empty vessels unable to affect their own destiny? Accountability has its limits under these circumstances. It can grow excessive and intrusive, burdening school boards with expectations outside their jurisdiction.

Sometimes, attempts by states to ensure school board accountability morph into micromanagement. When New Jersey's State Education Department adopted new accountability regulations in 2008, for example, it called for board members to receive permission in advance to get reimbursed for attending overnight events. It demanded that districts produce and distribute publications in the most cost-efficient manner, prohibiting multicolor, glossy materials, apparently because one large district had spent a fortune on such materials. It banned the employment of a staff member whose exclusive role is public relations. And apparently because at least one district had feted its board members with lavish dinners that provided enough food for leftovers, the state demanded that board members not take away any unconsumed refreshments at the end of an approved event. Imagine! A school board member walking off with a doughnut bought with public funds.

Federal agencies provide an onerous paradigm for the oppressive model that some states seem to try to replicate in the name of accountability. From 1981 to 2008, the number of hours that Americans spent filling out more than 8,000 government forms increased from one billion to 10 billion[18] despite the earlier passage of the Paperwork Reduction Act of 1980 by Congress. Pardon school boards if they think they face something like the fictional Circumlocution Office that Dickens conjured up in his novel *Little Dorrit*, a circuitous bureaucracy with little purpose beyond its own preservation.

It frequently feels to school board members like states aren't much better than the federal government. Gordon MacInnes, who served in New Jersey's legislature and later worked for the state education department, said that the department might more properly be called the "Regulation" Department. The education department, he came to feel, was more concerned with enforcing regulations than with promoting good educational practice. In Massachusetts, for example, school boards, administrators, and teachers complain about a system of accountability, assessment, and accreditation imposed from Boston and Washington that weighs them down with compliance provisions. At least 15 separate systems, on top of more than 100 reporting mandates, are meant to bolster the quality of instruction, but may be so cumbersome that they undermine educational efficiency and effectiveness.

On top of the federal government's No Child Left Behind and its many requirements, school systems throughout Massachusetts had to digest an alphabet soup of mandated assessments: MELA-O (Massachusetts English Language Assessment-Oral) for English language oral assessment; MEPA (Massachusetts English Proficiency Assessment) to assess proficiency in English; and general testing through MCAS (Massachusetts Comprehensive Assessment System) in several subjects at several grades. Furthermore, there were audits by the Massachusetts Department of Education and Secondary Education, program reviews that included audits in such areas as civil rights and food services, National Assessment of Educational Progress examinations, and the lengthy periodic process of accreditation by the New England Association of Schools and Colleges.

School boards tend to do the best they can under the circumstances, but members are mostly amateurs and volunteers. As such, they struggle to react to the pressures of parents, taxpayers without children in public schools, employee unions, and sometimes, students. On top of this, they constantly must fend off attacks from people who think that school taxes are too high. Accountability does not so easily fit into this complex set of demands.

# Chapter 12

# Other Ways to Govern Schools

If the school board is not the proper vehicle for looking after the educational interests of a community's children, then what is the alternative? There has been a range of other approaches across the country, though most school districts have been largely untouched by these experiments, and the traditional school board has continued to carry on unimpeded with business as usual in most locales. This could mean that no place has found a better form of governance or that the weight of the status quo is just too heavy to lift. Yet efforts to diminish board authority have a long history and remain viable. Various forms of school-based management during the final decades of the twentieth century enhanced the power of school communities, reducing the authority of central boards. The Chicago Reform Act, passed by the Illinois legislature in 1988, for instance, exemplifies this approach. It provided for governance through local school councils, empowering parents, other residents, and teachers to select principals and to have input.

The passage of charter school legislation in Minnesota in 1991 ushered in the most widely used method of loosening the jurisdiction of the school boards over individual schools. Boards surrender a portion of their control when charter schools come into existence, but continue to govern the rest of the system. President Barack Obama and his education secretary, Arne Duncan, promoted charter schools and even dangled stimulus funds in front of local and state officials to induce them to authorize more of them. Notably, in Massachusetts, Governor Deval Patrick and Boston Mayor Thomas M. Menino, strong union supporters who had been skeptical if not downright critical of charter schools, appeared together at a news conference in the summer of 2009 to indicate their newfound willingness to apply for federal aid to establish charter schools in low-achieving school systems. Standing at their side was Duncan, who had threatened to exclude states that did not expand access to charter schools from obtaining a share of billions in stimulus funds.

Mayoral control, another option, poses one of the greatest threats to school boards, which under this arrangement may end up serving no larger purpose than that of the body's appendix. The degree of authority over the public schools assumed by mayors in various cities that have adopted this approach varies. In

New York City, in its most extensive form, the mayor—through the chancellor that he appointed—assumed supreme control over education and the school board essentially disappeared.

State takeovers represent yet another neutering of school boards. Takeovers have occurred in districts around the country where dissatisfaction with school boards and their accomplishments was rife. Such school systems usually were ineffective, and—to put it harshly—children were cheated out of an education. Abysmal test scores and miserable fiscal management tend to be the hallmarks of leading candidates for takeovers in states with legislation allowing such intervention. The role of the school board becomes problematic when the state enters the picture.

Vouchers are an additional device for wresting away school board control over students. A voucher effectively removes a student from the jurisdiction of a particular board. The board remains, but the student moves on, cashing in the voucher to attend a school—usually a nonpublic one—not under the aegis of the previous school board.

All in all, whatever the instrument for altering the governance structure, it comes into play when a school board fails to improve its schools. During the last quarter of the twentieth century, Detroit represented a leading example of a district trying to improve education by changing governance. First, regional boards to oversee groups of schools replaced the authority of the city's central board, and then, individual schools got enhanced powers to control themselves. The school system only kept getting worse and worse, showing that changes in governance may not be the panacea that some advocates imagine them to be.

School boards give up some power when schools or groups of schools gain greater authority. This happened when the legislation in Illinois led to school-based decision making and when the legislature in New York State provided for the million-student New York City system to break itself into 31 community school districts (later amended to 32) that largely operated the elementary and middle schools. The central board retained ultimate jurisdiction over the community school districts and kept control of the high schools.

For the most part, though, these various options would be unnecessary and demand for them would diminish if school boards did their job—provide students with schools that work. It is intriguing to consider this fact when one watches mayors seek control over the public schools or when advocates of charter schools say that shifting students out of regular public schools is the only way to ensure a quality education. Even so extreme a step as a state takeover is necessitated by the failure of local school boards to provide children with the kind of education that they deserve.

## The Spread of Charter Schools Across the Country

Charter schools are, in fact, public schools and school boards retain nominal jurisdiction over them. But charter schools operate independently, usually with their
own governing boards that have decision-making power, giving them far more
latitude than the ordinary public school. They generally receive per-pupil assistance under a state-devised formula that diverts the money away from the school
district in which their students reside. There were more than 4,300 charter schools,
enrolling more than 1.2 million students in 40 states in 2008, by estimate of the
U.S. Department of Education.[1]

Though charter schools serve a relatively minuscule portion of the nation's students, some supporters see them as a vital element in the reform movement. These
backers maintain that labor contracts and various regulations burden public
schools and prevent them from performing as well as they might. "When parents
recognize which schools are failing to educate their children, they will demand
more effective options for their kids," Arne Duncan, the education secretary, wrote
in an op-ed opinion piece on school reform in *The Wall Street Journal*. "They
won't care whether they are charters, noncharters, or some other model."[2] On the
other hand—despite such pronouncements—charter schools remain an enigma
to many parents, who still don't understand whether they are public or private,
whether they charge tuition, or whether they teach religion.[3]

Given their autonomy and separate governing bodies, the question arises of
whether charter schools are a more thorough-going expression of democracy in
action than the public schools that remain under the authority of the local school
board. There are, after all, fewer layers between a charter school and the families it serves. Parents select these schools through a process that is perhaps more
democratic than the usual policy that compels students to attend schools merely
because they live in certain neighborhoods. But the governing boards of charter
schools and their administrators can be just as imperious as their counterparts in
the school system and there is no guarantee that propinquity produces democracy.

### *Obstacles to Charter Schools*

Some supporters consider the public school establishment, including school
boards, hostile to charter schools, which threaten the existing monopoly. "Teachers, administrators, school boards and vendors to schools are some of the long-
established power organized special interests that depend on and seek to exert
control over the public dollars," said Jessani Gordon, executive director of the New
Jersey Charter Public Schools Association. "So it is not surprising that a still-form-
ing sector of public schools—charter public schools—has had to fight year-in
and year-out for the legal entitlement of the children who are enrolled in charter
public schools."[4] Gordon maintained that though state law called for per-pupil

funding of charter school students at 90 percent of the amount in a traditional school district, some students were supported at as little as 65 percent of
that amount.

Teacher unions tend to see charters as a diversion of students and money that
rightfully belong to regular public schools. Julie Korenstein, a staunch union supporter and a long-time member of the Los Angeles school board, said: "My heart
sank into my stomach when Barack Obama said we should pursue reform by using
charter schools." When she retired from the school board in 2009, Korenstein was
concerned that with 160 charter schools that had about 58,000 students the system
was losing $300 million annually to the charter schools because of the drop in state
aid triggered by the movement of students. "Charter schools are destructive to
school districts," she told me.

Some critics worry about dwindling union membership if teachers in charter
schools do not have to belong to the union, as is frequently the case. They see the
independence of charter schools as a challenge to bargaining contracts that dictate
work rules that unions want applied to all teachers. Unions mute their opposition
when teachers in charter schools must belong to the union and follow provisions
of the contract. They approve of charter schools if the union itself operates them,
which is a contradiction of intent as charters are meant to circumvent bargaining
contracts with teacher unions and onerous regulations. The irony is that demand
for charter schools would not have arisen to the extent that it has if school boards
had not given up so much authority over the day-to-day operations of the schools
in collective-bargaining contracts.

Proponents of charter schools want to see schools in which the hours of the
work day are not so tightly constrained; hiring of personnel has fewer restrictions; people with needed skills but without state-mandate credentials can work;
a principal may not need a license to administer a school; it is easier to get rid of
nonperforming educators; and parents may assume some of the duties.

Besides objecting to the drain on money that charter schools represent, school
boards do not like to surrender authority over students who attend charter schools.
In Tulsa, the school board even sued to avoid having to comply with the Oklahoma
Charter Schools Act and put a moratorium on considering applications to establish charter schools. The school board relented only after a court ruled its actions
illegal. And finally, besides the other barriers, charter schools in most places have
little or no access to funds for facilities and capital improvements. Regulations
usually make no provision for such aid. Charter schools must rely on donors and
the questionable munificence of their school districts.

*Are Charter Schools Better?*

What impact do charter schools have on student learning? Surely, that is a critical question to ask about them. Some backers of charter schools speak of them as

an exit plan for squeezing out from under the thumb of the local school board. A change in governance, though, does not necessarily make a charter school better than an ordinary public school. Students gain little if charter schools do not take advantage of their greater leeway to enhance learning. The research on student outcomes at charter schools is mixed in its findings. "While many charter schools are performing at the highest levels, some struggle to provide the quality education our students deserve," a report from the federal government said in 2008.[5]

Results of three studies released in 2009 show the difficulty of trying to reach conclusions about the educational worth of charter schools. Stanford University's Center for Research and Education Outcomes found that gains reported in 17 percent of charter schools in several states were significantly better than those in traditional public schools, while 37 percent had lower gains, and gains were no different in 46 percent of charter schools. Meanwhile, researchers from Harvard and MIT, studying Boston schools, found that charter schools in the city outperformed traditional public schools. Another researcher, looking at charter schools in New York City, found that more often than not they were helping to close achievement gaps. Personally, I reserve judgment on the impact of charter schools on achievement, but they certainly do alter the governance structure.

Some staunch backers of charter schools maintain that autonomy should not serve as a shield to protect weak charters. Weeding out inadequate charter schools would not only benefit students they fail to educate, but also put more successful charter schools in a better light. The school board in Hillsborough County, Florida, in 2009 took over one charter school and closed two others for their inability to boost student performance. Education Secretary Duncan, at the same time that he promoted charter schools, warned that inferior charter schools taint the entire movement.

Regulations for establishing and monitoring charter schools vary. Such states as New York made it exceedingly difficult to create charter schools, while states like Arizona made it easy to set up these schools. Part of the difference among the states has to do with the entities empowered to authorize the creation of charter schools. Sometimes states charge special boards with this responsibility, while elsewhere, charter schools may be authorized by universities, local school boards, nonprofit organizations, and even by mayors. Once up and running, charter schools usually receive nowhere near the kind of scrutiny given to regular public schools. School boards tend to pay little attention to them as they have limited authority over them. Some observers say that a key to bolstering charter schools is for authorizers to exercise more rigor.

*Governance of Charter Schools*

Governing boards of charter schools resemble and differ from local school boards. They hire personnel, oversee finances, and set policies just as school boards do.

Usually, though, they govern a single school, not multiple schools. In some locales, there is considerable overlap among the members of charter school governing boards—a practice unknown in the world of local school boards. The top administrator with which a charter board works is generally a principal, not a superintendent. And very unlike a regular school board, a charter board usually must concern itself with fundraising to supplement the funds it gets from the local school district.

Founders of charter schools often put themselves on the boards and choose the remainder of the members. The boards may include as members parents whose children attend the school and teachers who work at the school. This may seem to make charter schools more democratic, bringing them closer to their immediate constituencies, but it could be an invitation for micromanagement. These tiny operations have few ways to resist interference by interested parties.

A major difference between the boards of school districts and those of charter schools has to do with training for the governance role. Members of the boards of charter schools have fewer opportunities and fewer requirements for training than members of regular school boards. Only one state, Florida, mandates by law that charter school board members undergo training. In 11 other states, state departments of education or charter school authorizers require this training of board members at charter schools, though the states have no legislation to this effect.[6] Organizations have arisen in some parts of the country to identify and cultivate candidates for charter school boards, producing pools from which the schools may select board members.

Imagine if each building in a school system had to have its own governing board? Given how few people seem interested in serving on district-wide school boards, a community would quickly run out of candidates for the boards of individual schools. This, essentially, is the situation that some charter schools face. "Research consistently has found that creating and sustaining high-quality boards is one of the most formidable challenges facing charter schools," a study found. "Charter schools don't typically fail because of their academic program. It's because their business and their oversight [are] not adequate."[7]

So while members of regular school boards certainly face challenges, the struggles of charter schools illustrate how much more troublesome it can be for a volunteer to serve on the board of a school with chronically inadequate funding, little access to money for facilities, teachers who must willingly submit themselves to overwork, and parents whom they must entice to send their children. Charter schools are the boutiques of the public education world, often tiny and dependent on just a few devoted souls to keep them from succumbing to a host of pressures.

There is a notable exception to the single struggling charter school and it may grow more prominent and alter the equation. Networks of charter schools formed under the leadership of a charter management organization have emerged and, like a group of chain stores, each unit draws on the strengths and resources of others. One of the best known of these networks, the Knowledge is Power Program (KIPP), has won wide acclaim for its success in inner-city neighborhoods. This may be the future of the charter school movement and local school boards had better take notice.

## Mayoral Control of Schools

Normally, a board of education governs the school system and a mayor governs the municipality. In almost no case has a school board taken over the governance of a municipality—although a few individual school board members and school superintendents have become mayors. Since the late twentieth century, though, the idea that mayors might govern school systems has grown more popular. Donald R. McAdams, president of the Center for Reform of School Systems, remarked,

> The move to mayoral control of urban districts happens not just because policy makers believe education is integral to the success of a city and must be aligned with the other functions of city government; it occurs also, perhaps primarily, because policy makers believe that elected boards bring personal and special interest agendas to the board table, micromanage, and make it almost impossible for superintendents to manage. Sadly, this is often the case, and one of the reasons such cities as New York, Chicago, Philadelphia, Detroit, Cleveland, and Boston, to name some of the most well-known cities with appointed boards, have chosen this governance model.[8]

Kalman "Buzzy" Hettleman, who served on the Baltimore school board from 2005 to 2008, concluded after he finished his term, "Mayors appear better positioned than anyone else—including state educators and local school boards and superintendents—to provide muscular executive authority that can take on the educational establishment . . . the most promising urban school reform battles are being fought by a new era of mayors who, unlike earlier counterparts, accept hands-on responsibility for public schools."

Clearly, the main motivation for putting school systems under the aegis of mayors is the failure, especially in big cities, of school boards to improve education. There are also reasons other than the pursuit of scholastic improvement for giving mayors this authority—to combat corruption, for example—but the goal of better learning is supposedly paramount. Mayoral control of public schools has been a largely urban phenomenon, occurring where schools tend to be worst and the most ungovernable.

In taking control of schools, mayors sometimes appoint noneducators to preside on their behalf. They look for good managers, not necessarily for people with educational credentials. Thus, Mayor Richard M. Daley, who gained authority over Chicago's schools from the state legislature in 1995, named his transit chief, Ron Huberman, as chief executive of the public schools when Arne Duncan left the post. Joel I. Klein, a lawyer without credentials as a superintendent, has been running the New York City public schools since Mayor Michael R. Bloomberg assumed control in 2002.

The more than two-thirds of the nation's school systems with enrollments of less than 2,500 almost certainly will not become candidates for mayoral control. There is probably less dissatisfaction with school boards in smaller settings and citizens would be more likely to oppose any move by a mayor to reduce the authority of the boards. Schools in such places tend not to ail to the degree that they do in large cities. Moreover, the boundaries of towns and municipalities do not always coincide with those of school districts.

Just knowing that a mayor controls a school system does not reveal the extent to which the arrangement involves a school board. Generally, it means the mayor appoints the school board (if there is one) and, to that extent, membership is somewhat similar to sitting on any appointed board. But whereas most appointed boards function with the same authority as elected boards, the power of a board controlled by a mayor can vary according to the wishes of the mayor and the laws and regulations that enable him or her to preside over the schools. At its most extreme, the board can be powerless, as in New York City. Indicative of its diminished role was the vote it took one February night in 2009 to ban homemade brownies from school fund-raisers but to allow the sale of such packaged foods as Doritos and Pop-Tarts.

Questions about democracy come full circle when mayors gain the upper hand over school boards. "For mayoral control to function effectively," wrote Joseph P. Viteritti, a scholar of school governance systems, "accountability must proceed on two levels: The school system must be answerable to the mayor, and the mayor must be answerable to the people. That is the way democracy is supposed to work."[9] As I have said repeatedly throughout this book, whatever the deficiencies of school board members, they are seen as the people's representatives and as the officials closest to the grass roots. The late Gerald Bracey, a commentator on education, went so far in an article in *The Huffington Post* as to label mayoral control "The New Tyranny," and to call it a power grab.[10]

On the other hand, mayors, too, represent the people. Citizens elect them to office, almost always by far larger turnouts than appear for a typical school board election. What some critics seem to have uppermost in mind when they portray mayoral control as undemocratic is the idea that members of the community, especially parents of schoolchildren, may not have as ready access to the school system. It is one thing to phone a neighbor who sits on the school board and quite another for a parent who wants to discuss a classroom problem to gain the ear of the mayor.

*Advantages and Disadvantages of Mayoral Control*

The plethora of problems in urban areas makes it difficult to separate low achievement in the public schools from the woes of public safety, housing, employment, and health care—all of which ultimately conflate the challenges faced by inner-city education. Theoretically, a mayor with influence in all these areas can more readily pursue solutions in collaboration with the public schools if they are under his control. Michael D. Usdan pointed out, given the realities of urban poverty, that political leaders increasingly recognize that attempts to ameliorate the social conditions in which children live must accompany efforts to bolster achievement.[11] Who is better positioned for this task than the mayor?

The mayor is the most directly accountable local official, far more so than members of an independent school board. When municipal bus service suffers, people blame the mayor. When snow removal lags, people blame the mayor. When the police abuse their power, people blame the mayor. Suddenly, if a mayor gains control over the operations of the school system, people have someone to blame if they believe their children are not learning.

Urban school superintendents come and go. Their typical tenure is less than five years. A mayor who remains in office for a couple of four-year terms can lend continuity to governance of the school system. In turn, a mayor who forms a good relationship with a superintendent, as happened in Boston from 1995 to 2006 between Mayor Menino and Superintendent Thomas W. Payzant, can shield him or her from some of the inevitable unrest and foster a situation in which an effective superintendent spends a longer time in the post than usual.

On the other hand, mayors are political animals. They conduct expensive, high-stakes races for their offices and try to retain those positions until term limits or the opportunity for higher office impels them to move on. Whatever they do or touch inevitably has political overtones. Regular school boards cannot guarantee that public school systems will not get enmeshed in politics, but chances of this happening grow when an elected politician controls the schools. The question of who could do more to improve education was, for example, a major campaign issue in New York City when Mayor Michael R. Bloomberg battled in 2009 for reelection with his challenger, City Comptroller William R. Thompson Jr., a former president of the school board.

Oversight of the public schools is but one item in the bulging portfolio of a mayor. The National School Boards Association (NSBA), unsurprisingly, adopted a statement at its 2009 convention in San Diego opposing mayoral control of schools. The resolution was prompted as a response to Education Secretary Duncan's endorsement of the arrangement. "It is too important to be added to the many responsibilities that mayors are asked to manage," said the NSBA. "School board members are directly accountable to their communities, based solely on the performance of the schools, while mayors are not elected solely on their management of education."

The school system dwarfs other departments already under the authority of most mayors. Giving the mayor authority over the public schools means concentrating power in the hands of one person. Democracy might be better served by spreading power. A weakness of regular school boards is the tendency of some to dispense jobs based on favoritism and nepotism. For a mayor, who has many more favors to repay, the school system could be a piggybank for patronage. Julie Korenstein, who spent 22 year on the Los Angeles school board before retiring, firmly opposed attempts to give more authority over the schools to the mayor. "Too much power in one person's hands is disconcerting to me," she said. "It's important to have a balance of power."

What counts most, whoever governs the schools, is the achievement of students. While researchers weigh in on both sides of the debate, there is no compelling evidence that youngsters fare better academically in schools that mayors control. "There is remarkably little evidence that mayors or appointed boards are more effective at governing schools than elected boards," concluded Frederick M. Hess, who studied the issue for the American Enterprise Institute.[12]

### Mayor Bloomberg's New York City

As the largest school system in the United States, the New York City Public Schools border on the unmanageable. The school decentralization that the system featured during the last third of the twentieth century created a situation in which a few of the community school districts were governed well by community school boards that hired exemplary community superintendents who presided over the schools in geographic chunks of the one-million-student system. Many of the other community districts were mediocre at best. System-wide test scores were in the basement by the time Michael Bloomberg was elected mayor in 2001.

Some observers thought he was out of his mind when he sought control of the school system, a request that the state legislature granted in 2002. The community school districts and their local boards essentially disappeared and a Panel for Educational Policy replaced the central board of education. The panel was altogether toothless and the stage was set for Bloomberg to become a one-man board of education. He selected Joel Klein as the city schools chancellor, a person who was a product of the school system and a former lawyer in the antitrust division of the U.S. Department of Justice.

Bloomberg insisted that placing the public schools under his aegis would automatically create accountability since his continuation as mayor depended on public approval. Bloomberg and Klein shook up a moribund bureaucracy and tried to institute unprecedented reforms. They created more charter schools, established an academy for training principals, weakened the practice by which veteran teachers could transfer from school to school and bump younger teachers, added many small high schools to the system with the help of a $100-million grant from the Gates Foundation, and did away with social promotion at certain grade levels. They also aroused the opposition of the teacher union by seeking to change policies on tenure and merit pay.

When the legislature renewed Bloomberg's control of the schools in 2009, he had to contend with foes who attacked him on several fronts. Bloomberg—and, by extension, Klein—had been somewhat arrogant and heavy-handed in running the schools. In particular, some critics felt that the duo had given short shrift to parents and not been sufficiently open on some financial matters. A rise in scores on state tests was less than it first appeared. Scores on the National Assessment of Educational Progress were mixed, showing in reading, for example, that blacks and lower-income fourth graders improved during the years of mayoral control but that achievement was flat for various groups of eighth graders.

There was criticism early on over the adoption of a reading program that supposedly downplayed phonics in favor of whole language and of a math program that some contended did not give enough attention to basics. The legislature kept most features of mayoral control intact, but made some changes that lawmakers said would lead to more oversight and transparency. They also parceled out some of the power to district superintendents and required more interaction with parents. For the most part, though, it was to be more of the same from 2010 through 2014.

### Harrisburg's Mayoral Takeover

The transfer of control from the board of education to the mayor in 2001 as the result of a legislative act in Pennsylvania was the key to efforts to improve public schools in the state capital, Harrisburg, where a legacy of corruption and ineptitude had doomed students to failure. For the longest time, legislators from around Pennsylvania simply ignored the dismal local school system as they went about the state's business under the Romanesque dome of one of the more beautiful capitol buildings in the country. Harrisburg's schools ranked last in the state and the situation was so bad that the president of the local teacher union told me it was "a miserable place to be a teacher or a student."[13]

One of the first steps that Stephen R. Reed, the mayor for two decades, took after wresting away control of education from the school board was to hire as superintendent Gerald Kohn, who had gained a reputation as a reformer in one of New Jersey's neediest school districts. Kohn, having to report only to the mayor, had a relatively free hand to mop up Pennsylvania's version of the Augean stables. He instituted changes in everything from business practices to early education to literacy instruction to central administration.

By the time that a team of consultants from the University of Pennsylvania studied the district in 2008, they concluded in a 183-page report that "having successfully navigated the first stage of reform, Harrisburg's leaders now face the even more difficult challenge of engaging the still skeptical, yet essentially receptive middle group of teachers in the district's reform efforts."[14] The report pointed out so far as the district's business practices were concerned, for instance, that before the takeover the system operated on a cash-and-carry basis with no balancing of accounts, no payroll controls, no verification of employment and attendance, and with violations of the code of the Internal Revenue Service.

A doctoral candidate at Temple University who studied the district for her dissertation found that the previous turbulence that marked the district had faded, job satisfaction among employees had risen, and public confidence in the system had increased. She determined that a committed group of school administrators, who saw the mayor's continued incumbency as crucial to the ability of the Harrisburg Public Schools to succeed in its mission, had emerged.[15] The mayor, though, lost the Democratic primary election in 2009 and a new mayor took office in 2010, when authorization for mayoral control was to end. The new mayor announced even before taking office that she would fire the superintendent. Reformers feared for the future, when power would revert to the school board. While mayoral control is no panacea for ailing schools, few authorities in Harrisburg thought the school system could have improved if it had remained under the jurisdiction of the school board.

## State Takeovers of Schools

States have assumed responsibility for school systems in instances of utter educational failure or when the school board has been unable to manage its finances or to root out corruption. States invoke the procedure reluctantly. Twenty-four states have legislation to permit such takeovers, according to the National School Boards Association. State governments generally don't relish this role and try to return a district to the control of the local board as quickly as possible, but some takeovers last for years. In the meantime, advisory boards—often made up of local people and appointed by the state—tend to replace the regular school boards. Most local educators remain in their jobs during a takeover, although the state may install a superintendent of its own choosing.

Since 1988, according to NSBA, 19 states have taken control of 49 school districts, a move that the school board group said has produced mixed results. NSBA is correct in this regard. A state takeover may be only a Band-Aid over a festering wound and long-standing problems may reappear once a local board regains control and the dressing is stripped away. There are also instances in which states take over operations of single schools, removing them from the oversight of the local school board.

*New Orleans: The Recovery School District*

Perhaps America's most unusual state takeover occurred when Louisiana assumed control of the public schools of New Orleans. The city's educational system, terrible to begin with, was obliterated by Hurricane Katrina and students scattered to the winds as families sought refuge elsewhere. Seldom has there been such an opportunity to start over from scratch.

The state school superintendent became overseer of what was left of the New Orleans public schools and he imported Paul G. Vallas, the patron saint of struggling school districts (in Chicago and Philadelphia), to patch this Humpty Dumpty together again. As the plan unfolded, all the schools judged as failing were to fall under the jurisdiction of Vallas and his Recovery School District, a double entendre pertaining both to the road back from natural disaster and the effort to resuscitate a disaster of a school system. The fewer than a half-dozen schools that were not underperforming—mostly selective-admission magnet schools—remained under the control of the local school board, an entity that became as vital as an eraser in a classroom without chalk boards.

Officials in many of the former buildings, as they returned to use, chose to convert them to charter schools, enrolling 60 percent of the city's public school students. This gave considerable autonomy to the schools while keeping them linked to the Recovery District in a loose relationship. Starting over also meant that former collective bargaining agreements and the salaries and working conditions that the teacher union had negotiated were washed away with Katrina's infamous floods. Parents had a wide variety of school choice. The schools set out in hot pursuit of avid novice teachers from Teach for America and other such programs.

"School leaders can no longer blame 'the system' if a teacher is not performing," Vallas and a co-writer said in an opinion piece for *Education Week*. "In all but a handful of schools, principals now have the autonomy to select and promote their staff members. This freedom, combined with the need to perform, has led to a laser-like focus on both teacher quality and mission alignment."[16]

Governance became key to the attempt to turn around low performing schools. In this instance, though, governance was entwined with the management of the schools, usually a no-no. But without a traditional board of education setting the policies this task fell mostly to individual schools, which were then accountable to Vallas, who reported to State Superintendent Paul Pastorek.

*New Jersey: The Long Good-Bye*

New Jersey ranks as a pioneer of modern takeovers, putting three of its largest urban school systems under the aegis of the state and drastically reducing the authority of their school boards. The legislature passed the law authorizing this far-reaching intervention in 1987 and two years later Jersey City became the first target of a takeover, followed by Paterson 1991, and Newark in 1995. Conditions were not the same in all three places, but—like the cities of which they are part—the school systems suffered from allegations of fraud and mismanagement. Students were drowning in a sea of neglect, virtually ignored in a state with some of the highest-achieving suburban school systems in the country. The state appointed executive superintendents to manage each of the districts and more or less swept the school boards into insignificance.

Researchers carried out surprisingly few studies to document the impact of New Jersey's takeovers even as student achievement in the state's urban areas continued to lag far behind the suburbs. Few, if any, families would have moved into the three cities to take advantage of the education offered by the public schools. Although state-appointed executive superintendents ran the schools in the three cities, New Jersey stopped calling the arrangements takeovers. The state adopted its Quality Single Accountability Continuum (NJQSAC) in 2005 and began to refer to the districts as school systems at various stages of measuring up to the standards that NJQSAC sets in five categories—operations management, personnel, instruction and program, governance, and fiscal management.

Performance reviews of the five areas under NJQSAC provided the evaluation criteria for restoring independence to the school districts. Jersey City, for example, made enough progress by 2009 to reinstate an elected school board. The evaluation of its fiscal management showed sufficient progress for the board to take control of its budget, but the system didn't receive high enough marks for the board to resume authority over personnel matters.

Paterson showed, in its NJQSAC evaluation, that it still had ground to make up before the school board could assume full control. Its score of 11 percent on governance was accompanied by findings of an evaluation team from Montclair State University that said the school board still had to articulate a clear mission statement with a "buy-in" by stakeholders and that some board members were uncertain as to the status of the district's equity plan. The evaluation also found that the school board and administration still had to ensure that the screening, hiring, and monitoring of all district personnel was performed on an ongoing and systematic basis to avoid future violations of the law and of public trust. The team pointed out that in 2006 two former district administrators pled guilty to accepting bribes from contractors.

Some members of Paterson's school board, which functioned as an advisory body while waiting to regain control of the system, expressed frustration at their lack of authority to become more involved in decisions regarding personnel. They thought that the New Jersey Department of Education needed to provide more guidance as to the board's role under circumscribed circumstances. This absence of clarity is a reason why states are not eager to take over local school districts.

*St. Louis: Dueling Boards*

The state appointed a Special Administrative Board (SAB) to assume governance of the St. Louis Public Schools in 2007 with the mayor, the board of aldermen, and the governor naming the three members. The state created a curious tandem, allowing the city's elected school board to continue in office along side the SAB, holding monthly meetings even though it was stripped of power. Adding to the confusion, the same person served as secretary to both boards. The seven-member elected school board, arguing in part that the takeover denied the voting rights of the citizens of St. Louis, lost in court when it sued to remove the SAB and reverse the takeover. "A large portion of the population considers them [the SAB] illegitimate and a board of occupation," Peter Downs, president of the elected board, told me.

Whatever the feelings of those for whom Downs spoke, the SAB named a superintendent and carried out the governance tasks that normally fall to a regular school board. The district remained unaccredited—one of the failures that occasioned the takeover—and had to deal with a declining student population as families worried about keeping their children in the schools of an unaccredited system with an unbalanced budget. The enrollment, which peaked at 115,000 in 1967, had dropped to 33,000 and the quality of the system declined along with the number of students. This happened after almost three decades of court-ordered desegregation that ended in 1998. Then, through the first half of the first decade of the 2000s, two factions of citizens squared off over their visions of public education and battled for seats on the school board, a dispute that most of the elected school board contended set the stage for the state takeover.

The law authorizing a stake takeover charged the Special Administrative Board with monitoring the school system, but the two boards disagreed on what this meant. The SAB rebuffed requests for information from the elected school board, but some odd aspects of tacit collaboration emerged. The elected board objected to the SAB's proposal to close 28 mostly underutilized schools, saying that some of the buildings could be converted to full-service schools offering social services, adult education, and other programs in the extra space, while continuing to serve students. After a public response favoring the elected board's proposal, the district closed fewer schools and designated some of the remaining ones as pilots for the full-service concept.

The Danforth-Freeman committee, which issued the report that led to the state takeover, was reconvened at the end of 2009 to spend the next year analyzing the district's governance under the takeover. The committee was expected to provide another report looking to the future of the governance of the St. Louis Public Schools after the authority of the Special Administrative Board's authority was due to expire in June 2011.

## Other Threats to School Board Authority

There are yet other approaches that loosen the reins of governance by local school boards. By far the most extensive manner in which elementary and secondary school students slip out from under the jurisdiction of their school boards is by enrolling in parochial and private schools. It is a form of choice that we take for granted and which has not grown appreciably in recent years. Catholic schools alone during the 2008 through 2009 school year enrolled 2,192,531 students, 14.9 percent of whom were non-Catholic. School boards become conduits for channeling small amounts of public funds on behalf of nonpublic school students for such legally approved purposes as transportation and textbooks. But such schools, which altogether enroll more than 5 million students, operate independent of local school boards. Nonpublic schools are in one respect a boon to local school districts in that families pay taxes to support public education but do not use it.

Vouchers and tax credits promote choice, making it possible for students to attend parochial and private schools at some degree of public expense. There were 171,332 students in 18 choice programs in 10 states using such programs, according to the Alliance for School Choice, based in Washington DC, Milwaukee had the largest of the voucher programs. School boards and teacher unions detest vouchers and tax credits as devices that drain off money and students from public schools.

Then, there is home schooling, which accounts for the education of about one million students who receive their education outside the control of local school boards. Sometimes such students have a relationship with their local public schools that enables them to take some of the courses and participate in some cocurricular activities. For the most part, though, students educated at home remain beyond the purview of local school boards.

Online learning looms as one of the greatest threats to school boards, which have been slow to exploit the instructional advantages of the Internet. It plays a much larger role in higher education, where students are older and more mature and more inclined to pursue courses on their own. School boards ought to do more to incorporate online features into secondary schools and develop the sort of hybrid courses so prevalent at colleges and universities, letting students pursue part of their education in classrooms and part online. Otherwise, a version of the model pioneered by Florida Virtual School may eventually put more high school students out of the reach of school boards. Online learning, home schooling, and charter schools have led to amalgamations that raise questions about the future of and the need for school boards.

Schools without school boards have long existed in the United States in one form or another, though on a modest scale. Some colleges and universities have run laboratory schools, primarily as venues in which to train future teachers. In more recent years, institutions of higher education in the cities have taken responsibility for individual urban public schools where students foundered and where school boards seemed unable to bring improvement. Most notably, Boston University assumed control of an entire school system in Chelsea, Massachusetts.

*Education Management Organizations*

While charter schools pretty much escape the control of school boards, another— perhaps intermediate step—involves turning over the operation of a public school to an educational management organization (EMO) that reports to the district administration. Such an organization may be either a for-profit or non-profit entity. Philadelphia has been among the leaders in giving private managers the chance to run some of its schools. This happened after the state removed the school board and a School Reform Commission (SRC) assumed control of the city's public schools in 2001. The governor appointed three members of the commission and the mayor appointed two. It was called a state-city partnership, but given that the governor intervened to dismiss the school board and create the arrangement, it resembled a state takeover. One of the first moves by the SRC was to award contracts to outside groups to manage 45 of Philadelphia's worst schools, beginning in the fall of 2002.

By 2009, some private managers had pulled out or been asked to depart, leaving 28 schools run by two for-profit organizations and three nonprofit groups at a total cost to the district of $6.7 million. After seven years, it was unclear just how much value the city got for its money. Two researchers who examined achievement in Philadelphia concluded that schools under for-profit organizations did better than schools under nonprofit managers and better than regular district schools.[17]

In general, though, the impact of private management remained uncertain. Some members of the School Reform Commission—the city still had no board of education—expressed disappointment with the outside groups. A new school administration that took office in 2008 seemed to have reservations about private management. One contemplated change would have made the private groups consultants—in charge of certain aspects of a school rather than running the whole operation.

Philadelphia's path was one that the school board in Los Angeles voted in 2009 to follow. Prodded by Mayor Antonio Villaraigosa, the school board said it would give outside groups control of 250 underperforming schools, as well as let such groups take over 51 new schools scheduled to open in coming years. The *Los Angeles Times* called this move "a startling acknowledgement that the Los Angeles school system cannot improve enough schools on its own."[18] But by the time in 2010 when the Los Angeles Board of Education decided to award contracts for running the schools, the list had been slashed to 12 existing schools and 18 new ones. The biggest surprise was the setback to charter-school boosters embodied in a decision to turn over the operation of 22 of the schools to groups of teachers. By all accounts, board members sympathetic to the district's teacher union played a key role in bypassing charter operators.

When school boards give control of schools in such cities as Los Angeles or Philadelphia to educational management organizations, it is a tacit admission of the inability of the boards to carry out the mission with which the public entrusts them. School boards in such settings have sometimes allowed themselves to be tied down by bargaining agreements, compromised by political circumstances, and stuck in tired old ways. It remains to be seen on any large scale, though, if private management of public schools will enhance student achievement.

### An EMO in Philadelphia

Martin Luther King High School, a sprawling three-story structure in northwest Philadelphia in what was once a relatively affluent neighborhood, typified the schools that educational management organizations operated. Poverty had made inroads by the time MLK opened in 1972. The school evolved into a series of houses, each occupying a different floor and each with its own principal. The school system classified the house principals as assistant principals and paid them accordingly. Foundations, Inc., a nonprofit group that in 2002 got the contract to run the school, supplemented the pay of the school's heads so that they received salaries equivalent to those of the system's principals, an example of what an EMO can do for a school.

Early on, Foundations arranged for a series of focus groups by Public Agenda, an opinion research organization, that revealed that students, teachers, and parents viewed MLK as an "out-of-control, unsafe, even violent school," where some observers thought that teachers and administrators were "at best ineffective, possibly even negligent." Three years later, other focus groups found a feeling that the school was "turning the corner on the most pressing issue it had been facing— safety and security." Many people seemed ready to shift the discussion to questions of student achievement.

The two classes that had spent the most time at King under the aegis of Foundations had remarkably low dropout rates by the fall of 2007, when I visited the school. Foundations had established a small mentoring program that appeared to help keep students from dropping out. The school also created Upgrade! Academy to provide counseling and intervention for students after two consultants paid by Foundations reviewed students' records and identified the number of credits each still needed to earn a diploma. King became more successful in graduating students than Germantown High or Olney High, two comparable nearby schools.

Poor attendance still plagued the school, with about one of every four students absent each day. Nevertheless, math scores for 2006 through 2007 reflected the influence of several instructional innovations by Foundations. The percentage of students proficient in math doubled and the percentage below basic declined.

Foundations encouraged students to take the SAT examination and their performance on the SAT improved relative to 17 other large, comprehensive high schools
in Philadelphia. The school offered its first Advanced Placement courses under
the auspices of Foundations. In addition, two programs designed to promote college attendance received side-by-side offices and the school pointed more students toward postsecondary education. Foundations also invited the Job Resource
Development Center to relocate in MLK from a neighborhood office, offering students training in life skills and career skills and using a donated van to take them
on job searches.

Modest success, however, brought greater challenges. The school district withdrew some services from the school on the assumption that the largesse of Foundations would fill the void. The district also reduced the per-student amount it paid
Foundations to operate the school. Sixty-four percent of the seniors were still below
the basic level in reading and 72 percent in math. The high school was a work in
progress despite some improvements and remained an underperforming school.

In the final analysis, what does it mean to democracy when elementary and
secondary students receive an education not directly under the control of a local
school board? Is this any less democratic? Some people think so. Education historian Diane Ravitch worried about any approach that weakens local school governance by turning over control of public schools and the youngsters they educate to
outside groups. She deemed school boards "the first line of defense for public education" and said that the responsibility for providing good public schools should
not be given over to the free market.[19]

This is a proposition likely to be subjected to increasing debate as pressure
builds to raise achievement among students who traditionally have not fared well
in the public schools and as their numbers increase. What may be most important
to the preservation of democracy is not so much who governs elementary and secondary schools, but whether those who govern them do so in ways that ensure the
best possible education for every child. School boards governing districts where
students have been least successful can do more to resolve the issue by demonstrating their ability to improve the public schools under their jurisdiction.

# Chapter 13

# Do School Boards Have a Future?

Someone must govern elementary and secondary education. If not school boards, then what arrangement should there be? Local control of schools implies to many Americans a board of fellow citizens from the community whose sole concern is the welfare of students. This idealized picture of the school board does not necessarily comport with reality but it is synonymous with democracy in the minds of many people.

In part, the issue of responsibility revolves around who serves on school boards and how they attain those positions. There are few tests for service other than the usual requirements that a member of the board of education reside in the district and be a citizen. Members may have doctoral degrees or may not have even completed high school. They may have intimate knowledge of education or be ignorant of anything concerning the schools other than what they gleaned during their own school days. More than 90 percent of them gain their positions through school board elections and fewer than 10 percent are appointed.

## Qualifications of Members

I have devoted my career to dissecting and writing about education policy and ran for the school board with a pretty good understanding of how schools work. Even this background, though, might not have given me an edge in the view of some people. I can still remember the person whose doorbell I rang only to hear him tell me: "You may be overqualified for this position." Interesting!

No one is too qualified for membership on a school board. Schoolchildren ought to have benefit of knowledgeable people making decisions about elementary and secondary education. Nobel laureate Peter Agre, a biochemist, when asked in 2009 about whether scientists should run for public office, opined that probably the U.S. Senate is too lofty a goal for a first-time scientist-politician. "There are other places for scientists to serve," he said, "school boards, town councils, state legislatures, even Congress."[1]

Indeed, insight and intelligence suit school board members very well. Everyone who serves need not be a scientist or hold a PhD, but the qualifications of school board members have not received sufficient attention. Even in the nation's earliest days, Benjamin Franklin recognized that the citizens who governed the schools should be a cut above others. When he proposed the establishment of the Philadelphia Academy, Franklin said he wanted prominent and influential men of Philadelphia to serve as trustees. In fact, of the original 24 trustees, 15 were titled and eight were wealthy merchants.[2] Supposedly, the process of getting elected or winning an appointment to one of today's school boards includes an examination of one's qualifications, but still school boards are graced by some members who have no business on such bodies.

*Sorting Out Who Makes the Best Board Member*

In a 1954 book, Charles Everand Reeves, an expert on educational administration, listed more than a page of qualities he thought a good school board member should possess. Among them were interest in the development of children; willingness to subordinate personal, political, and religious interests to the good of the larger group; not wanting to adopt changes of unproven merit except for purposes of experimentation; success in one's own occupation; a willingness to devote time and energy to the work of the board; loyalty to the democratic process; tolerance in dealing with people with opposite opinions to one's own; unsusceptibility to intimidation; openness to changing one's mind when proved wrong; readiness to accept responsibility for personal and board mistakes; and a reputation for integrity and good judgment.[3]

Another author, Lynn Hamilton, who spent 15 years on the school board in North Little Rock, Arkansas, wrote a book about his experiences and set out what he deemed the personal characteristics of successful school board members. The following are among his admonitions to school board members:

- Don't publicly or privately criticize the schools or school employees.
- Respond quickly to problems.
- Don't be evasive with people.
- Make the hard decisions even though you find them distasteful.
- Be humble.
- Learn the art of apologizing.
- Develop and use your sense of humor.
- Dress in a manner that invites respect.[4]

The problem is who, other than the voters, will say which candidate is unqualified and what criteria exist for making such a judgment. There are few criteria for most public positions other than possibly judgeships. Certainly, every school board ought to have some members whose children attend the public schools, but all such men and women are not necessarily highly qualified for these positions. The well-being of the school system may be at stake when people who care about only a single issue or have no motivation but to restrain spending exercise their democratic right to run for the school board.

In years past, school boards more frequently attracted leading citizens, socially prominent people, and professionals who accepted positions as a responsibility that enabled them to give something back to their communities. They had a sense of noblesse oblige, viewing themselves as role models whose public service was part of what they owed others. There was more than a hint of elitism to their board membership and white males disproportionately held seats on school boards. In such places as the posh suburbs north of Chicago, a citizens' caucus would select a slate of upstanding individuals to run for the school board with popular support and without having to dirty their hands by knocking on doors and distributing position statements in a contested election. But members generally were committed, knowledgeable, honest people who accepted the responsibility with a sense of dedication.

The question now is whether democracy has improved the situation or made it worse. Service on school boards has become less attractive to many qualified people who would have much to contribute, according to Meredith Mountford and C. Cryss Brunner, who studied the motivations of board members. They wrote that candidates ran unchallenged in half of the country's elections for school board seats and that in many other instances boards appointed members to fill out vacated terms, presumably positioning them to run as incumbents.[5]

Today, fewer paragons of the community serve on school boards as the nation itself has grown more egalitarian and diverse. In many ways, this has made school boards more democratic, more representative of the population at large. The downside, though, is that more men and women may pursue seats on school boards and seek to retain those positions not so much to contribute to the next generation as to enhance their own standing and, perhaps, as a launching pad to further opportunities. Board membership, for some, is the only source of influence and prestige that they will ever have, and they are reluctant to surrender their seats once they have attained them.

When he wrote his classic book about American democracy, Alexis de Tocqueville spoke of "the defects and weaknesses of a democratic government" and said that those "entrusted with the direction of public affairs in the United States are frequently inferior, in both capacity and morality." He offered the backhanded compliment "that the great advantage of the Americans consists in their being able to commit faults, which they may afterwards repair."[6] Tocqueville had observed the institutions of this country during the first half of the nineteenth century, but critics of today's school boards might find resonance in his words.

John DeFlaminis, an academic at the University of Pennsylvania who previously spent 17 years as the superintendent of one of the leading school districts in suburban Philadelphia, was struck by the scrupulous process of being appointed to the board of a top private school. He was recruited for the post. Yes, recruited because of his expertise, something that occurs far less often with elected public school boards. He endured five levels of screening. In turns, he was quizzed about what he considered micromanagement by a board member, what he knew and didn't know about education, what he considered the role of a board member, and his attitude toward private education. Once selected, he was involved in three days of training with a distinguished expert. If only something like this happened with those joining public school boards.

### Elected vs. Appointed

One way to get better qualified, more ethical people on school boards might be to appoint them. This appears to be a ready solution for weeding out those with the least to contribute and those with less than pure motives for serving. Elections are affected by money, popularity (not to be confused with ability), lethargy of the electorate, and lack of knowledge about candidates' qualifications. Single-issue candidates may have more appeal to the electorate than in some other kinds of elections, and groups that promote and support candidates, as teacher unions do, exert an overpowering effect. Nevertheless, fewer than 10 percent of the nation's school board members gain their positions through appointment.

When citizens in Missouri grew fed up with the domination of politics in the selection of judges throughout the state they voted in 1940 for an amendment to the state constitution that they thought would introduce more merit into the process. The amendment established a procedure for the nonpartisan selection of a group of candidates, called a panel, for each judgeship and allowed the governor to choose the judge from that panel. About 30 other states eventually adopted this approach, which became known as the Missouri Plan.

Years later, though, conservatives maintained that the Missouri Plan despite its ostensible safeguards could nonetheless fall under the control of those whom some might consider partisan. *The Wall Street Journal* in 2009 supported an effort in Missouri to modify the plan. "The judicial nominating commissions have given disproportionate influence to lawyers' groups, which tend to favor elite fellow lawyers, the tort bar and liberal candidates," the newspaper charged in an editorial. It also stated that the same trend existed in such a state as Tennessee, where since 1995, "67 percent of appellate nominees more often voted in Democratic primaries" than the 33 percent who voted in Republican primaries.[7] Some people, though, still believed that appointing judges on the basis of merit could work and Sandra Day O'Connor, the former U.S. Supreme Court associate justice, agreed in 2009 to become chair of the O'Connor Judicial Selection Initiative to promote this proposition.

The debate continues over whether to elect or appoint school boards. In Montclair, New Jersey, the long-time appointed board periodically faces challenges from residents who would prefer an elected board in the town of 38,000 just 12 miles west of New York City, where many residents commute to prestigious jobs on Wall Street, in publishing, and at venerable law firms. In 2009, the battle was joined again with mailings and lawn signs proliferating in behalf of one side or the other as Montclair voted anew on whether to scrap its appointed board.

Mayor Jerry Fried told me that the process under which he and members of the Town Council selected the seven school board members allowed the town to create a "leadership team" that blended "different parts of our diverse community." This meant, he said, avoiding extreme single-issue candidates and balancing skills sets so that various members have some degree of expertise in finance, curriculum, management, and possess other characteristics that benefit the schools.

Diversity and balance are particularly important in Montclair, where all education below high school occurs in magnet schools that families choose, not necessarily the school closest to home. This is a special place—a community that has striven assiduously to promote racial integration—where the population ranges economically from the impoverished to the affluent and where the numbers of whites and blacks are about evenly divided in the high school with its Advanced Placement courses in 15 subject areas.

Under Montclair's approach, a committee created and prioritized questions for school board applicants, who responded to a written questionnaire. The committee used the responses to rank the candidates and select finalists who were interviewed face-to-face and ranked again. Nonetheless, opponents of the appointed board complained that its members communicated poorly with the public, always provided the superintendent with knee-jerk support, and did not exercise sufficient fiscal restraint in budgeting—criticisms that people elsewhere just as readily lodge against elected boards. Montclair voted 58 percent to 42 percent to keep appointing the members to its school board.

Beyond the question of whether an appointive process produces better school board members than an election is the issue of whether bypassing elections is democratic. Eileen Cooper Reed, a retired lawyer who became president of the board in Cincinnati in 2010, told me, "I'm glad that we have an elected school board. It's important as a part of democracy. An elected school board models democracy in terms of how it comes to be."

Many Americans consider the ballot box a guarantor of democracy. Indeed, voters in a school district always have the chance to install the candidates they most want on a board and to deny reelection to those with whom they are dissatisfied.

As in most elections, though, the process may prove a less than perfect form of democracy. The turnout for school board elections can be minuscule—in the single digits—leaving the election outcome in the hands of relatively few individuals. More typically, the turnout is slightly better, from the low teens to at least 20 percent of the eligible voters participating, still not great. Anne L. Bryant and Michael A. Resnick, the two highest-ranking officials of the National School Boards

Association, said that finding ways to bolster voter turnout for local board elections would strengthen education and democracy.[8]

Reformers in many parts of the United States thought they could separate school boards from politics by having candidates run without party labels and by conducting elections at a time when they would not be swept into the frenzy of electoral politics.

Thus, at least one-third of school districts hold their elections on days and times of the year, typically in the spring, when no other elections occur. This practice tends to insulate school elections, but it contributes to low voter participation. Does it serve democracy best to hold an election at a time when, predictably, fewer people will vote but partisan politics will have less of a role or by scheduling the balloting at a time—say, November—when larger turnouts are more likely but when partisan politics are more apt to intervene?

A bill to shift school board elections from the spring to the fall got serious consideration in the New Jersey legislature in 2009. Proponents sweetened the proposal by tying it to a provision eliminating a public vote on school budgets below state caps in an effort to win the support of the New Jersey School Boards Association. Ultimately, the legislation did not pass, but the attempt to change the date so that more people would vote in conjunction with other elections held in the fall underscores the issues in the debate over how democracy is best served.

### Training School Board Members

Chances are that few men and women take positions on school boards hoping to make their lives more complicated. It is a near given, though, that such service, carried out conscientiously, will be sometimes frustrating and exasperating and subject one to criticism and sometimes even to name-calling. It will consume huge chunks of one's time, often leaving one feeling unrewarded. Stress is almost a certainty.

Board members face the challenge of becoming public figures, a strange, new role for people not accustomed to spending time in the public eye. "When your local paper runs your obituary, it will surely mention your board service," wrote Gary Lister, chairman of a Georgia school board. "Informed readers will realize that citizen oversight of local government is one of the corner stones of democracy in America, and school boards have their roots in the earliest town hall meeting when our young country founded."[9]

#### A Need for Professional Development of Board Members

Most school board members are unpaid volunteers, but their performance may be scrutinized and as widely commented upon as the work of salaried politicians. They are guppies dropped into a fishbowl, unaccustomed to being objects of attention. Many school board members are unprepared for their 15 minutes in the spotlight. They need training for this role as much as they need knowledge that deepens their understanding of cognitive issues. Thus, steps that make the job easier and less fraught with tension are welcome.

School boards have a common problem in that so many members take their seats with virtually no preparation for the tasks that await them. Moreover, even during their continued service on a board, few delve in a deeply sustained way into the manner in which a school board should operate and how they might be most effective as members. Actually, it's not all that different from being a parent: Not many people are ready for the role and few bolster their skills as parents through formal training.

Service on school boards varies, depending on the size and complexity of school systems. But the challenges may have more in common than some people realize. A study carried out by the Institute for Educational Leadership in 1986 found many more similarities than differences, regardless of demographics, when respondents rated boards for effectiveness. Boards serving districts of various sizes tended to rank similarly when it came to strategies for communicating with their constituencies, capacity of board members to make informed decisions, board-superintendent relationships, and use of time.[10] Therefore, there is overlap in the kinds of training appropriate for board members. They are most likely to receive training in understanding their role and responsibilities in governing a school system. They feel most in need of additional training on student achievement issues and in how to collaborate with the community.[11]

School boards might be better if there were more opportunities for training when people join boards and more continuing education. In a growing number of districts, board members must prepare themselves to govern systems serving students from ethnic minority groups that are fast becoming the majority in some of these districts. Proper training would help board members meet the needs of such youngsters. A lack of sensitivity to cultural differences provides a recipe for disaster. Public schools are learning organizations. Board members usually understand the imperative to provide professional development for the educators they employ, but do not as readily recognize their own need for training. Professional development for board members, though, ought to be more central to the mission of the public schools so that those entrusted with governance can do the best possible job.

The importance of training was underscored, for instance, by the reforms instituted to improve one of the country's most dysfunctional school boards, the Clayton County board in Georgia described earlier. After the Southern Association of Schools and Colleges threatened to revoke the school system's accreditation, the school board proposed to make itself more capable of fulfilling its roles and responsibilities through a program that would "train board members on matters of board operation, board governance, meeting techniques, parliamentary procedures, power and influence strategies, ethics and ethical decision-making, along with board policy development and enforcement."[12] Responding to the actions of the rogue school board, Georgia's state legislature proposed a statute requiring the state board of education to adopt a training program for members of all local school boards. The bill's language mandated that local school boards use the training program. Such training is not unusual in many states, where state school board associations often oversee training that one or another state entity requires.

Such states as New Jersey, where board terms run for three years, mandate training for board members and the New Jersey School Boards Association oversees the training. Newly elected members must attend an orientation. In their second year, board members must undergo training on governance and in their third year, more training in governance and school finance. Reelected or reappointed members have to attend a session for advanced training and a legal update. Unfortunately, New Jersey's legislature in a misguided attempt to tighten financial accountability limited the ability of school board members to get reimbursed for overnight expenses associated with training.

### Preparing Board Members for New Realities

Even when and where training exists, however, it tends to focus on areas tangential to the classroom. Board members, unless they have had careers in education, seldom possess substantial knowledge of issues involving learning itself. Some would say that this omission doesn't matter as it is up to the superintendent and the professionals employed by the district to have this expertise. Maybe so, but many of the policies and decisions for which school boards take responsibility inevitably bear upon student learning. I wonder about the qualifications of some board members for approving these policies.

There is, for instance, the question of whether board members, born and raised decades earlier than today's students, comprehend the implications for education of the technological universe that took form during the first decade of this century. By 2009, the average American from 8 to 18 years of age spent 10 hours and 45 minutes a day immersed in technology, more than three hours more than a counterpart in 1999.[13] These are youngsters for whom the television provides constant background sound; music has to be portable; texting is as normal as speaking; video games have replaced outdoor play; social networking defines one's essence; film has broken loose from the boundaries of the big screen; cell phones are owned by 20 percent of children as young as ages 6 to 11[14]; and computers—large and small—are so ordinary as to be passé.

Public schools, given these realities, cannot afford to ignore the many ways in which technology expresses itself in the lives of the young. Teaching and learning should take these monumental changes into consideration. Online learning is just another form in which to deliver education. Open source courseware brings the lectures of the greatest teachers in the country to the fingertips of students. You-Tube, iTunes, Facebook, and social networking sites offer possibilities for collaboration and for enhancing the globalization of learning. The primacy of textbooks and other teaching materials and even the library are challenged by Google and the ability to download information from the Internet. Cell phones have many applications that can promote instruction and these gadgets get "smarter" every year. Even Twitter with its succinct messages can play a role in education.

The issue revolves not just around technology but involves communication, as well. Board members need to realize that cutting off schools from these developments is as dangerous to education as it would have been to ignore the implications of Gutenberg's printing press with its movable type. Today's students grow up in a culture so different from that which board members knew as students that it is easy for boards to make mistakes about students' interests, motivations, and ambitions—all of which affect their learning. It may well be that the intimate experiences of young people with technology affect their attention span, the way they approach reading, and even their thinking processes. Much of their learning occurs outside classrooms and teachers are no longer as dominant as purveyors of information. School boards that set policies without proper regard for these dynamics may fail to make the schools that they govern in sync with the twenty-first century.

### The Center for Reform of School Systems

Don McAdams, a former president of the school board in Houston with experience as a college professor and as a college president, recognized the flaws in the preparation of school board members. "Most people come on a school board not having a clue as to what they are supposed to do," McAdams told me. He set out to remedy the situation and to help school board members improve their abilities to handle the responsibilities that they assume. Aided by $800,000 from the Broad Foundation and mostly smaller grants from foundations in Texas, he created the Center for Reform of School Systems (CRSS) in 1999. CRSS evolved into one of the nation's best examples of an organization devoted to seeking reforms in elementary and secondary education by equipping board members to function better in governing their school systems. From the start, CRSS sought to apply this expertise to urban schools, but the approach was appropriate for school boards in districts in all settings.

Associations of school boards in counties and states around the country frequently offer—and sometimes use the compulsion of state regulations to require—professional development for school board members in their locales. Seldom, though, do these sessions offer the depth and intensity of what CRSS tried to provide. Furthermore, CRSS had a reform agenda that county and school board associations were not inclined to promote.

The center operated mainly by bringing together school board members for sessions that normally extended over several days. CRSS made extensive use of the case method, an instructional approach in which participants read carefully documented, real life stories of school boards' experiences. Board members dissected these cases and extracted lessons from how peers on other boards dealt with various situations. The model illustrates the possibilities for improving school boards by engaging members in meaningful learning. Members participated in CRSS institutes as a group from the same school board along with their superintendent. Given the symbiotic relationship between a school board and its superintendent and the difficulty of carrying out work if the board and superintendent are not on the same page, this kind of approach has more promise than one in which board members attend sessions without the superintendent.

The basic format for CRSS was an induction model that focused on governance. Four or five school boards and their superintendents went through training together. McAdams found that about 30 participants was an optimum number for examining a case. The entire group holed up in a hotel and had four consecutive days of no-nonsense training. The program emphasized what board members, working in unison, can achieve through leadership built around change.

McAdams took the position that board members, especially in urban districts, must be "reform leaders committed to high achievement," and that practicing good governance means striving to narrow the achievement gap that exists between and among ethnic groups of students. Thus, what the center called Reform Governance embodied a framework that began with the board's core beliefs and commitments, which then translated into a theory of action. The process extended to developing policies for reform; examining the board's rules, responsibilities, and relationships; building civic capacity; and planning for transitions. All of this informed the work of the superintendent and the superintendent, in turn, informed the work of the school board.

Generally, CRSS followed up initial training with on-site visits to participating school districts by consultants who worked with boards on policies for promoting change. In addition, board members attended more institutes to build their capacity for sustaining change and managing the inevitable transition of board members and superintendents. CRSS worked mostly with school boards in Texas, but it also served boards in such places as Denver, Charlotte-Mecklenburg, Gwinnett County, Georgia, Atlanta, Memphis, Harford, and Elizabeth, New Jersey. In addition, the center sent consultants into districts that requested assistance even if board members had not gone through the formal training. CRSS, a nonprofit entity, charged for such services and sought to become less reliant on foundation grants. Drawing on the modules it developed for the multiday institutes, CRSS provided training for a day or even a half-day on whatever topic district officials said they wanted to study.

### Fewer School Boards or None At All

Is there a better way to oversee the local school system? Is it really necessary to have a board of education? Richard F. Elmore, a Harvard scholar, said that in his work in Australia he found that schools in the State of Victoria did not have school boards or any local governance structure. The state itself governed the schools through a lean regional structure.[15] Some advocates of mayoral control seem to have such an approach in mind. The notion that schools might be better off without school boards is not a new one. As long ago as the 1930s, when there were still tens of thousands of boards of education, some prominent educators proposed abolishing school boards and suggested that superintendents assume most of the responsibilities of board members.[16]

The criticism has continued ever since. Matt Miller wrote in an *Atlantic* article in 2008: "Many reformers across the political spectrum agree that local control has become a disaster for our schools. But the case against it is almost never articulated. Public officials are loath to take on powerful school-board associations and teachers' unions; foundations and advocacy groups, who must work with the boards and unions, also pull their punches. For these reasons, as well as our natural preference for having things done nearby, support for local control still lingers, largely unexamined, among the public."[17]

Whatever one's attitude about school boards, the trend is clear: There has been an inexorable consolidation of school districts and, in turn, fewer school boards. As recently as 1950, there were 83,237 school districts, according to the former U.S. Office (now Department) of Education. Now, there are 13,862, and that is probably too many. There are even so-called nonoperating districts that don't have schools. Usually, these districts serve small towns and their boards exist to oversee arrangements for sending students to schools in a neighboring district and to collect taxes to pay for their tuition and transportation.

New Jersey had 26 such nonoperating districts, each with its own school board, when the state in 2009 ordered them to prepare to merge with neighboring districts. Furthermore, the state dictated that its elementary-only and high-school-only districts should merge into neighboring K-12 districts. Such moves, while welcomed by those who want to reduce the number of school boards, are not without complications. The districts involved in a merger are likely to have different tax structures and some residents of merged districts would probably have to pay higher taxes to bring revenues in line. In any event, consolidation would reduce the number of school boards. The ultimate merger would be to combine all the districts within a given state as Hawaii did.

Louis V. Gerstner Jr., the former chief executive of IBM and a long-time advocate of school reform, argued for no more than 70 school districts in the entire country as a way to improve governance. Each of the 50 states would have a school board, as well as each of the country's 20 largest districts. As matters now stand, according to Gerstner, every school board "is involved in standards, curriculum, teacher selection, classroom rules, and so on"—which he calls an "unbelievably unwieldy structure ... incapable of executing a program of fundamental change."[18] Yet consolidation is controversial whenever and wherever someone proposes it. Issues of democracy get conflated with those involving differing tax wealth, questions of status, the value of physical plants, employee pay scales, and existing contracts—all of which figure into discussions of consolidation.

### Making the Best of What We Have

The bottom line reveals that none of the various methods to weaken school boards or to banish them altogether is a sure-fire way to raise student achievement, which, really, ought to be the most important reason for favoring one type of governance over another. It is entirely understandable that the search for a better way to govern schools in a district where failure has followed failure often focuses on board members. They deserve to have their performance scrutinized, but their role most likely is largely tangential to educational outcomes.

Even with greater intrusion by state and federal governments into the operations of local school systems and the perception of declining influence by school board members, such writers as William Hayes insist there is still a vital role for local school boards. "Officials in Washington, D.C., or the state capital cannot effectively determine an acceptable property tax rate for a community, what interscholastic sports should be offered . . . who should serve as superintendent of schools. Bus routes, discipline policies and the maintenance of buildings and grounds are examples of other issues that are best determined at the local level," he said.[19]

There is scant evidence that school systems would be better served if school boards did not exist, whatever alternative might arise. Phillip C. Schlechty, a veteran consultant and author of books and articles on school reform, observed that critics should seek ways to cause school boards to operate differently rather than "use the dysfunctional nature of many school boards as a convenient rationale for removing the control of school from local communities."[20]

Furthermore, as matters now stand, even the loss of some control to the state and federal levels does not deprive school boards of the ability to make a difference in student outcomes. The school board continues to select the superintendent, the most important person in the administration. Then, working with the superintendent, the board can adopt policies that encourage the employment of the most highly qualified educators, affect how the district makes use of those educators, and support steps to link professional development ever more tightly to student achievement.

Sarah C. Glover, who visited school districts as a consultant for the previously mentioned Center for Reform of School Systems felt that school boards are essential for leading reform. She said that boards have the potential to hold schools accountable for student achievement and to ensure the efficient expenditure of tax dollars—two hallmarks of reform. She acknowledged "missteps by school boards," but maintained that some form of governance is essential and that other individuals and entities are not in positions to provide it. Superintendents, she said, move from place to place and rarely commit themselves to a long-term vision, mayors cannot maintain a focus on education, and leadership from business is uneven and crisis-driven. "That leaves school boards," she wrote.[21]

On the other hand, Glover's own experience as a member of the school board that serves 5,000 students in Bozeman, the home of Montana State University, did not leave her confident that all school boards will provide the kind of leadership that she envisioned. She quit the board after one term, disenchanted because her colleagues "were not ready to ask bigger questions." She told me that her board came together on a vision for the district, but didn't assign measurable objectives so that they could trace their progress and did not provide sufficient resources to fulfilling the vision. "This should have been an opportunity to create a school system that is vibrant, relevant, and important," she lamented.

Could it be that school boards might be more valuable and effective if they were charged with fewer duties? They could sharpen their focus on student achievement, for example, if their members did not have to worry about such areas as maintenance and facilities. A county or regional authority could take on these responsibilities. Transportation, too, could be placed with such an entity so that school boards would no longer buy or rent vehicles or hire drivers and attendants to work on those vehicles.

"Districts are forced to try to build expertise in a vast number of specialties and services," pointed out Frederick M. Hess, who raised the possibility of regionalizing some such activities, including even some involving pedagogy, so that every school district would not have "to meet every need of every single child in a given area."[22] My point is that the citizen volunteers who represent the community on school boards should not be distracted from their most important task, namely, concentrating on what occurs in the classroom.

Whatever may happen to change governance, it is almost certain that local school boards will not vanish—even if, eventually, consolidation leaves fewer of them. By and large, the public wants local school boards and state legislators are not about to eliminate them despite the flaws. The idea of governing from the grass roots adds to the appeal that local school boards have with the public. Too many Americans would consider any other arrangement as undemocratic, however inaccurate this notion of democracy may be.

# Notes

## Chapter 1

1. Chester E. Finn Jr., "Reinventing Local Control," in *School Boards: Changing Local Control*, ed. Patricia F. First and Herbert J. Walberg (Berkeley, CA: McCuthan Publishing, 1992), 21.
2. Ronald W. Rebore, *A Handbook for School Board Members* (Englewood Cliffs, NJ: Prentice-Hall, 1984), 5.
3. Carl F. Kaestle, "Equal Educational Opportunity and the Federal Government: A Response to Goodwin Liu," *Yale Law Journal* 116 (November 21, 2006): 152–56, http://www.yalelawjournal.org/the-yale-law-journal-pocket-part/constitutional-law/equal-educational-opportunity-and-the-federal-government:-a-response-to-goodwin-liu.
4. Charles Everand Reeves, *School Boards: Their Status, Functions and Activities* (Westport, CT: Greenwood, 1954), 10.
5. Patricia F. First, "Evaluating School Boards: Looking Through Next-Generation Lenses," in *School Boards: Changing Local Control*, ed. Patricia F. First and Herbert J. Walberg (Berkeley, CA: McCutchan Publishing, 1992), 178.
6. Jacqueline P. Danzberger and Michael D. Usdan, "How Boards See Themselves and How Their Policies See Them," in *School Boards: Changing Local Control*, ed. Patricia F. First and Herbert J. Walberg (Berkeley, CA: McCutchan Publishing, 1992), 98.
7. Agnes Repplier, "Americanism," *The Atlantic*, March 1916.
8. Sean Loughlin, "Rumsfeld on Looting in Iraq, 'Stuff Happens,'" *CNN.com*, April 12, 2003, http://www.cnn.com/2003/US/04/11/sprj.irq.pentagon.
9. The quote from Twain comes from the opening epigraph to chapter 61 of his *Following the Equator: A Journey Around the World*, available at the Electronic Text Center at the University of Virginia, http://etext.lib.virginia.edu/etcbin/toccer-new2?id=TwaEqua.xml&images=images/modeng&data=/texts/english/modeng/parsed&tag=public∂=61&division=div1 (accessed July 22, 2010). The quote from Shaw is widely believed to be his but is apocryphal.
10. Sean Wilentz, *The Rise of American Democracy* (New York: W. W. Norton, 2005).
11. Henry H. Brickell and Regina H. Paul, *Time for Curriculum: How School Board Members Should Think About Curriculum* (Alexandria, VA: National School Boards Association, 1988), 9.
12. G. Thomas Bellamy and John I. Goodlad, "Continuity and Change in Pursuit of a Democratic Public Mission," *Phi Delta Kappan* 89, no. 8 (2008): 565–71.
13. Charles Everand Reeves, *School Boards: Their Status*, 18
14. David Tyack, "Democracy in Education—Who Needs It?" *Education Week*, November 17, 1999, commentary page.

15. Robert W. Flinchbaugh, *The 21st Century Board of Education: Planning, Leading, Transforming* (Lancaster, PA: Technomic Publishing, 1993), 1.
16. Iowa Association of School Boards, "IASB Lighthouse Research Report," *IASB Compass*, September 2000.
17. Stephen J. Carroll and Ethan Scherer, *The Impact of Educational Quality on the Community* (Santa Monica, CA: RAND Corporation, 2008).
18. Thomas L. Alsbury, "Hitting a Moving Target: How Politics Determines the Changing Roles of Superintendents and School Boards," in *Handbook of Education Politics and Policy*, ed. Bruce S. Cooper, James G. Cibulka, and Lance D. Fusarelli (New York: Routledge, 2008), 131–32.
19. John Dewey, *Democracy and Education* (New York: Free Press, 1944), 20.
20. Margot Stern Strom, "Education, Democracy, and Rights," *Boston Globe*, November 20, 2008.
21. Peter Beilenson and Helen Beilenson, eds., *The Wisdom and Wit of Franklin Delano Roosevelt* (White Plains, NY: Peter Pauper, 1982), 29.
22. Diane Ravitch, "Now Is the Time to Teach Democracy," *Hoover Digest* (Hoover Institution, Stanford University), no. 1 (2002).

## Chapter 2

1. Frederick M. Hess, *School Boards at the Dawn of the 21st Century* (Alexandria, VA: National School Boards Association, 2002), 4.
2. Martha Abele Mac Iver, Robert Balfanz, and Vaughan Byrnes, *Dropouts in the Denver Public Schools: Early Warning Signals and Possibilities for Prevention and Recovery* (Baltimore, MD: The Center for the Social Organization of Schools, Johns Hopkins University, 2009).
3. Strategic Support Team of the Council of the Great City Schools. *Accelerating Achievement in the Denver Public Schools, 2008–09* (Washington, DC: Council of Great City Schools, 2009), 107.
4. Jeremy Meyer, "DPS Graduation Rate Higher, But Only About Half Finish on Time," *Denver Post*, December 18, 2009.
5. Henry H. Brickell and Regina H. Paul, *Time for Curriculum: How School Board Members Should Think About Curriculum* (Alexandria, VA: National School Boards Association): 146.
6. Debra Viadero, "Early-Algebra Push Seen to Be Flawed," *Education Week*, February 10, 2010, 1.
7. Ann Duffett and Steve Farkas, *Growing Pains in the Advanced Placement Program: Do Tough Trade-Offs Lie Ahead?* (Washington, DC: Thomas B. Fordham Institute, 2009).
8. Dave E. Marcotte and Steven W. Hemelt, "Unscheduled School Closings and Student Performance," *Education Finance and Policy* 3, no. 3 (2008): 316–38.
9. Rick Fry and Felisa Gonzales, *One-in-Five and Growing Fast: A Profile of Hispanic Public School Students* (Washington, DC: Pew Hispanic Center, 2008).
10. James Vaznis, "City Schools Challenged by Shifting Ethnic Mix," *Boston Globe*, April 19, 2009.
11. "Moving Toward Language Proficiency," *Education Week*, January 8, 2009, 32.
12. Debra Viadero, "Research Hones Focus on ELLs," *Education Week*, January 8, 2009, 22.
13. Mauricio Gaston Institute for Latin Community Development and Public Policy, *English Language Learners in Massachusetts: Trends in Enrollments and Outcomes* (Boston:

Mauricio Gaston Institute for Latin Community Development and Public Policy, University of Massachusetts at Boston, 2009), 1–2.

14. E. D. Hirsch Jr., "How Schools Fail Democracy," *Chronicle Review*, September 29, 2009.

15. Sam Dillon, "New Push Seeks to End Need for Pre-College Remedial Classes," *New York Times*, May 28, 2009, A14.

16. North Carolina Justice Center, "This Academic Genocide Must End," *Legislative Bulletin*, April 28, 2009.

17. "The Lighthouse Inquiry: School Board/Superintendent Team Behaviors in School Districts with Extreme Differences in Student Achievement" (paper, Iowa Association of School Boards, April 10–14, 2001), 7–8.

18. Georgia General Assembly, Substitute to SB 84 (LC 33 3538S), April 22, 2010, http://www.legis.state.ga.us/legis/2009_10/sum/sb84.htm.

19. Michael D. Usdan, "School Boards: A Neglected Component of School Reform," *ECS Governance Notes*, March–April 2005.

## Chapter 3

1. Education Commission of the States, "Taxation and Spending Policies," *State Notes*, June 2004, http://www.ecs.org/clearinghouse/52/94/5294.htm.

2. *Health, United States, 2008* (Hyattsville, MD: U.S. Department of Health and Human Services, Centers for Disease Control and Prevention, National Center for Health Statistics, 2008).

3. *Geography Matters: Child Well-Being in the States* (Washington, DC: Every Child Matters Education Fund, 2008).

4. Adam Liptak, "Inmate Count in U.S. Dwarfs Other Nations,'" *New York Times*, April 23, 2008, 1.

5. Tom Carroll, "Education Beats Incarceration," *Education Week*, March 26, 2008, 32.

6. Susan Tave Zelman and Christopher T. Cross, "Systems, Not Superheroes," *AASA Journal of Scholarship and Practice* 4, no. 4 (2008): 33–38.

7. Robert H. Frank, "Don't Blame All Borrowers," *Washington Post*, April 27, 2008, B7.

8. Goodwin Liu, "Interstate Inequality in Educational Opportunity," *NYU Law Review* 81, no. 6 (2006): 2068.

9. Ibid.

10. Ibid., 2061.

11. Ibid., 2047.

12. *Digest for Education Statistics 2008* (Washington, DC: Institute for Education Sciences, National Center for Education Statistics, 2009), 262.

13. Bruce J. Biddle and David C. Berliner, *What Research Says About Unequal Funding for Schools in America* (Los Alamitos, CA: West Ed, 2003), 3.

14. Carmen G. Arroyo, *The Funding Gap* (Washington, DC: Education Trust, 2008).

15. Goodwin Liu, "Interstate Inequality," 2094.

16. Rachel B. Tompkins, "Rural Schools: Growing, Diverse, and . . . Complicated," *Education Week*, January 2008, 24.

17. Christopher B. Swanson, *Cities in Crisis: A Special Analytic Report on High School Graduation* (Bethesda, MD: Editorial Projects in Education Research Center, 2008), 14.

18. James B. Hunt Jr. and Thomas H. Kean, "A New National Strategy for Improving Teaching in High-Need Schools," *Education Week*, March 5, 2008, 36.

19. Sarah Saxton-Frump, "Bridging the Poverty Gap in Education," *Star-Ledger*, March 23, 2008.

20. McKinsey & Company, *How the World's Best Performing School Systems Come Out on Top* (Paris, Organization for Economic Cooperation and Development, 2007).

21. *Knocking at the College Door* (Boulder, CO: Western Interstate Commission for Higher Education, 2008), xiv.

22. Sam Roberts, "Births to Minorities Approach a Majority," *New York Times*, February 12, 2010.

23. William G. Howell and Martin R. West, "Educating the Public," *Education Next*, Summer 2009, 41–47.

24. *Digest of Education Statistics, 2007* (Washington, DC: Institute for Education Sciences, National Center for Education Statistics, 2008).

25. Peter Eisler, Blake Morrison, and Anthony DeBarros, "Schools Don't Meet Fast-Food Standards," *USA Today*, December 9, 2009, 1.

26. U.S. Department of Agriculture, Food and Nutrition Service, Office of Research and Analysis *Analyses of Verification Summary Data School Year 2007–08*, Executive Summary, October 2009.

27. Michael Eugene et al., *Managing for Results in America's Great City Schools: Report of the Performance Measurement and Benchmarking Project of the Council of the Great City Schools* (Washington, DC: Council of the Great City Schools, 2009).

28. Paul Hill, Marguerite Roza, and James Harvey, *Facing the Future: Financing Productive Schools* (Seattle, WA: Center on Reinventing Public Education, 2008), 50.

29. Ibid., 51.

30. Paul T. Hill and Marguerite Roza, "The End of School Finance As We Know It," *Education Week*, April 30, 2008, 36.

31. Marguerite Roza, "Breaking Down School Budgets," *Education Next* 9, no. 3 (Summer 2009): 30.

32. Winnie Hu, "Auditors Peering into Finances of Public School Districts Across the State," *New York Times*, February 27, 2009.

33. Jennifer Mrozowski, "State to Take Over DPS Finances," *Detroit News*, December 8, 2008.

34. Dakarai I. Aarons, "Decline and Fall," *Education Week*, August 12, 2009, 24.

35. John Merrow, "Interview: Fixing Detroit Public Schools and The 'Cosby Effect,'" *Taking Note*, http://learningmatters.tv/blog/op-ed/interview-fixing-detroit-public -schools-the-cosby-effect/3182.

36. Robert W. Flinchbaugh, *The 21st Century Board of Education: Planning, Leading, Transforming* (Lancaster, PA: Technomic Publishing, 1993), 270.

37. Michael Yaple, New Jersey School Boards Association, "Building a Better Bond Referendum," *School Leader* (March–April 2009): 22–23.

## Chapter 4

1. Paul E. Peterson, "What Is Good For General Motors . . . Is Good for Education," *Education Next* 9, no. 2 (Spring 2009): 5.

2. Jennifer Medina and Robert Gebeloff, "With More Money, City Schools Added Jobs, Many at Top Dollar," *New York Times*, July 1, 2009, 1.

3. Mary McCain, *Serving Students: A Survey of Contracted Food Service Work in New Jersey's K-12 Public Schools* (New Bunswick, NJ: Rutgers Center for Women and Work, Rutgers University, 2009).

4. Eleanor Chute, "Advantages Aside, Montour Troubled," *Post-Gazette*, September 28, 2009.

5. Brian C. Rittmeyer, "Party Boss Is Said to Have Dominated Montour Board," *Tribune-Review*, November 9, 2003.

6. Joseph Tanfani and Mark Fazlollah, "A Drain on City's Struggling Schools," *Philadelphia Inquirer*, May 4, 2009, A5.

7. Charles J. Russo, "The Legal Status of School Boards in the Intergovernmental System," in *School Boards: Changing Local Control*, ed. Patricia F. First and Herbert J. Walberg (Berkeley, CA: McCutchan Publishing, 1992), 13–14.

8. Jonah E. Rockoff, et al., "Can You Recognize an Effective Teacher When You Recruit One?" (working paper, Cambridge, MA: National Bureau of Economic Research, 2008).

9. Keren Brooking, "Future Challenge of Principal Succession in New Zealand Schools: Implications of Quality and Gender," *International Studies in Educational Administration* 36, no. 1 (2008): 41–55.

10. Summerford Accountancy PC, *Report prepared for Wake County Board of Education* (Birmingham, AL: Summerford Accountancy PC, 2006.).

11. Nate Carlisle, "2nd Guilty Plea Made in Davis Schools Scam," *Salt Lake Tribune*, October 2, 2009.

12. New Jersey School Board Association, "School Ethics Commission Issues Decisions on Board Member Conduct," *School Board Notes*, November 14, 2008.

13. "College President, Teach Thyself," *Boston Globe*, December 1, 2008, editorial.

14. Susan Black, "Out of Bounds," *American School Board Journal* 196, no. 1 (January 2009): 37.

15. Raegen Miller and Robin Chait, *Teacher Turnover, Tenure Policies, and the Distribution of Teacher Quality* (Washington, DC: Center for American Progress, 2008), 16.

16. National Council on Teacher Quality, *State Teacher Quality Yearbook* (Washington, DC: National Council on Teacher Quality, 2009).

17. The Center for Greater Philadelphia, "Value-Added Assessment," Operation Public Education, http://www.cgp.upenn.edu/ope_value.html.

18. Jennifer Medina, "Progress Slow in Bloomberg Goal to Rid Schools of Bad Teachers," *New York Times*, February 24, 2010,1.

19. Jason Song, "Firing Tenured Teachers Can Be A Costly and Tortuous Task," *Los Angeles Times*, May 3, 2009.

20. Jason Song, "Los Angeles Teacher Should Be Fired Immediately, Judge Again Rules," *Los Angeles Times*, January 13, 2010.

21. Jason Song, "L.A. Unified Pays Teachers Not to Teach," *Los Angeles Times*, May 6, 2009.

22. Javier C. Hernandez, "Budget Bind Turns Spotlight on Reserve Teacher Policy," *New York Times*, September 26, 2008, B3.

23. *Sharon A. Lucero v. Nettle Creek School Corp. et al.*, 566 F.3d 720 (7th Cir. 2009).

24. Del Stover and Glenn Cook, "Legal List: Top 10 Issues," *American School Board Journal* 196, no. 2 (February 2009): 16–25.

25. Ting-Yi Oei, "My Students, My Cellphone, My Ordeal," *Washington Post*, April 19, 2009.

26. U.S. Department of Labor, *Employee Benefits in the United States* (Washington, DC: U.S. Department of Labor, 2009).

27. Raegen T. Miller, Richard J. Murnane, and John B. Willett, *Do Teacher Absences Impact Student Achievement? Longitudinal Evidence from One Urban School District* (Cambridge, MA: National Bureau of Economic Research, 2007).

28. Il Hwan Chung, et al., *Documenting Variation in Teacher Contract Provisions Across New York School Districts* (Syracuse, NY: Education and Finance Accountability Program, Syracuse University, 2008), ii.

29. Employee Benefits Research Institute, *Facts from EBRI* (Washington, DC: Employee Benefits Research Institute, 2007), 2.

## Chapter 5

1. Doug Eadie, "Governance: A Superintendent's View," *American School Boards Journal* 196 no. 5 (May 2009): 46.

2. John Carver, *Boards That Make a Difference* (San Francisco, CA: Jossey-Bass, 2006), 174.

3. James H. Lytle, "Report on School Boards Elicits Opposing Views," *Education Week*, November 4, 2009, 26.

4. Thomas E. Glass and Louis A. Franceschini, *The State of the American Superintendency: A Mid-Decade Study* (Summit, PA: Rowan & Littlefield Education), 2007.

5. Educational Research Service, *Salaries and Wages Paid Professional and Support Personnel in Public Schools, 2006–2007* (Alexandria, VA: Educational Research Service for the American Association of Supervisors and Administrators, 2007).

6. Frederick M. Hess, *School Boards at the Dawn of the 21st Century* (Alexandria, VA: National School Boards Association, 2002), 22.

7. Ibid., 23.

8. Robert W. Flinchbaugh, *The 21st Century Board of Education: Planning, Leading, Transforming* (Lancaster, PA: Technomic Publishing, 1993), 390.

9. American Institutes for Research, *Findings and Recommendations of the Citizens' Task Force on Charlotte-Mecklenburg Schools* (Washington, DC: American Institutes for Research, 2005), 7–8.

10. Ann Doss Helms, "Scores Up for Black, Poor Teens," *Charlotte Observer*, November 5, 2009.

11. Harry Hodges, *City Management* (New York: F. S. Crofts, 1939), 680–81.

12. National School Boards Association, *CUBE Survey Report: Superintendent Tenure* (Alexandria, VA: National School Boards Association, 2002).

13. Joseph M. Cronin, "Reallocating the Power of Urban School Boards," in *School Boards: Changing Local Control*, ed. Patricia F. First and Herbert J. Walberg (Berkeley, CA: McCutchan Publishing, 1992), 68.

14. Richard Lee Colvin, *Leadership and Learning* (New York: The Hechinger Institute on Education and the Media, 2008), 9.

15. Michael D. Usdan, "A Story of School Governance," *American School Board Journal* 192, no. 4 (April 2005): 32–36.

16. Howard Blume, "Cortines at the Helm," *Los Angeles Times*, December 21, 2008.

17. Kathleen McGrory, Laura Isensee, and Jennifer Lebovich, "Dade Schools Superintendent Hangs on By One Vote," *Miami Herald*, August 5, 2008.

18. Kathleen McGrory, "Report: Costly Plan Failed to Improve Schools," *Miami Herald*, May 15, 2009.

19. Council of Chief State School Officers, *Educational Leadership Policy Standards: ISLLC 2008* (Washington, DC: Council of Chief State School Officers, 2008).

20. Arthur Levine, *Educating School Leaders* (Washington, DC: The Education Schools Project, 2005), 12.

21. Carver, *Boards*, 161.

## Chapter 6

1. Terry M. Moe, "The Union Label on the Ballot Box: How School Employees Help Choose Their Bosses," *Education Next*, Summer 2006, 58–66.
2. Curt Wary, "Redefining the Bargaining Environment," *School Leader*, July/August 2008, 12.
3. Gene I. Maeroff, *Don't Blame the Kids: The Trouble with America's Public Schools* (New York: McGraw-Hill, 1982), 159.
4. Javier C. Hernandez, "Judge Says No to Teachers' Campaign Buttons, but Yes to Certain Politicking," *New York Times*, October 18, 2008, A20.
5. U.S. Department of Labor, Bureau of Labor Statistics, "Union Members 2009," news release, January 22, 2010.
6. David Streitfeld, "Is Steel's Revival a Model for Detroit," Week in Review, *New York Times*, November 23, 2008, 3.
7. Jim Siegel and Catherine Candisky, "Teacher Salaries Raising Eyebrows," *Columbus Dispatch*, August 16, 2009.
8. Andrew J. Rotherham, "Teaching Change," *The New York Times*, March 10, 2008, A17.
9. Marguerite Roza, *Frozen Assets: Rethinking Contracts Could Free Billions for School Reform* (Washington, DC: Education Sector, 2007).
10. Frederick M. Hess and Martin R. West, *A Better Bargain: Overhauling Teacher Collective Bargaining for the 21st Century* (Cambridge, MA: Program on Education, Policy and Governance, Harvard University, 2006).
11. Marguerite Roza and Raegen Miller, *Schools in Crisis: Making Ends Meet* (Seattle, WA: Center on Reinventing Public Education, University of Washington, 2009), 1.
12. Maria Sacchetti, "Springfield Teachers OK Merit Pay Contract," *Boston Globe*, September 9, 2006.
13. John Dewey, *Democracy and Education* (New York: The Free Press, 1944), 3.
14. Lesli A. Maxwell, "Human Capital Key Worry for Reformers," *Education Week*, December 3, 2008, 1.
15. Tabitha Grossman, *Building a High-Quality Education Workforce* (Washington, DC: National Governors Association Center for Best Practices, 2009).
16. School Redesign Network, *Professional Learning in the Learning Profession: A Status Report of Teacher Development in the United States and Abroad* (Stanford, CA: School Redesign Network, Stanford University, 2009), 5.
17. Hayes Mizell, "School Boards Should Focus on Learning for All," *Phi Delta Kappan*, March 2010, 20–23.
18. Jacob Vigdor, "Scrap the Sacrosanct Salary Schedule," *Education Next*, Fall 2008, 38.
19. National Council on Teacher Quality, *Human Capital in Boston Public Schools: Rethinking How to Attract, Develop, and Retain Effective Teachers* (Boston, MA: Massachusetts Business Alliance for Education, 2010).
20. Thomas Toch and Robert Rotherman, *Rush to Judgment: Teacher Evaluation in Public Education* (Washington, DC: Education Sector, 2008), 1.
21. Ibid., 2.

## Chapter 7

1. William Hayes, *So You Want to Be a School Board Member?* (Lanham, MD: Scarecrow Press, 2001), viii.
2. C. Emily Feistritzer, *Profile of School Board Presidents in the United States* (Washington, DC: National Center for Education Information, 1989).
3. *Out of Many, One: Toward Rigorous Common Core Standards from the Ground Up* (Washington, DC: Achieve, 2008).
4. Barbara Hoberock, "Henry Urged to Sign School Board Control Measure," *Tulsa World*, May 6, 2009.
5. Dalia Zabala, et al., *State High School Exit Exams: Moving Toward End-of-Course Exams* (Washington, DC: Center on Education Policy, 2008).
6. Carl F. Kaestle, *Equal Educational Opportunity, the Federal Government, and the United States Constitution: An Interpretive Synthesis* (Atlanta, GA: Southern Education Foundation, 2006), 21–22.
7. NCSL Task Force on Federal Education Policy, *Education at a Crossroads: A New Direction for Federal and State Education Policy* (Washington, DC: National Conference of State Legislators, 2010).

## Chapter 8

1. Kate Zernike, "Palin Promises Choice for Disabled Students," *New York Times*, October 25, 2008, A13.
2. Amanda M. Fairbanks, "Tug of War over Costs to Educate the Autistic," *New York Times*, April 19, 2009, 28.
3. Associated Press, "Settlement Reached in Baltimore Special Ed. Lawsuit," *Education Week*, March 9, 2010.
4. Randy Ariey, "Care to Teach My Special-Ed Class? . . . I Thought Not," *Wall Street Journal*, December 5, 2008.
5. *Daniel R.R. v. State Board of Education*, 874 F.2d 1036 (5th Cir. 1989).
6. Bruce Mohl and Jack Sullivan, "Spending Spiral," *CommonWealth*, April 15, 2009.
7. Mari Molenaar and Michael Luciano, *Financing Special Education in New Jersey* (Trenton, NJ: New Jersey School Boards Association, 2007).
8. *Board of Education of the Hendrick Hudson Central School District v. Amy Rowley*, 458 U.S. 176 (U.S. Supreme Court, 1982).
9. *Burlington School Committee v. Massachusetts Department of Education*, 471 U.S. 359 (U.S. Supreme Court, 1985).
10. Peter Wright and Pamela Wright, "Supreme Court Issues Pro-Child Decision in *Forest Grove School District v. T. A.*," *Wrightslaw.com*, http://www.wrightslaw.com/law/art/forestgrove.ta.analysis.htm.
11. *Honig v. Doe*, 484 U.S. 305 (U.S. Supreme Court, 1988).
12. *Irvington Independent School District v. Tatro.* 468 U.S. 883 (U.S. Supreme Court, 1984).
13. *Cedar Rapids Community School District v. Garret F.* 526 U.S. 66 (U.S. Supreme Court, 1999).
14. Tamar Lewin, "Court Backs Repayment for Special Education," *New York Times*, June 23, 2009, A16.
15. *Zachary Deal v. Hamilton County Board of Education.* 392 F.3d 840 (6th Cir., 2004.)

16. "FAPE: Free and Appropriate Education, Deal v. Hamilton County Board of Education, 392 F.3d 840 (6th Cir., 2004)," *Tennessee School Law Quarterly* 5, no. 1 (2005): 3.

17. Committee on Labor and Public Welfare, Subcommittee on the Handicapped, *Education of All Handicapped Children, 1973–74. Part 2 Hearings*, 93rd Cong., 1st sess., 1973, 1154.

## Chapter 9

1. Doug Eadie, "Governance: A Superintendent's View," *American School Boards Journal* 196, no. 5 (May 2009): 46–47.

2. Frederick M. Hess, *School Boards at the Dawn of the 21st Century* (Alexandria, VA: National School Boards Association, 2002), 25–28.

3. Ibid., 25.

4. Ibid., 33–37.

5. Robert W. Flinchbaugh, *The 21st Century Board of Education: Planning, Leading, Transforming* (Lancaster, PA: Technomic Publishing, 1993), 148.

6. Donald R. McAdams, *What School Boards Can Do: Reform Governance for Urban Schools* (New York: Teachers College Press, 2006), 23.

7. Hess, *School Boards*, 29.

8. A survey by Ingersoll Rand Security Technologies in conjunction with RETA Security, Inc. and American Association of School Administrators. Ingersoll Rand, *2009 Sustainability Report: Inspiring Progress in Sustainability* (Davidson, NC: Ingersoll Rand, 2009).

## Chapter 10

1. Doug Eadie, "Governance: A Superintendent's View," *American School Boards Journal* 196, no. 5 (May 2009): 46–47.

2. Robert W. Flinchbaugh, *The 21st Century Board of Education: Planning, Leading, Transforming* (Lancaster, PA: Technomic Publishing, 1993), 107.

3. Ibid., 131.

4. Georgia General Assembly, Substitute to SB 84 (LC 33 3538S), April 22, 2010, http://www.legis.state.ga.us/legis/2009_10/sum/sb84.htm.

5. Bob Utter and Denny Heck, *Report of the Governor's Special Masters on the Marysville School District Strike* (Marysville, WA: Marysville Education Association, 2003).

6. John Carver, *Boards That Make a Difference* (San Francisco: Jossey-Bass, 2006), 81.

7. Frederick M. Hess, *School Boards at the Dawn of the 21st Century* (Alexandria, VA: National School Boards Association, 2002), 17.

8. Association of Governing Boards, *Survey of Higher Education Governance* (Washington, DC: Association of Governing Boards, 2009).

9. Jerry Grillo, "Holding School Boards Accountable," *Georgia Trend*, June 2009.

10. Gregory Goyert, "The Principles that Guide Our Work," *American School Boards Journal* 196, no. 5 (May 2009): 49.

11. C. Emily Feistritzer, *Profile of School Board Presidents in the United States* (Washington, DC: National Center for Education Information, 1989).

12. Jim Willse, remarks at "The Newspaper Crisis," a conference at the Woodrow Wilson School, Princeton University, Princeton, NJ, May 1, 2009.

13. Darrell M. West, Grover J. Whitehurst, and E. J. Dionne Jr, *Invisible: 1.4 Percent Coverage for Education Is Not Enough* (Washington, DC: Brookings Institution, 2009).

## Chapter 11

1. David Mathews, "The Public and the Public Schools," *Phi Delta Kappan*, April 2008.
2. Scott Osborn, "Nebraska Sets the Standard on Government Accountability," *Wall Street Journal*, March 14, 2009, A7.
3. McAdams, *What School Boards Can Do: Reform Governance for Urban Schools* (New York: Teachers College Press, 2006), 57–58.
4. Daniel Weisberg, et al., *The Widget Effect: Our National Failure to Acknowledge and Act on Differences in Teacher Effectiveness* (Brooklyn, NY: The New Teacher Project, 2009), 1–2.
5. Jay Mathews, "Educators Resist Even Good Ideas from Outsiders," *Washington Post*, January 12, 2008.
6. Jennifer Medina, "Cost of Grading Schools Is Said to Be $130 Million," *New York Times*, November 14, 2008, A28.
7. Joseph Berryhill, Jean Ann Linney, and Jill Fromewick, "The Effects of Education Accountability on Teachers: Are Policies Too Stress Provoking for Their Own Good?" *International Journal of Education Policy and Leadership* 4, no. 5 (June 8, 2009): 1–14.
8. David J. Hoff, "Schools Struggling to Meet Key Goal on Accountability," *Education Week*, January 7, 2009, 1.
9. Alyson Klein, "Spellings' Worldview: There's No Going Back on K-12 Accountability," *Education Week*, December 10, 2008, 17.
10. Jean Johnson, *A Mission of the Heart: What Does It Take to Transform a School?* (New York: Public Agenda, 2007), 3.
11. Linda Ocasio, "Newark Schools Chief Reflects on His First Year," *Star-Ledger*, August 9, 2009, 19.
12. John Carver, *Boards That Make a Difference* (San Francisco: Jossey-Bass, 2006), 159.
13. Barack Obama, "Prepared remarks of President Obama: Back to school event, Arlington, VA," news release, September 8, 2009.
14. James S. Coleman, "Families and Schools," *Educational Researcher* 16, no. 6 (1987): 32–38.
15. Marguerite Roza and Raegen Miller, *Schools in Crisis: Making Ends Meet* (Seattle, WA: Center on Reinventing Public Education, University of Washington, 2009), 1.
16. Christopher Berry and William G. Howell, "Accountability Lost," *Education Next* 8, no. 1 (Winter 2008): 66–72.
17. William Hayes, *So You Want to Be a School Board Member?* (Lanham, MD: Scarecrow, 2001), 6–7.
18. Alison Leigh Cowan, "8,000 Federal Forms, 10 Billion Hours, In Spite of Paperwork Reduction Effort," *New York Times*, July 13, 2009, A13.

## Chapter 12

1. *A Commitment to Quality: National Charter School Policy* (Washington, DC: U.S. Department of Education, Office of Innovation and Improvement, 2008), 1.
2. Arne Duncan, "School Reform Means Doing What's Best for Kids," *Wall Street Journal*, April 22, 2009, editorial.

3. 41st Annual Phi Delta Kappan/Gallup Poll, September 2009, http://www.pdkintl.org/Kappan/poll.htm (site discontinued).
4. Jessani Gordon, "State Continues Shortchanging Charter School Children," *Star-Ledger*, May 14, 2009, 15.
5. Ibid., 1.
6. *Creating and Sustaining High-Quality Charter School Governing Boards* (Washington, DC: National Resource Center on Charter School Finance and Governance, Center on Educational Governance, University of Southern California, 2008), 1.
7. Ibid., 4.
8. Donald R. McAdams, *What School Boards Can Do: Reform Governance for Urban Schools* (New York: Teachers College Press, 2006), 10.
9. Joseph P. Viteritti, "Should Mayors Run Schools?" *Education Week*, April 8, 2009, 32.
10. Gerald Bracey, "Mayoral Control of Schools: The New Tyranny," *Huffington Post*, July 21, 2009.
11. Michael D. Usdan, "Mayors and Public Education: The Case for Greater Involvement," *Harvard Educational Review*, Summer 2006, 149.
12. Frederick M. Hess, *Assessing the Case for Mayoral Control of Urban Schools* (Washington, DC: American Enterprise Institute for Public Policy Research, 2008), 3.
13. Gene I. Maeroff, *Building Blocks: Making Children Successful in the Early Years of School* (New York: Palgrave Macmillan, 2006).
14. *The Harrisburg School District: A Snapshot of Implementation Progress* (Philadelphia: Penn Center for Educational Leadership, University of Pennsylvania, 2008), 1.
15. Jenry Goodrich-Small, "The Impact of the Mayoral Takeover on the Attitudes of Administrators in the Harrisburg School District" (PhD diss., Temple University, May 2009).
16. Paul G. Vallas and Leslie R. Jacobs, "'Race to the Top' Lessons from New Orleans," *Education Week*, September 2, 2009, 26.
17. Paul E. Peterson and Matthew M. Chingos, "For-Profit and Nonprofit Management in Philadelphia Schools," *Education Next* 9, no. 2 (Spring 2009): 65–70.
18. Howard Blume and Jason Song, "Vote Could Open 250 L.A. Schools to Outside Operators," *Los Angeles Times*, August 25, 2009.
19. Diane Ravitch, "Why Public Schools Need Democratic Governance," *Phi Delta Kappan* 91, no. 6 (March 2010): 24–27.

## Chapter 13

1. Claudia Dreifus, "'There Are Other Places for Scientists to Serve: School Boards, Town Councils, State Legislatures, Even Congress,'" *New York Times*, January 27, 2009, D2.
2. Robert W. Flinchbaugh, *The 21st Century Board of Education: Planning, Leading, Transforming* (Lancaster, PA: Technomic Publishing, 1993), 12.
3. Charles Everand Reeves, *School Boards: Their Status, Functions and Activities* (Westport, CT: Greenwood Press, 1954), 103.
4. Lynn Hamilton, *The Secrets of School Board Success* (Lanham, MD: Rowman & Littlefield Education), 2008.
5. Meredith Mountford and C. Cryss Brunner, "Motivations for School Board Membership: Implications for Decision Making," in *The New Superintendency*, ed. C. Cryss Brunner and Lars G. Bj√∂rk (Bingley, UK: Emerald Group Press, 2001), 135.
6. Alexis de Tocqueville, *Democracy in America* (New York: HarperCollins, 2006).
7. "Missouri Brakes," *Wall Street Journal*, April 18, 2009, editorial.

8. Michael A. Resnick and Anne L. Bryant, "School Boards: Why American Education Needs Them," *Phi Delta Kappan* 91, no. 6 (March 2010): 14.

9. Gary Lister, "Does Your Resume Define Your Life?" *American School Board Journal* 195, no. 12 (December 2008): 50–51.

10. Jacqueline P. Danzberger and Michael D. Usdan, "How Boards See Themselves and How Their Policies See Them," in *School Boards: Changing Local Control*, ed. Patricia F. First and Herbert J. Walberg (Berkeley, CA: McCutchan Publishing, 1992), 115–16.

11. Frederick M. Hess, *School Boards at the Dawn of the 21st Century* (Alexandria, VA: National School Boards Association, 2002), 19.

12. Southern Association of Colleges and Schools, *Southern Association of Colleges and Schools Accreditation Report* (Tempe, AZ: Southern Association of Colleges and Schools, 2008), 4.

13. Victoria J. Rideout, Ulla G. Foehr, and Donald F. Roberts, *Generation M2: Media in the Lives of 8- to 18-Year-Olds* (Menlo Park, CA: Kaiser Family Foundation, 2010).

14. Mediamark Research & Intelligence, *America Kids Study* (New York: Mediamark Research & Intelligence, 2010).

15. Richard F. Elmore, foreword to Nancy Walser's *The Essential School Board Book: Better Governance in the Age Accountability* (Cambridge, MA: Harvard Education Press, 2009), xi–xii.

16. Reeves, *School Boards*, 5.

17. Matt Miller, "First, Kill All the School Boards," *The Atlantic*, January 2008, 94.

18. Louis V. Gerstner Jr., "Lesson from 40 Years of Education 'Reform,'" *Wall Street Journal*, December 1, 2008, A23.

19. William Hayes, *So You Want to Be a School Board Member?* (Lanham, MD: Scarecrow, 2001), 111.

20. Phillip C. Schlechty, "No Community Left Behind." *Phi Delta Kappan* 89, no. 8 (April 2008): 552–59.

21. Sarah C. Glover, "Steering a True Course," *Education Next* 4, no. 3 (Summer 2004): 10.

22. Frederick M. Hess, "Weighing the Case for School Boards," *Phi Delta Kappan* 91, no. 6 (March 2010): 18.

# Bibliography

Aarons, Dakarai I. "Decline and Fall." *Education Week*, Aug. 12, 2009, 24.

Achieve. *Out of Many, One: Toward Rigorous Common Core Standards from the Ground Up.* Washington, DC: Achieve, 2008.

Alsbury, Thomas L. "Hitting a Moving Target: How Politics Determines the Changing Roles of Superintendents and School Boards." In *Handbook of Education Politics and Policy*, edited by Bruce S. Cooper, James G. Cibulka, and Lance D. Fusarelli, 131–32. New York: Routledge, 2008.

American Institutes for Research. *Findings and Recommendations of the Citizens' Task Force on Charlotte-Mecklenburg Schools.* Washington, DC: American Institutes for Research, 2005.

Ariey, Randy. "Care to Teach My Special-Ed Class? . . . I Thought Not." *Wall Street Journal*, December 5, 2008.

Arroyo, Carmen G. *The Funding Gap.* Washington, DC: Education Trust, 2008.

Associated Press. "Settlement Reached in Baltimore Special Ed. Lawsuit." *Education Week*, March 9, 2010, http://www.edweek.org/search.html?qs=special+education+blog.

Association of Governing Boards. *Survey of Higher Education Governance.* Washington, DC: Association of Governing Boards, 2009.

Beilenson, Helen. *The Wisdom and Wit of Franklin D. Roosevelt*, edited by Peter Beilenson. White Plains, NY: Peter Pauper, 1982.

Berry, Christopher R., and William G. Howell. "Accountability Lost." *Education Next* 8, no. 1 (Winter 2008): 66–72.

Berryhill, Joseph, Jean Ann Linney, and Jill Fromewick. "The Effects of Education Accountability on Teachers: Are Policies Too Stress Provoking for Their Own Good?" *International Journal of Education Policy & Leadership* 4, no. 5 (June 8, 2009): 1–14.

Biddle, Bruce J., and David C. Berliner. *What Research Says About Unequal Funding for Schools in America.* Los Alamitos, CA: West Ed, 2003.

Black, Susan. "Out of Bounds." *American School Board Journal* 196, no. 1 (January 2009): 37–38.

Blume, Howard. "Cortines at the Helm." *Los Angeles Times*, December 21, 2008.

———, and Jason Song. "Vote Could Open 250 L.A. Schools to Outside Operators." *Los Angeles Times*, Aug. 25, 2009.

*Board of Education of the Hendrick Hudson Central School District v. Amy Rowley.* 458 U.S. 176 (1982). http://www.wrightslaw.com/law/caselaw/ussupct.rowley.htm.

Bracey, Gerald. "Mayoral Control of Schools: The New Tyranny." *Huffington Post*, July 21, 2009.

Brickell, Henry H., and Regina H. Paul. *Time for Curriculum: How School Board Members Should Think About Curriculum.* Alexandria, VA: National School Boards Association, 1988.

Brooking, Keren. "Future Chalenge of Principal Succession in New Zealand Schools: Implications of Quality and Gender." *International Studies in Educational Administration* 36, no. 1, 2008, 41–55.

*Burlington School Committee v. Massachusetts Department of Education.* 471 U.S. 359 (U.S. Supreme Court, 1985). http://www.wrightslaw.com/law/caselaw/ussupct.burlington.htm.

Carlisle, Nate. "2nd Guilty Plea Made in Davis Schools Scam." *Salt Lake Tribune,* October 2, 2009.

Carroll, Stephen J., and Ethan Scherer. *The Impact of Educational Quality on the Community.* Santa Monica, CA: RAND Corporation, 2008.

Carroll, Tom. "Education Beats Incarceration." *Education Week,* March 26, 2008, 32.

Carver, John. *Boards That Make a Difference.* San Francisco: Jossey-Bass, 2006.

*Cedar Rapids Community School District v. Garret F.* 526 U.S. 66 (U.S. Supreme Court, 1999). http://www.wrightslaw.com/law/caselaw/97.garret.cedar.rapids.htm.

The Center for Greater Philadelphia. "Value-Added Assessment." Operation Public Education. http://www.cgp.upenn.edu/ope_value.html.

Chung, Il Hwan, William Duncombe, Lisa Melamed, and John Yinger. *Documenting Variation in Teacher Contract Provisions Across New York School Districts.* Syracuse, NY: Education and Finance Accountability Program, Syracuse University, 2008.

Chute, Eleanor. "Advantages Aside, Montour Troubled." *Post-Gazette,* September 28, 2009.

Citizens Facilities Advisory Committee of Wake County. *Report on the Wake County Building Program: County Facilities.* Wake County, NC: Citizens Facilities Advisory Committee of Wake County, 2008.

Coleman, James S. "Families and Schools." *Educational Researcher* 16, no. 6, (1987): 32–38.

"College President, Teach Thyself." *Boston Globe,* December 1, 2008.

Colvin, Richard Lee. *Leadership and Learning.* New York: The Hechinger Institute on Education and the Media, 2008.

Council of Chief State School Officers. *Educational Leadership Policy Standards: ISLLC 2008.* Washington, DC: Council of Chief State School Officers, 2008.

Cowan, Alison Leigh. "8,000 Federal Forms, 10 Billion Hours, In Spite of Paperwork Reduction Effort." *New York Times,* July 13, 2009.

Cronin, Joseph M. "Reallocating the Power of Urban School Boards." In *School Boards: Changing Local Control,* edited by Patricia F. First and Herbert J. Walberg. Berkeley, CA: McCutchan Publishing, 1992.

*Daniel R. R. v. State Board of Education.* 874 F.2d 1036 (5th Cir. 1989).

Danzberger, Jacqueline P., and Michael D. Usdan. "How Boards See Themselves and How Their Policies See Them." In *School Boards: Changing Local Control,* edited by Patricia F. First and Herbert Walberg. Berkeley, CA: McCutchan Publishing, 1992.

de Tocqueville, Alexis. *Democracy in America.* New York: HarperCollins, 2006.

Dewey, John. *Democracy and Education.* New York: The Free Press, 1944.

Dillon, Sam. "New Push Seeks to End Need for Pre-College Remedial Classes." *New York Times,* May 28, 2009.

Dreifus, Claudia. "'There Are Other Places for Scientists to Serve: School Boards, Town Councils, State Legislatures, Even Congress.'" *New York Times,* January 27, 2009.

Duncan, Arne. "School Reform Means Doing What's Best for Kids." *Wall Street Journal,* April 22, 2009.

Eadie, Doug. "Governance: A Superintendent's View." *American School Boards Journal* 196, no. 5 (May 2009): 46–47.

Education Commission of the States. "Taxation and Spending Policies." *State Notes,* June 2004, http://www.ecs.org/clearinghouse/52/94/5294.htm.

Educational Research Service. *Salaries and Wages Paid Professional and Support Personnel in Public Schools, 2006–2007*. Alexandria, VA: Educational Research Service for the American Association of Supervisors and Administrators, 2007.

Eisler, Peter, Blake Morrison, and Anthony DeBarros. "Schools Don't Meet Fast-Food Standards." *USA Today*, December 9, 2009.

Elmore, Richard F. Foreword in *The Essential School Board Book: Better Governance in the Age Accountability*, by Nancy Walser, xi–xii. Cambridge, MA.: Harvard Education Press, 2009.

Employee Benefits Research Institute. *Facts from EBRI*. Washington, DC: Employee Benefits Research Institute, 2007.

Eugene, Michael, Robert Carlson, Heidi Hrowal, John Fahey, Jean Ronnei, Steve Young, Joseph Gomez et al. *Managing for Results in America's Great City Schools: Report of the Performance Measurement and Benchmarking Project of the Council of the Great City Schools*. Washington, DC: Council of the Greater City Schools, 2009.

Every Child Matters Education Fund. *Geography Matters: Child Well-Being in the States*. Washington, DC: Every Child Matters Education Fund, 2008.

Fairbanks, Amanda M. "Tug of War over Costs to Educate the Autistic." *New York Times*, April 19, 2009.

"FAPE: Free and Appropriate Education, *Deal v. Hamilton County Board of Education*, 392 F.3d 840, (6th Cir. 2004)." *Tennessee School Law Quarterly* 5, no. 1 (Winter 2005): 3.

Feistritzer, C. Emily. *Profile of School Board Presidents in the United States*. Washington, DC: National Center for Education Information, 1989.

Finn, Chester E. "Reinventing Local Control." In *School Boards: Changing Local Control*, edited by Patricia F. First and Herbert J. Walberg, 21. Berkeley, CA: McCuthan Publishing, 1992.

First, Patricia F. "Evaluating School Boards: Looking Through Next-Generation Lenses." In *School Boards: Changing Local Control*, edited by Patricia F. First and Herbert J. Walberg, 178. Berkeley, CA: McCutchan Publishing, 1992.

Flinchbaugh, Robert W. *The 21st Century Board of Education: Planning, Leading, Transforming*. Lancaster, PA: Technomic Publishing, 1993.

41st Annual Phi Delta Kappan/Gallup Poll, September 2009, http://www.pdkintl.org/Kappan/poll.htm (site discontinued).

Frank, Robert H. "Don't Blame All Borrowers." *Washington Post*, April 27, 2008.

Fry, Rick, and Felisa Gonzales. *One-in-Five and Growing Fast: A Profile of Hispanic Public School Students*. Washington, DC: Pew Hispanic Center, 2008.

Gerstner Jr., Louis V. "Lesson from 40 Years of Education 'Reform.'" *Wall Street Journal*, December 1, 2008.

Georgia General Assembly, Substitute to SB 84 (LC 33 3538S), April 22, 2010, http://www.legis.state.ga.us/legis/2009_10/sum/sb84.htm.

Glass, Thomas E., and Louis A. Franceschini. *The State of the American Superintendency: A Mid-Decade Study*. Summit, PA: Rowan & Littlefield Education, 2007.

Glover, Sarah C. "Steering a True Course." *Education Next* 4, no. 3 (Summer 2004): 10.

Goodrich-Small, Jenry. "The Impact of the Mayoral Takeover on the Attitudes of Administrators in the Harrisburg School District." diss., Temple University Graduate Board, 2009.

Gordon, Jessani. "State Continues Shortchanging Charter School Children." *Star-Ledger*, May 14, 2009.

Goyert, Gregory. "The Principles that Guide Our Work." *American School Boards Journal* 196 no. 5 (May 2009): 48–49.

Grossman, Tabitha. *Building a High-Quality Education Workforce*. Washington, DC: National Governors Association Center for Best Practices, 2009.

Hamilton, Lynn. *The Secrets of School Board Success*. Lanham, MD: Rowman & Littlefield Education, 2008.

Hayes, William. *So You Want to Be a School Board Member?* Lanham, MD: Scarecrow, 2001.

The Hechinger Institute on Education and the Media. *Leadership and Learning*. New York: The Hechinger Institute on Education and the Media, n.d.

Helms, Ann Doss Helms. "Scores Up for Black, Poor Teens." *Charlotte Observer*, November 5, 2009.

Hernandez, Javier C. "Budget Bind Turns Spotlight on Reserve Teacher Policy." *New York Times*, September 26, 2008.

———. "Judge Says No to Teachers' Campaign Buttons, but Yes to Certain Politicking." *New York Times*, October 18, 2008.

Hess, Frederick M. *Assessing the Case for Mayoral Control of Urban Schools*. Washington, DC: American Enterprise Institute for Public Policy Research, 2008.

———. *School Boards at the Dawn of the 21st Century*. Alexandria, VA: National School Boards Association, 2002.

———. "Weighing the Case for School Boards." *Phi Delta Kappan* 91, no. 6 (March 2010): 18.

———, and Martin R. West. *A Better Bargain: Overhauling Teacher Collective Bargaining for the 21st Century*. Cambridge, MA: Program on Education, Policy & Governance, Harvard University, 2006.

Hill, Paul, and Marguerite Roza. "The End of School Finance As We Know It." *Education Week*, April 30, 2008, 36.

———, Marguerite Roza, and James Harvey. *Facing the Future: Financing Productive Schools*. Seattle, WA: Center on Reinventing Public Education, 2008.

Hirsch, E. D., Jr. "How Schools Fail Democracy." *Chronicle Review*, September 29, 2009.

Hoberock, Barbara. "Henry Urged to Sign School Board Control Measure." *Tulsa World*, May 6, 2009.

Hodges, Harry. *City Management*. New York: F. S. Crofts, 1939.

Hoff, David J. "Schools Struggling to Meet Key Goal on Accountability." *Education Week*, January 7, 2009, 1.

*Honig v. Doe*. 484 U.S. 305 (U.S. Supreme Court, 1988). http://www.wrightslaw.com/law/caselaw/ussupct.honig.doe.htm.

Howell, William G., and Martin R. West. "Educating the Public." *Education Next* 9, no. 3 (Summer 2009): 41–47.

Hu, Winnie. "Auditors Peering into Finances of Public School Districts Across the State." *New York Times*, February 27, 2009.

Hunt, James B., and Thomas H. Kean. "A New National Strategy for Improving Teaching in High-Need Schools." *Education Week*, March 5, 2008, 36.

"IASB Lighthouse Research Report." *IASB Compass*, September 2000.

Ingersoll Rand. *2009 Sustainability Report: Inspiring Progress in Sustainability*. Davidson, NC: Ingersoll Rand, 2009.

Institute for Education Sciences. *Digest for Education Statistics 2008*. Washington, DC: Institute for Education Sciences, National Center for Education Statistics, 2009.

———. *Digest of Education Statistics, 2007*. Washington, DC: Institute for Education Sciences, National Center for Education Statistics, 2008.

Iowa Association of School Boards. "The Lighthouse Inquiry: School Board/Superintendent Team Behaviors in School Districts with Extreme Differences in Student

Achievement." Paper, American Educational Research Association 2001 Annual Meeting, Apr. 10–14, 2001, 7–8.

Irvington Independent School District v. Amber Tatro. 468 U.S. 883 (U.S. Supreme Court, 1984). http://www.wrightslaw.com/law/caselaw/ussupct.tatro.htm.

Iver, Martha Abele Mac, Robert Balfanz, and Vaughan Byrnes. *Dropouts in the Denver Public Schools: Early Warning Signals and Possibilities for Prevention and Recovery.* Baltimore, MD: The Center for the Social Organization of Schools, Johns Hopkins University, 2009.

Johnson, Jean. *A Mission of the Heart: What Does It Take to Transform a School?* New York: Public Agenda, 2007.

Kaestle, Carl F. "Equal Educational Opportunity and the Federal Government: A Response to Goodwin Liu." *Yale Law Journal* 116 (Nov. 21, 2006): 152–56. http://www.yalelawjournal.org/the-yale-law-journal-pocket-part/constitutional-law/equal-educational-opportunity-and-the-federal-government:-a-response-to-goodwin-liu.

———. *Equal Educational Opportunity, the Federal Government, and the United States Constitution: An Interpretive Synthesis.* Atlanta, GA: Southern Education Foundation, 2006.

Klein, Alyson. "Spellings' Worldview: There's No Going Back on K-12 Accountability." *Education Week*, December 10, 2008, 17.

Levine, Arthur. *Educating School Leaders.* Washington, DC: The Education Schools Project, 2005.

Lewin, Tamar. "Court Backs Repayment for Special Education." *New York Times*, June 23, 2009.

Liptak, Adam. "Inmate Count in U.S. Dwarfs Other Nations.'" *New York Times*, April 23, 2008.

Lister, Gary. "Does Your Resume Define Your Life?" *American School Board Journal* 195, no. 12 (December 2008): 50–51.

Liu, Goodwin. "Interstate Inequality in Educational Opportunity." *NYU Law Review* 81, no. 6, 2006, 2068.

Loughlin, Sean. "Rumsfeld on Looting in Iraq, 'Stuff Happens.'" *CNN.com*, April 12, 2003. http://www.cnn.com/2003/US/04/11/sprj.irq.pentagon.

Lytle, James H. "Report on School Boards Elicits Opposing Views." *Education Week*, November 4, 2009, 26.

Maeroff, Gene I. *Don't Blame the Kids: The Trouble with America's Public Schools.* New York: McGraw-Hill., 1982.

———. *Building Blocks: Making Children Successful in the Early Years of School.* New York: Palgrave Macmillan, 2006.

Marcotte, Dave E., and Steven W. Hemelt. "Unscheduled School Closings and Student Performance." *Education Finance and Policy.* Summer 2008, 316–38.

Mathews, David. "The Public and the Public Schools." *Phi Delta Kappan*, April 2008.

Mathews, Jay. "Educators Resist Even Good Ideas from Outsiders." *Washington Post*, January 12, 2008.

Mauricio Gaston Institute for Latin Community Development and Public Policy. *English Language Learners in Massachusetts: Trends in Enrollments and Outcomes.* Boston, MA: Mauricio Gaston Institute for Latin Community Development and Public Policy, University of Massachusetts at Boston, 2009.

Maxwell, Lesli A. "Human Capital Key Worry for Reformers." *Education Week.* December 3, 2008, 1.

McAdams, Donald R. *What School Boards Can Do: Reform Governance for Urban Schools.* New York: Teachers College Press, 2006.

McCain, Mary. *Serving Students: A Survey of Contracted Food Service Work in New Jersey's K-12 Public Schools.* New Brunswick, NJ: Rutgers Center for Women and Work, Rutgers University, 2009.

McGrory, Kathleen. "Report: Costly Plan Failed to Improve Schools." *Miami Herald,* May 15, 2009.

McGrory, Kathleen, Laura Isensee, and Jennifer Lebovich. "Dade Schools Superintendent Hangs on By One Vote." *Miami Herald,* August 5, 2008.

McKinsey & Company. *How the World's Best Performing School Systems Come Out on Top.* Paris: Organization for Economic Cooperation and Development, 2007.

Mediamark Research & Intelligence. *America Kids Study.* New York: Mediamark Research & Intelligence, 2010.

Medina, Jennifer. "Progress Slow in Bloomberg Goal to Rid Schools of Bad Teachers." *New York Times,* February 24, 2010.

———. "Cost of Grading Schools Is Said to Be $130 Million." *New York Times,* November 14, 2008.

———, and Robert Gebeloff. "With More Money, City Schools Added Jobs, Many at Top Dollar." *New York Times,* July 1, 2009.

Merrow, John. "Interview: Fixing Detroit Public Schools & The 'Cosby Effect.'" Taking Note. http://learningmatters.tv/blog/op-ed/interview-fixing-detroit-public-schools-the-cos by-effect/3182.

Meyer, Jeremy. "DPS Graduation Rate Higher, But Only About Half Finish on Time." *Denver Post,* December 18, 2009.

Miller, Matt. "First, Kill All the School Boards." *The Atlantic,* January 2008, 94.

Miller, Raegen, and Robin Chait. *Teacher Turnover, Tenure Policies, and the Distribution of Teacher Quality.* Washington, DC: Center for American Progress, 2008.

Miller, Raegen T., Richard J. Murnane, and John B. Willett. *Do Teacher Absences Impact Student Achievement? Longitudinal Evidence from One Urban School District.* Cambridge, MA: National Bureau of Economic Research, 2007.

"Missouri Brakes." *Wall Street Journal,* April 18, 2009.

Mizell, Hayes. "School Boards Should Focus on Learning for All." *Phi Delta Kappan,* March 2010, 20–23.

Moe, Terry M. "The Union Label on the Ballot Box: How School Employees Help Choose Their Bosses." *Education Next* 6, no. 3 (Summer 2006): 58–66.

Mohl, Bruce, and Jack Sullivan. "Spending Spiral." *CommonWealth,* Spring 2009, 34–48.

Molenar, Mari, and Michael Luciano. *Financing Special Education in New Jersey.* Trenton, NJ: New Jersey School Boards Association, 2007.

Mountford, Meredith, and C. Cryss Brunner. "Motivations for School Board Membership: Implications for Decision Making." In *The New Superintendency,* edited by C. Cryss Brunner and Lars G. Björk, 135–52. Bingley, United Kingdom: Emerald Group, 2001.

"Moving Toward Language Proficiency." *Education Week,* January 8, 2009, 32.

Mrozowski, Jennifer. "State to Take Over DPS Finances." *Detroit News,* December 8, 2008.

New Jersey School Board Association. "School Ethics Commission Issues Decisions on Board Member Conduct." *School Board Notes.,* November 14, 2008.

National Conference of State Legislators. *Education at a Crossroads: A New Direction for Federal and State Education Policy.* Washington, DC: National Conference of State Legislators, 2010.

National Council on Teacher Quality. *Human Capital in Boston Public Schools: Rethinking How to Attract, Develop, and Retain Effective Teachers.* Boston, MA: Massachusetts Business Alliance for Education, 2010.

———. *State Teacher Quality Yearbook*. Washington, DC: National Council on Teacher Quality, 2009.

National School Boards Association. *CUBE Survey Report: Superintendent Tenure*. Alexandria, VA: National School Boards Association, 2002.

National Resource Center on Charter School Finance and Governance. *Creating and Sustaining High-Quality Charter School Governing Boards*. Washington, DC: National Resource Center on Charter School Finance and Governance, 2008.

North Carolina Justice Center. "This Academic Genocide Must End," *Legislative Bulletin*, April 28, 2009.

Obama, Barack. "Prepared remarks of President Obama: Back to school event: Arlington, VA." news release, September 8, 2009.

Ocasio, Linda. "Newark Schools Chief Reflects on His First Year." *Star-Ledger*, August 9, 2009.

Oei, Ting-Yi. "My Students, My Cellphone, My Ordeal." *Washington Post*, April 19, 2009.

Osborn, Scott. "Nebraska Sets the Standard on Government Accountability." *Wall Street Journal*, March 14, 2009.

Penn Center for Educational Leadership. *The Harrisburg School District: A Snapshot of Implementation Progress*. Philadelphia, PA: Penn Center for Educational Leadership, University of Pennsylvania, 2008.

Peterson, Paul E. "What Is Good For General Motors . . . Is Good for Education." *Education Next* 9, no. 2 (Spring 2009): 5.

———, and Matthew M. Chingos. "For-Profit and Nonprofit Management in Philadelphia Schools." *Education Next* 9, no. 2 (Spring 2009): 65–70.

Ravitch, Diane. "Now Is the Time to Teach Democracy." *Hoover Digest* 2002, no. 1. http://www.hoover.org/publications/hoover-digest/article/6366.

———. "Why Public Schools Need Democratic Governance." *Phi Delta Kappan* 91, no. 6 (March 2010): 24–27.

Rebore, Ronald W. *A Handbook for School Board Members*. Englewood Cliffs, NJ: Prentice-Hall, 1984.

Reeves, Charles Everand. *School Boards: Their Status, Functions and Activities*. Westport, CT: Greenwood Press, 1954.

Repplier, Agnes. "Americanism." *The Atlantic*, March 1916.

Resnick, Michael A., and Anne L. Bryant. "School Boards: Why American Education Needs Them." *Phi Delta Kappan* 91, no. 6 (March 2010): 11–14.

Rideout, Victoria J., Ulla G. Foehr, and Donald F. Roberts. *Generation M2: Media in the Lives of 8- to 18-Year-Olds*. Menlo Park, CA: Kaiser Family Foundation, 2010.

Rittmeyer, Brian C. "Party Boss Is Said to Have Dominated Montour Board." *Tribune-Review*, November 9, 2003.

Roberts, Sam. "Births to Minorities Approach a Majority." *New York Times*, February 12, 2010.

Rockoff, Jonah E., Brian A. Jacob, Thomas J. Kane, and Douglas O. Staiger. "Can You Recognize and Effective Teacher When You Recruit One?" Working paper. Cambridge, MA: National Bureau of Economic Research, 2008.

Rotherham, Andrew J. "Teaching Change." *New York Times*, March 10, 2008.

Roza, Marguerite. "Breaking Down School Budgets." *Education Next* 9, no. 3 (Summer 2009): 28–33.

———. *Frozen Assets: Rethinking Contracts Could Free Billions for School Reform*. Washington, DC: Education Sector, 2007.

———, and Raegen Miller. *Schools in Crisis: Making Ends Meet*. Seattle, WA: Center on Reinventing Public Education, University of Washington, 2009, 1.

Russo, Charles J. "The Legal Status of School Boards in the Intergovernmental System." In *School Boards: Changing Local Control*, edited by Patricia F. First and Herbert J. Walberg, 13–14. Berkeley, CA: McCutchan Publishing, 1992.

Sacchetti, Maria. "Springfield Teachers OK Merit Pay Contract." *Boston Globe*, September 9, 2006.

Saxton-Frump, Sarah. "Bridging the Poverty Gap in Education." *Star-Ledger*, March 23, 2008.

Schlechty, Phillip C. "No Community Left Behind." *Phi Delta Kappan* 89, no. 8 (April 2008): 552–59.

School Redesign Network. *Professional Learning in the Learning Profession: A Status Report of Teacher Development in the United States and Abroad.* Stanford, CA: School Redesign Network, Stanford University, 2009.

Siegel, Jim, and Catherine Candisky. "Teacher Salaries Raising Eyebrows." *Columbus Dispatch*, August 16, 2009.

Song, Jason. "Los Angeles Teacher Should Be Fired Immediately, Judge Again Rules." *Los Angeles Times*, January 13, 2010.

———. "L.A. Unified Pays Teachers Not to Teach." *Los Angeles Times*, May 6, 2009.

———. "Firing Tenured Teachers Can Be A Costly and Tortuous Task." *Los Angeles Times*, May 3, 2009.

Southern Association of Colleges and Schools. *Southern Association of Colleges and Schools Accreditation Report.* Tempe, AZ: Southern Association of Colleges and Schools, 2008.

Stover, Del, and Glenn Cook. "Legal List: Top 10 Issues." *American School Board Journal* 196, no. 2 (February 2009): 16–25.

Strategic Support Team of the Council of the Great City Schools. *Accelerating Achievement in the Denver Public Schools, 2008–09.* Washington, DC: Council of Great City Schools, 2009.

Streitfeld, David. Week in Review. "Is Steel's Revival a Model for Detroit." *New York Times*, November 23, 2008.

Strom, Margot Stern. "Education, Democracy, and Rights." *Boston Globe*, November 20, 2008.

Summerford Accountancy PC. *Report prepared for Wake County Board of Education*, Birmingham, AL: Summerford Accountancy PC, 2006.

Swanson, Christopher B. *Cities in Crisis: A Special Analytic Report on High School Graduation.* Bethesda, MD: Editorial Projects in Education Research Center, 2008.

Tanfani, Joseph, and Mark Fazlollah. "A Drain on City's Struggling Schools." *Philadelphia Inquirer*, May 4, 2009.

Thomas B. Fordham Institute. *Growing Pains in the Advanced Placement Program: Do Tough Trade-Offs Lie Ahead?* Washington, DC: Thomas B. Fordham Institute, 2009.

Toch, Thomas, and Robert Rotherman. *Rush to Judgment: Teacher Evaluation in Public Education.* Washington, DC: Education Sector, 2008.

Tompkins, Rachel B. "Rural Schools: Growing, Diverse, and . . . Complicated." *Education Week*, January 16, 2008, 24.

Twain, Mark. *Following the Equator: A Journey Around the World.* Available at http://etext.lib .virginia.edu/etcbin/toccer-new2?id=TwaEqua.xml&images=images/modeng&data=/ texts/english/modeng/parsed&tag=public∂=61&division=div1.

Tyack, David. "Democracy in Education—Who Needs It?" *Education Week*, November 17, 1999.

U.S. Congress. Senate. Committee on Labor and Public Welfare, Subcommittee on the Handicapped. *Education of All Handicapped Children, 1973–74.* 93rd Cong., 1st sess., Oct. 19, 1973.

U.S. Department of Agriculture. Food and Nutrition Service, Office of Research and Analysis. *Analyses of Verification Summary Data School Year 2007–08*. Executive Summary, October 2009.

U.S. Department of Education. *A Commitment to Quality: National Charter School Policy*. Washington, DC: U.S. Department of Education, Office of Innovation and Improvement, 2008.

U.S. Department of Health and Human Services. *Health, United States, 2008*. Hyattsville, MD: U.S. Department of Health and Human Services, Centers for Disease Control and Prevention, National Center for Health Statistics, 2008.

U.S. Department of Labor. *Employee Benefits in the United States*. Washington, DC: U.S. Department of Labor, 2009.

U.S. Department of Labor, Bureau of Labor Statistics. "Union Members 2009." news release January 22, 2010.

Usdan, Michael D. *School Boards: A Neglected Component of School Reform*. Denver, CO: Education Commission of the States, 2005.

———. "A Story of School Governance." *American School Board Journal* 192, no. 4 (April 2005): 32–36.

Utter, Bob, and Denny Heck. *Report of the Governor's Special Masters on the Marysville School District Strike*. Marysville, WA: Marysville Education Association, 2003.

Vallas, Paul G., and Leslie R. Jacobs. "'Race to the Top' Lessons from New Orleans." *Education Week*, September 2, 2009, 26.

Vaznis, James. "City Schools Challenged by Shifting Ethnic Mix." *Boston Globe*, April 19, 2009.

Viadero, Debra. "Early-Algebra Push Seen to Be Flawed." *Education Week*, February 10, 2010, 1.

———. "Research Hones Focus on ELLs." *Education Week*, January 8, 2009, 22.

Vigdor, Jacob. "Scrap the Sacrosanct Salary Schedule." *Education Next* 8, no. 4 (Fall 2008): 38.

Viteritti, Joseph P. "Should Mayors Run Schools?" *Education Week*, April 8, 2009, 32.

Wary, Curt. "Redefining the Bargaining Environment." *School Leader* (New Jersey School Boards Association) (July/August 2008): 12. http://www.njsba.org/school-leader/mayjune09.html#top.

Weisberg, Daniel, Susan Sexton, Jennifer Mulhern, and David Keeling. *The Widget Effect: Our National Failure to Acknowledge and Act on Differences in Teacher Effectiveness*. Brooklyn, NY: The New Teacher Project, 2009.

West, Darrell M., Grover J. Whitehurst, and E. J. Dionne Jr. *Invisible: 1.4 Percent Coverage for Education Is Not Enough*. Washington, DC: Brookings Institution, 2009.

Western Interstate Commission for Higher Education. *Knocking at the College Door*. Boulder, CO: Western Interstate Commission for Higher Education, 2008.

Wilentz, Sean. *The Rise of American Democracy*. New York: W. W. Norton, 2005.

Willse, Jim. Remarks at "The Newspaper Crisis," a conference at the Woodrow Wilson School, Princeton University, May 1, 2009.

Wright, Peter, and Pamela Wright, "Supreme Court Issues Pro-Child Decision in *Forest Grove School District v. T. A.*," Wrightslaw, http://www.wrightslaw.com/law/art/forestgrove.ta.analysis.htm.

Yaple, Michael. "Building a Better Bond Referendum." *School Leader* (March/April 2009): 22–23. http://www.njsba.org/school-leader/marapr09.html#bond

Zabala, Dalia, Angela Minnici, Jennifer McMurrer, and Liza Briggs. *State High School Exit Exams: Moving Toward End-of-Course Exams*. Washington, DC: Center on Education Policy, 2008.

*Zachary Deal v. Hamilton County Board of Education.* 392 F.3d 840 (6th Circuit, 2004). http://www.wrightslaw.com/law/caselaw/04/6th.deal.hamilton.tn.htm.

Zelman, Susan Tave, and Christopher T. Cross. "Systems, Not Superheroes." *AASA Journal of Scholarship and Practice* 4, no. 4 (Winter 2008): 33–38.

Zernike, Kate. "Palin Promises Choice for Disabled Students." *New York Times*, October 25, 2008.

# Index